i

Sidnie Manton:
Letters and Diaries

Sidnie Manton: Letters and Diaries

Expedition to the Great Barrier Reef 1928-1929

Sidnie Drinking from a Coconut Shell
Bali 1929

TABLE OF CONTENTS

Page Number	
xi	Introduction
xiii	Preface
xv	List of Letters
xix	Calendar of her Expedition
xxix	Personnel of The Expedition
xxxiii	C.M. Yonge and the Diving Apparatus
xxxv	Map of Sidnie's Journey
1	THE LETTERS
147	THE DIARIES
283	Sidnie's Photograph Album
301	Biography of Sidnie Manton
303	Bibliography
305	Appendix
307	Editing Notes

INTRODUCTION

100 years ago the Barrier Reef was a very different place from now. Pearl fishers and turtle soup canners had exploited the Reef almost to extinction. Scientists realised they didn't have enough knowledge of the whole ecological picture to know what action would be appropriate. A unique place was being spoiled by ignorance. A decade in the planning, the Great Barrier Reef Expedition 1928-29 attracted worldwide interest with newspaper articles appearing across the globe.

The Expedition was established on Low Isle, near Port Douglas. It was the base for the first such scientific study of a coral reef anywhere in the world: an eminent group of biologists, geographers and oceanographers examined the structure and ecology of the surrounding reef. Many current theories of coral reef ecology are based on the findings of this early expedition. Their pioneering discoveries are still used to provide base-line data for research today. The underwater studies involved donning a primitive diving helmet resembling a dustbin with a handle on top and a window on the front, constructed at Plymouth Marine Laboratory.

Sidnie Manton, a woman of great determination and academic brilliance, had been selected at the age of 26 to become a member of the Expedition, to join a group of some of the best scientists Britain could find.

She wrote letters home and kept a diary 1928-29 whilst travelling from London to the research station on Low Island, Great Barrier Reef and back. She wrote well and included amusing sketches to illustrate her activities and surroundings. On her month long voyage on the ocean liner SS Mooltan to Australia, she taught elderly passengers to dance, was a winner at deck tennis (she had been a Cambridge Blue for various sports) and knitted socks for her father which she posted home as she finished them.

xi

She travelled mainly alone by ocean liner, train, car, post bus, small boats, horse and on foot, accompanied by numerous packing cases containing 3 hundredweight of scientific apparatus, photographic gear including darkroom equipment as well as her own personal belongings.

Her first assignment in Australia was to start a research station on Mount Wellington in Tasmania. She spent 5 weeks collecting *Anaspides* (a crustacean extinct in the rest of the world). She searched remote streams and set up a breeding colony on the mountainside and in a hotel bedroom. These studies were continued by students from Hobart University.

She next travelled for two weeks by a second magnificent liner SS Orford and finally a long train journey with all her luggage to join the other members of the Great Barrier Reef Expedition on Low Island where she remained for 4 months. She investigated the growth of corals and breeding of reef animals and did some primitive diving and much drawing and photography. They were very isolated on Low Island, relying on weekly food deliveries and communicating in emergencies by flashing a morse lamp from the top of the lighthouse at night or by heliography in sunlight.

They made boat journeys to other islands and reefs which were often dangerous, she described having to sleep rolled in a blanket strapped to the hatch between two other scientists with a tarpaulin lashed over all three of them whilst anchored at sea with a strong gale worsening the Pacific swell.

Her return journey was made alone through Bali, Java and Sumatra where she relates vivid details of village life with dancing, shadow puppets, ceremonies, markets, temples, volcanoes, travels and hotels. She also witnessed the remarkable Balinese custom of cremation in which the corpse is burnt inside a massive wooden cow.

PREFACE

We started transcribing these documents over 5 years ago because we wanted to read them ourselves and they were too fragile and illegible for this to be easy.

The text that follows is a complete transcription of her records from these times. The letters are on various qualities of paper loose in a folder, labelled in her husband's writing, whilst the diary is in a rather tight ring binder. The pages are difficult to handle and the handwriting is often illegible and incomprehensible, containing Latin names of organisms and place names that have totally changed or which are now spelt very differently.

The transcript is illustrated with letterheads from ships and hotels and with samples of her handwriting and all the various drawings which she put in. These are included in order to give the reader more of the direct experience of seeing the originals than is provided by the printed words alone. The black and white photos are from Sidnie's photo albums and the post cards, maps and Malay phrase book were found tucked in with the folder of diaries.

We were greatly encouraged and helped by Elaine Charwat, when she was deputy librarian at The Linnean Society of London, and by Paula Napier and Tricia Grassi, to whom are due huge thanks. Our contact with Professor Ove Hoegh-Guldberg of the University of Queensland, Australia and Professor Maoz Fine of Bar-Ilan University, Israel (who have both recently researched on Low Island and so are familiar with the base line work of the 1928-1929 expedition) and Trisha Fielding (historian at James Cook University) gave us much excitement and support by their enthusiasm and determination that this book should be published.

The photograph for the front cover is of Low Isle with its iconic lighthouse and was kindly provided by Professors Ove Hoegh-Guldberg and Maoz Fine.

This book has been prepared by her daughter Elizabeth Clifford and granddaughter Jeanie Clifford (Teasdale) with IT support from great grandchildren Hannah and Simon Teasdale.

LIST OF LETTERS

No.	Date	Location	Addressee
1	Dec 21 1928	S.S. Mooltan	Dear Family
2	Christmas Day	S.S. Mooltan	Dear Family
3	Dec 30	S.S. Mooltan	Dear Family
4	Jan 4 1929	S.S. Mooltan	Dear Family
5	Jan 4	S.S. Mooltan	Dear Stubbins
6	Jan 6	Columbo	Dear Daddy
7	Jan 8 and 15	S.S. Mooltan	Dear Daddy
8	Jan 19	S.S. Mooltan	Dear Family
9	Jan 22	The Astor, Hobart	Dear Family
10	Jan 27	Springs Hotel	Dear Family
11	Feb 4	Springs Hotel	Dear Family
12	Feb 10	Springs Hotel	Stubbins
13	Feb 12	Springs Hotel	Dear Family
14	Feb 25	Springs Hotel	Dear Family
15	Feb 27	Mt Wellington	Dearest Daddy
16	Mar 4	Brisbane Hotel	Dear Family
17	Mar 12	S.S. Orford	Dear Family
18	Mar 13	S.S. Orford	Dear Stubbins
19	Mar 13	S.S. Orford	Dear Family
20	Mar 17	S.S. Orford	Dear Family
21	Mar 18	Womens' College Brisbane	What ho Folks

22	Mar 22	Strand Hotel Cairns	What ho Folks
23	Mar 25	Strand Hotel	Dear Family
24	Mar 30	Low Island	Well Folks
25	Apr 6	Low Island	Dear Family
26	Apr 14	Low Island	Dear Family
27	Apr 17	Low Island	Dearest Daddy
28	Apr 17	Low Island	Dear Stubbins
29	May 3	Low Island	Dear Family
30	May 12	Low Island	Dear Family
31	May 19	Low Island	Dear Family
32	May 24	Low Island	Dear Family
33	May 31	Low Island	Dear Family
34	June 16	Low Island	Dear Family
35	June 23	GREAT BARRIER REEF EXPEDITION	Dear Family
36	June 30	Luana, Daintree River	Dear Family
37	July 8	GREAT BARRIER REEF EXPEDITION	Dear Family
38	July 17	Cairns	Dear Daddy
39	July 21	Brisbane	Dear Family
40	July 22	S.S. Nieuw Holland	Dear Family
41	July 31	Oranje Hotel Makassar	Dear Family

42	Aug 8	Hotel Ngemplak	Dear Family
43	Aug 13	Hotel Boroboedoer	Dear Family
44	Aug 17	Hotel Villa Dolce-Garoet (Java)	Dearly Beloveds
45	Aug 21	Batavia	Dearest Folks
46	Aug 22	S.S. Melchior Treub Near Pedang	Dear Family

EXPEDITION CALENDAR

Main stops underlined, arrival at Barrier Reef shown in bold type.

December 1928
20 Left Victoria station, <u>London</u> at 1:40 by the boat train.
     Left Boulogne at 6:20 pm
21 Arrived <u>Marseilles</u>. Boarded S.S. Mooltan
22 Departed Marseilles 7 am. Passed Corsica
23 At sea, passed Straits of Messina
24 At sea, played 8 sets of deck tennis
25 At sea, prolonged dinner and concert
26 Port Said 12:30, left 4:30, entered Suez Canal at sunset
27 At sea, Gulf of Suez
28 At sea, Red Sea
29 At sea
30 Reached Aden 8 pm
31 Left Aden 3:30. Fancy dress dance

January 1929
 1 At sea, Arabian coast in sight all day
 2 At sea
 3 At sea
 4 Arrived Bombay 5 pm Left 9:30 pm
 5 At sea, shoals of flying fish seen
 6 At sea
 7 Colombo 6 am, left 1 pm
 8 At sea crossed Equator
 9 At sea
10 At sea
11 At sea, passed Cocos Islands
12 At sea
13 At sea
14 At Sea, cloudy, rough, cool and very boring
15 At Sea

16 Disembarked <u>Freemantle</u>, mobbed by reporters, motored
to Perth Zoo, sailed at 5 pm
17 At Sea. First Albatross seen
18 At Sea
19 At Sea
20 Reached Adelaide 1 pm, end of voyage on S.S. Mooltan,
   caught train to Melbourne
21 Arrived Melbourne 8:15 am. Caught boat Nairana for
   Tasmania
22 Arrived <u>Launceston, Tasmania</u> ; train to Hobart,
   Astor Hotel
23 Hobart, two-horse cab to Springs Hotel
   (half way up Mount Wellington)
24 At Springs Hotel, to Diamond Springs,
   found *Anaspides* on plains
25 At Springs Hotel, collected live specimens of *Anaspides*
26 At Springs Hotel
27 At Springs Hotel
28 At Springs Hotel
29 At Springs Hotel
30 At Springs Hotel
31 At Springs Hotel

February
 1 At Springs Hotel, Walked to Hobart University
 2 At Springs Hotel
 3 At Springs Hotel, photographing *Anaspides*
 4 At Springs Hotel
 5 At Springs Hotel
 6 At Springs Hotel
 7 At Springs Hotel
 8 At Springs Hotel to Hobart Zoo, saw last *Thylacines*
   (Tasmanian wolf/tiger, extinct in 1933)
 9 At Springs Hotel
10 At Springs Hotel, spent day painting *Anaspides*
11 At Springs Hotel, unwell
12 At Springs Hotel, unwell

13 At Springs Hotel, better
14 At Springs Hotel, hunting for giant crayfish *(Astacopsis)*
15 At Springs Hotel, to Kingston and Browns River
   hunting crayfish
16 At Springs Hotel
17 At Springs Hotel, bad weather, writing day
18 To Great Lake by mail van, staying in a hut,
   to search for *Paranaspides*
19 Great Lake, bad weather
20 Great Lake
21 Great Lake
22 Great Lake
23 Back to Springs Hotel via New Norfolk and
   Derwent Valley
24 At Springs Hotel
25 At Springs Hotel drawing *Anaspides*
26 To Hartz Mountains by car then pack horse to stay in a hut
27 To top of Hartz Mountains, 4,260 feet, back to
   Springs Hotel
28 At Springs Hotel

March
 1 To Astor Hotel
 2 Sandy Bay, up Mt Nelson
 3 Visited University. Brisbane Hotel, Launceston
 4 Wet day
 5 Up to gorge. Left Launceston on Naiana
 6 Rough crossing to Melbourne. University.
   Motored to Ringwood
 7 Shopping. University Reception
 8 To Red Hill apple orchards
 9 To National Museum
10 To Botanic Gardens
11 University. Met Mrs Manton
12 Last day in Melbourne. Sailed on S.S. Orford
13 On board S.S. Orford

14 Arrived <u>Sydney</u> Harbour 8.30 am. To University,
   Museum and Zoo
15 In Sydney. Shopped in rain. Evening dance,
   caught boat by 7 mins
16 On board
17 Arrived <u>Brisbane</u> 2 pm
18 University of Brisbane
19 University of Brisbane
20 1.45 train
21 On train
22 Changed trains at Townsville
23 Arrived <u>Cairns</u>. Strand Hotel
24 Train to Kuanda and Baron Falls
25 In Cairns
26 Motor boat to Port Douglas - 3 1/2 hour trip.
Arrived on Low Island, Great Barrier Reef at dusk
27 On Low Island. Settled plans of work. Explored
28 General survey. Learnt fauna
29 Looked for Sea cucumbers
30 Learnt corals and gathered cauliflower coral colonies
31 Diving

April
 1 Drawing cauliflower corals
 2 Studied sea urchin gonads
 3 (No entry)
 4 Surveyed flats
 5 Surveyed mangroves
 6 Surveyed mangroves
 7 Surveyed
 8 Surveyed detailed strip
 9 Surveyed detailed strip
10 Surveyed detailed strip
11 Surveyed detailed strip
12 Changed all formalin in pots and jars
13 Cured coral
14 Diving in the anchorage

15 Cured corals, photographing and drawing
16 'Donkey jobs'
17 Mangrove pond
18 Drawing and curing corals
19 Survey
20 Break in the trade winds. 85° F
21 Photography, survey
22 Mapped the pen
23 Survey of anchorage started
24 Surveyed anchorage, up to necks in water
25 Surveyed last yards of anchorage, finished mapping pen
26 Neaps beginning. Debearding coral party at work
27 'Cold' 77° F
28 Diving after pots, letter writing
29 Rowed in 'Flattie' to collect *Symphyllia*
30 Ink drawing of Coral Pen Map

May
1 Party of 6 left for Three Isles on Luana. SMM left in
 charge of tide gauge, housekeeping, aboriginal cook etc
2 Printing coral photos
3 Coral redrawing and curing
4 Had two birthday cakes
5 Redrawing, letters, photography
6 Spring tide at last, deep anchorage traverse begun
7 Continued traverse in anchorage
8 Continued traverse of outside rampart
9 Continued traverse ending on Boulder Zone.
 Corals spawning
10 Continued traverse anchorage traverse
11 Corals still spawning
12 Coral curing and crab gonads
13 Bad weather - heliographed Port Douglas to find
 whereabouts of Luana
14 Still no Luana
15 Three set out in dingy and outboard for Port Douglas
searching Luana

16 Two parties return in Merinda
17 Committee meeting about Lizard island. Coral and crab
  gonads
18 Coral gonads and photography
19 Boat trip all round island seeing deep water coral
20 Traverse in the anchorage
21 Surveying NW rampart
22 Mapping a rock
23 Diving in helmet, finished traverse
24 Cleaning corals
25 Finished *Favia* gonads
26 Coral cleaning, photography and identifying corals
27 Cleaned corals
28 Drawing coral gonads with camera lucida
29 Diving for clam shells, pipes and rock
30 Finished *Symphyllia* gonads, packing for Lizard Island
31 Tivoli departed 6:30 am with some of the party.

June
 1 SMM on Low Island, coral cleaning
 2 Day trip to Snapper Island in Luana and Garnett
 3 Boiled corals
 4 Further party set out in Luana for Port Douglas,
   transhipped to Merinda, to Cooktown, stayed in
   Seaview Hotel
 5 Left at 5 am for Lizard Island arrived 11 am,
   set up camp for whole party
 6 Off in Tivoli to June Reef and back to Lizard Island
 7 Another day trip to June Reef (12 miles)
 8 To north end of June Reef and back to Lizard Island
 9 To a nearby reef, weather deteriorating
10 Stormy night straining tent, dived at fringing reef
11 Casuarina Beach, coral packing, pressing plants
12 Very windy night, packed Tivoli and then Merinda.
   Depart in howling gale for Cooktown (6 hrs),
   Seaview Hotel
13 On Merinda to Low Island. Rough Sea

14 Preparations for packing. Gonads, maps
15 Tivoli returned to Low Island
16 Unpacked Tivoli, corals from Lizard Island etc.
   Printed Outer Barrier photos
17 Finished muddy end of traverse
18 Finished gonads
19 Coral labelling and cataloguing
20 Chores and coral packing
21 Foul wind, lab day cataloguing etc
22 Map making
23 Walked right round island, more mapping
24 Bad weather, mapping and indoor jobs
25 Mapping
26 450 crates labelled and catalogued
27 Studied growing *Pocillopore*
28 Health problems
29 Continuing health problems
30 Five members departed for Daintree,
   up river to settlement

July
 1 Mouth of Daintree River and inland, forest and mangrove
 2 Left for Port Douglas to visit two members in hospital
 3 Writing up, photo printing
 4 Further member ill. Outside edge work
 5 On board Daintree (20 ton cargo boat)
   anchored in Bloomfield River
 6 To Ruby Reef, spent night lashed to hatch of boat
 7 To Escape Reef
 8 To Undine Reef, back to Low Island
 9 Developed films
10 Chores, notes, packing, printing photos
11 Developed colour plates
12 Packing corals
13 Notes of reef work
14 Panorama from Lighthouse assembled
15 Last day at Low island, chores, printing

16 Left in starlight at 5:40 am in Luana for Port Douglas.
   Shopping. On Daintree for Cairns
17 To Townsville by train, slept on train overnight
18 On train
19 Train arrived Brisbane
20 Addressed graduates at Lyceum, picnic at Moreton Bay.
   Dr F to hospital with acute appendicitis.
21 Dr F operated on successfully. Letters and packing.
22 Left Brisbane aboard S.S. Nieuw Holland,
   crossed Moreton Bay
23 Reached beginning of Great Barrier Reef
24 Had pleasant tea with Captain Bauer on the Bridge.
25 Passed Low Island at 4 am.
26 Passed Mount Adolphus Isles and entered Torres Straits
27 No land in sight
28 Flying fish, flat calm
29 Passed Timor
30 No land in sight till late afternoon.
   Salayer Straits and Celebes
31 Spectacular sunrise entering Makassar Harbour, Celebes.
   Orange Hotel

August
 1 Motored to Dongaÿa Tombs and to Soenggoominassee
   Bazaar
 2 Rowed in harbour. Motored to native kampongs
 3 Horse races, left at 5 pm on S.S. Melchior Treube
 4 Bali, landed at 4 pm. Stayed at Government Rest House at
   Kintamassi
 5 To Bangklet Village, Temple of Soekawati,
   Funeral with wooden cow,
 6 To Kedaton to see Balinese dancing, to tombs at
   Goenoeng Kawi
 7 A day of temples. Left Bali on the "Pig Express"
 8 Arrived on Java - Sourabaya. Hotel Ngemplak
 9 Walked to Mount Bromo
10 Went to Malang and Sourabaya

11 Train to Djarkarta
12 Train to Moentilar
13 Saw Merapi volcano at sunrise, visited many temples
14 Train to Garoet
15 Climbed the Papandayan volcano
16 Walked to Lake Bagendit, train to Bandoeng
17 Car to Lembang village, Train to Buitenzorg
18 To zoological museum and botanic gardens in Buitenzorg
19 Two day trip by boat from Batavia to reefs and islands
20 Swimming around Onrust Reef recording corals
21 Motored to Tangjong Priok, sailed on Melchior Treub,
    passed Krakatoa
22 At sea past coast of Sumatra
23 Arrived at Emmahaven, Sumatra. 6 hour train ride to
    Fort de Kock
24 Fort de Kock market
25 Drove to Matoer and Lake Manindjan
26 Left Fort de Kock by post bus to Kota-Nopan,
    a 9 hour journey
27 Back on the bus to Sibolga
28 Bus to Lake Toba
29 Spent day at Balige
30 Climbed 5,000' mountain, Dolok Tolong.
    Bad hotel in Pematang Siantar
31 Train across Medan plains

September
 1 Visited Kabandjahe, views of volcanoes
 2 To Lao Simono, a leper colony,
    weekly market at Kabandjahe
 3 Bus to Brastagi, walked to craters of Sibajak
 4 Rode a horse on the Karo plains
 5 Bus to Medan, train to harbour, boarded
    Duymaen van Twist
 6 Arrived George Town on island of Penang
 7 Rickshaw to Air Itam temple
 8 Tram to Air Itam

9 <u>Return journey starts</u> aboard 8,000 ton boat
   (S.S. Kashmir).
   Passed Sumatra.
10 At sea
11 At sea
12 Arrived Colombo
13 Sailed 6 am - rolling boat
14 Passed Minicoy
15 At sea
16 At sea - calm
17 At sea - rough sea, monsoon winds
18 At sea - calmer, near coast of Africa
19 Arrived Aden
20 At sea
21 At sea
22 At sea
23 Gulf of Suez
24 Up Suez Canal to Port Said
25 Mediterranean Sea
26 At sea
27 Passed Messina
28 Passed Corsica and Sardinia
29 Boat-Train from <u>Marseille to London</u>

PERSONNEL OF THE GREAT BARRIER REEF EXPEDITION 1928-1929

as listed by C.M.Yonge in his book "A year on the Great Barrier Reef"
Published by Putnam November 1930

The expedition consisted of Biological and Geographical Sections, the former being divided into three parties. The composition of each of these is given below, the months that each member spent with the expedition being indicated in parentheses.

A.BIOLOGICAL SECTION

1. *Boat Party.*
F.S. Russell, D.S.C., D.F.C., B.A., of Plymouth, who was in charge during the first five months and who worked on the animal plankton (5).
A.P. Orr, M.A., B.Sc., A.I.C., of Millport, who succeeded Mr Russell in charge of the party and who worked on the chemistry and hydrography of the sea water and the conditions over the reef flat and within the mangrove (12½).
Miss S.M. Marshall, B.Sc., of Millport, who worked on the plant plankton and on the effect of sediment on corals (12½).
J.S. Colman, B.A., of Oxford, who assisted Mr Russell and later continued his work on the animal plankton (10½).
Mrs F.S. Russell, M.B.E., of Plymouth who assisted Mr Russell in his laboratory work (5).

2. *Shore Party.*
T.A. Stephenson, D.Sc., of London who was in charge of this party, and who worked on the ecology of the reefs and on the breeding, development and growth of corals (11½).
G. Tandy, B.A., of the British Museum, who was the botanist (5).

Mrs T.A. Stephenson of London, who worked on the breeding of reef animals and assisted in the ecological work (11½).

F.W. Moorhouse, B.Sc., of Brisbane, who assisted in the work of the party, but was especially concerned with the animals of direct economic value (12½).

Miss E.A. Fraser, D.Sc, of London who assisted with the ecological work and with the observations on the breeding of reef animals (4).

Miss S.M. Manton, M.A., Ph.D., of Cambridge who assisted with the ecological work and with the observations on the growth of corals and the breeding of reef animals (4).

3. *Physiological (experimental) Party.*

C.M. Yonge, D.Sc., Ph.D., of Cambridge, who was in charge, and worked on the feeding and digestion of corals and other reef animals and on the significance in the life of corals of their contained algae, and who was also in charge of dredging and trawling operations (12½).

Mrs C.M. Yonge, M.B., Ch.B., of Cambridge, who was Medical Officer, and assisted in the chemical analyses necessitated by the work of this party (12½).

A.G. Nicholls, B.Sc., of Perth, W.A., who assisted the leader of this party throughout and also did work on the growth and breeding of the black-lip pearl oyster and on the manner in which corals form their skeletons (12½).

G.W. Otter, B.A., of Cambridge, who assisted generally in the work of this party, but was particularly concerned with the animals which bore into coral rock (11).

B GEOGRAPHICAL SECTION

J.A. Steers, M.A., of Cambridge led this section, which was largely separate from the Biological Section during the period he was in Australia, when an extensive cruise was made on the M.I. Tivoli from Townsville northward to the Flinders Islands returning as far as Mackay. The Tivoli called at Low Isles on the outward and return voyages. Mr Steers made a general geographical reconnaissance of the Great Barrier and the Queensland coast, and left Australia at the end of November 1928.

M.A. Spender B.A., of Oxford who assisted Mr Steers, and later spent 8 months on Low Isles, where he made accurate surveys of the islands and reef and later of other regions, working throughout in conjunction with the Shore Party.

E.C.Marchant B.A., of Cambridge, who accompanied Mr Steers during the latter half of his cruise, and later spent six weeks on Low Isles assisting in the geographical work

C.M. Yonge and the Diving Apparatus- air was pumped down the length of garden hose by a member of the party in a small boat

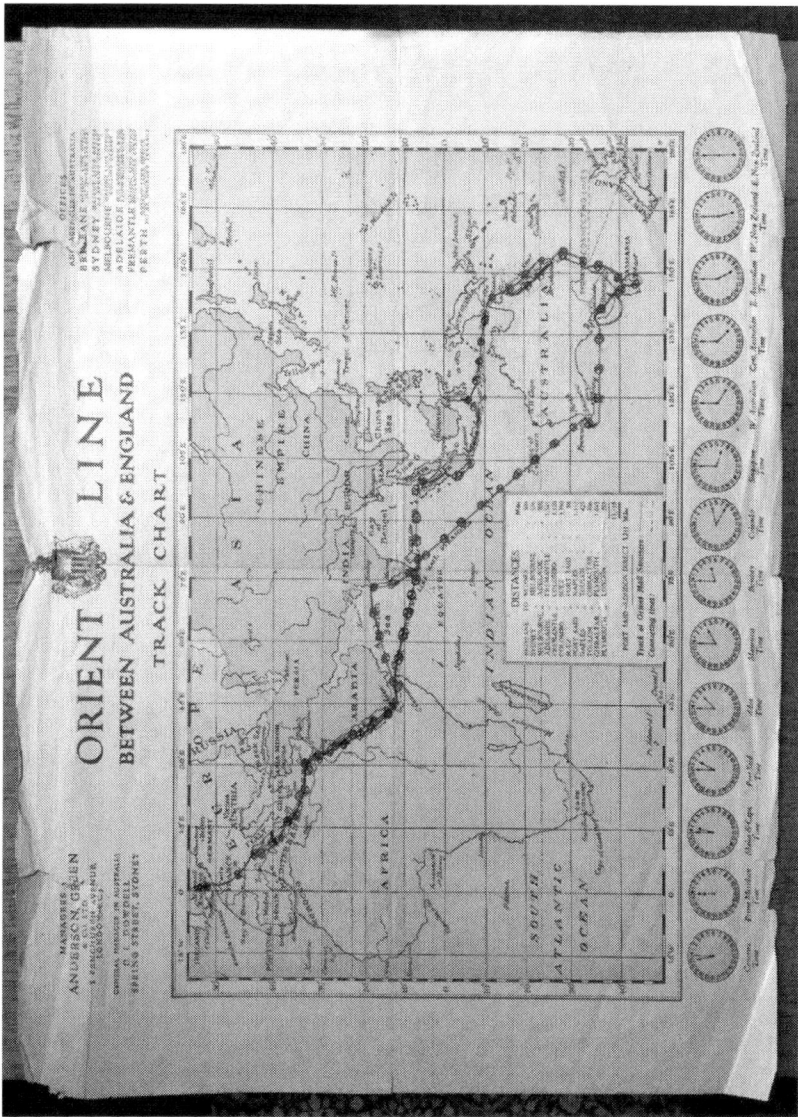

Map of Sidnie's Journey

XXXV

THE
LETTERS

P & O. S. N. Co.
S.S. Mooltan.
Dec. 21th. 1978

Dear Family,

In spite of all the nasty things
Bibs said about impending disorders internal,
I had a very good crossing. I was on the "Maid
of Orleans" a 1918 boat, which has been tinkered
up & the lower deck walled & glassed in at the
sides, covered with a rubber floor, and sprinkled
with leather upholstered seats for 2 put
across the boat as on the top of a bus. I have
scored heavily on the P&O train folk. Their
train arrived after mine at Folkestone, & all
the padded seats etc were then occupied, while
I sat in a fine seat in the middle of the boat
& gloated over their discomfort. I then proceeded

The First Letter

2

Letter 1

P&O.S.N.Co.
S.S. Mooltan
December 21 1928

Dear Family,

In spite of all the nasty things Bibs said about impending disorders internal, I had a very good crossing. I was on the 'Maid of Orleans' a 1918 boat, which has been tinkered up and the lower deck walled and glassed in at the sides, covered with a rubber floor, and sprinkled with leather upholstered seats for two put across the boat as in the top of a bus. I have scored heavily on the P&O train folk. Their train arrived after mine at Folkestone, and all the padded seats etc were then occupied, while I sat in a fine seat in the middle of the boat and gloated over their discomfort. I then proceeded to have a very good night with two and a half seats to spread over in a corner. I was on the boat by 11:45 am, having taken a horse cab which was just about to break in half, how it held together was a marvel. I find to my disgust that there is a howling infant of five months cutting its teeth in my cabin, and the cabin is hung about with washing. I shall be able to move into a 4 berth cabin tomorrow or after Port Said I gather. The baby is a blight as the two berth cabin is much the nicest. I have explored the second class part of the boat, it's not as spacious as I expected, and the lounge drawing room effect is rather small with only about 4 armchairs and 2 chesterfields in it. My deckchair has gone astray, but possibly it has been left in the luggage room, which they won't open till tomorrow after the boat leaves, so that if it's lost I shall have to do without till Egypt. However I expect it is there all right if Bibs did not put a 'wanted at Marseilles' label on it, without that label they would put it in the hold.

I don't think I shall bother to explore Marseilles this afternoon, as the quay is miles from the town.

I have not tracked down the "F" woman yet, I shall doubtless see her at lunch shortly.

Nearly all the stewards and boat hands appear to be black. The blackest and politest person looks after my cabin.

There appear to be a lot of babies and children on the boat – I do think they might park them all together to annoy each other.

I don't like the looks of the assembled passengers at the moment, they are a painted faced squiffy eyed selection here at the moment, and they doubtless think the same of me. However perhaps it is a bad sample.

I must now go to lunch – I am very hungry.

- had a very good lunch – and the P&O train people have just arrived – two hours <u>after</u> me – and three quarters of an hour late for lunch – I've found "Dr F" and we are going in search of a stamp and a pillar box –

Lots of love,
S

Letter 2

P&O.S.N.Co.
S.S. Mooltan
Christmas Day 1928

Dear Family,

I am now one day off Port Said. We are only stopping there for four hours and not at all at Suez. It is an oil ship and it stopped for 2½ days at Marseilles.

Last night and yesterday we had an awful sea, much worse than the Bay of Biscay. The boat rolled and pitched like a cork and you could have put the Earls Court Road in the furrows between the waves. I played deck tennis till 4 pm, and then it became impossible to walk about easily. I went to bed at 5 pm and had a huge tea and dinner and was perfectly well. Today is calmer and I am very stiff after 8 sets of deck tennis yesterday. The creaks of the ship and the way it quivers as a wave hits it is extraordinary.

Owing to the ship leaving Marseilles 7 hours late we passed between Corsica and Sardinia the first night and the Straits of Messina the second so saw nothing of the view. I shall not see Egypt either. I am thinking of leaving out Ceylon in favour of Egypt on the way back.

The air gets appreciably warmer all the time. Only the first day was beastly cold on deck. We have not had much sun yet.

The second class sitting room is most inadequate, the motion there is awful when rough, (my hand keeps on bouncing off the paper even now, and it's not very rough here) and there are five armchairs and two sofas for 275 passengers.

My cabin is always full of a baby being ill etc so I sit on deck or play games.

I've refooted a pair of socks which I will post from Port Said. You might acknowledge them, as if they don't arrive I won't post any more.

5

The second class top deck is much bigger than the first class one, in fact all the second class part of the boat except the lounge is very good.

I haven't seen your patient yet – was it Mrs Wilson? There are several Mrs Wilsons on the boat. Prof Dakin – the zoo. professor of Liverpool is in the first class part – I never expected to see him here.

It is getting rougher again so I will move to a better part of the boat than this beastly lounge.

I hope you are having a decent time in Belgium and that things will sort themselves out fairly decently.

Lots of Love,
S

Can you give me the formula of your fly mosquito oil which keeps them off? It might be very useful in Java which is infested with mosquitoes.

Letter 3

P&O.S.N.Co.
S.S. Mooltan
December 30 1928
Sunday

Dear Family,

This is my third day in the Red Sea, and we are due at Aden at 8 pm. The temperature is just fine warm and sunny with a light breeze. The first day in the Red Sea had an air temp. of 74° and a water temp. of 78°, but it has been warmer since then.

Everything has been very delightful since Port Said. The canal by night was great. A fine sunset over the canal and lakes and a full moon at its zenith at 11 pm lighting up the desert wonderfully. Some camels heavily packed going along the road at the side of the canal were fascinated by the ship's lights and noise and galloped along level with us for miles. We spent about 14 hours in the canal and I arose at 5 pm to see the Bitter Lake as we crossed it. The 15 miles near Suez were fine – vast expanses of desert with a brilliant oasis close by and fine distant mountains wonderfully weathered and bare.

The next 24 hours were spent in the Gulf of Suez, which was truly marvellous, rugged weathered ridges and mountains one behind another, arising directly out of the sea on either side for the most part. All ruddy brown with no speck of vegetation or habitation – a majestic type of scenery quite new to me. The sea was calm and we did a record run for this trip of 392 miles in 24 hours, the slowest was 324 in the rough Mediterranean. The sunsets in the Red Sea itself are quite unlike anything I've seen and are truly glorious. We saw no land for 2 days in the Red Sea, but some very fine ridges one behind the other are now visible to the East.

I spent 2 hours yesterday morning going over the ship's engines. The propellers are 19 foot across and rotate 81.5 times a minute! Their shafts are 26 feet below water and the ship leaves very little disturbance in the water behind and a

7

small wash from the front. The efficiency of the oil engine is 7% against 6.5% of the coal type. They refill with oil in 4 hours instead of 2 days, so we get no time to stray far on port days and I shall not be able to go to Kandy. The heat below among the engines isn't at all bad, only 110° in the boiler rooms among the furnaces with inside temperatures of 1900°.

The sea is getting rougher and I am on the top deck near the end there is a good deal of motion. I hope you can read this, I could write legibly in the saloon, but it is nicer outside.

No sea birds follow the ship at all, except for some gulls for a few hours near Suez.

There are some atrocious folk on the boat, and some very nice ones. The time passes extraordinarily there is no apparent time except meal times! I sit about and boil myself in the sun and read and knit and play tennis and dance in the evenings. We dance on deck to the world's worst band for about 1½ hours. Somehow I seem to have collected some pleasant grey headed old cronies who insist on being taught to dance. One long and thin retired colonel and one large and fat jolly old soul. They enjoy their efforts so much that it is quite a pleasure to try and dance with them.

I very much enjoyed going ashore at Port Said. Its flavours of the East so markedly compared with anything else I've seen. My legs were so used to the boat, that I was quite unstable on firm land. How these native women stick being wrapped up with heavy black cloths with only their eyes showing and their noses and foreheads covered with a bamboo stick I can't imagine. The pedlars with carpets of Egyptian and Syrian make and other goods probably made in Birmingham swarmed in boats around the ship trying to sell their wares. It was great fun looking down on them from the ship. I was much taken with some Syrian blue carpets, the quality is all right and the same as some Syrian carpets which Dr Thomas brought back from these regions. However I'm collecting no goods whatever on the outward journey.

I've met a very useful Australian who knows the Dutch East Indies inside out and have acquired lots of useful information. Our provisional plan is –

Leave Brisbane July 24. arrive Sourabaya Aug 4th. Proceed by car etc through the island (Java) to Batavia, taking 10 days. Leave by a local steamer for Palembang in Sumatra and work up Sumatra, mainly by water and get a Dutch mail boat which calls at the north end of Sumatra after leaving Singapore. This leaves on August 24th and gets to Suez on Sept 7th. Then I want to stay in Egypt for a week to 10 days and get any old boat home.

I hope that all is well with you.

Lots of love,
Sidnie
(PS I'm posting a second pair of refooted socks at Aden.)

9

Letter 4

P&O S.N.Co.
Approaching Bombay
She put Dec 4 1928, she must mean
Jan 4 1929

Dear Family,

I seem to be sending you such lots of letters, but I shall not hear from you for simply ages. The voyage so far has been the coolest on record for some time for the ship. I've had summer clothes on since Port Said, and one is quite warm at night in evening dress on the top deck in the wind. I got very sun burned the second day in the Red Sea and am only just recovering. I boiled myself in the sun for a morning, being fanned by the wind, but two days later I realised the full potency of the extra ultra violet light or whatever it is.

We reached Aden at night, and I went a drive in a car to see the famous water tanks for collecting the rainfall in a rocky gully. The whole place subsists on distilled water for all purposes. The whole place is scented of camel and Arab, but I found it vastly interesting. The way the Arabs live in one roomed square houses containing practically no furniture and lit by an oil lamp on the floor is amazing. Everything was bare and dusty with no speck of anything growing through the ten miles which we motored.

Since Aden it has been cooler. We put the clocks on half to one hour every day, a great strain on one's getting up. I usually sleep most of the afternoon as it is so pleasant to be up late at night these starry moonlight nights. I'm getting quite fat too.

We had a very good show on New Year's night even a fancy dress dance. My Colonel and the fat man are getting quite good! Nearly all the pleasant folk are getting off the boat at Bombay, and these noisy disgusting Australians will be left supreme, swollen in numbers by another hundred from India.

I have got some very useful information from a charming lady here about Egypt. She has lived there for

11

some time and has been everywhere and done everything and has been very interesting to talk to about the Near East.

There isn't much to write about, we have been out of sight of land for ages – I won the sac race this morning and got into several semi finals in a deck tennis tournament – the other deck games aren't worth playing. I expect the ten days between Colombo and Freemantle will be rather dull, as they expect it hot and rough, and all the nice folk on the boat will have gone. It's just as well that I did get my drawings done before leaving, as it is not steady enough here.

I'm posting you another pair of socks from Bombay, that is the third pair. You now ought to have enough to last till I get back. I haven't seen your patient yet, or rather she hasn't seen me.

It's funny how one meets folk one knows directly or indirectly, there are several people who know old Newnham friends of mine and who were at Homerton training college etc.

There isn't any more news, so I may as well stop. I expect you will be about done with E.C. by the time this reaches you – I do hope that all is going well. I've been sending postcards to mother from the ports of call.

Lots of love,
Sidnie

Letter 5

P&O S.N.Co.
S.S. Moultan
Bombay (nearly)
January 4 1929

Dear Stubbins, [her sister]

I've been writing to Daddy and I suppose that he is sending on my letters as he did yours – not that there is anything to say much as yet.

I do hope that things are turning out pleasant and bearable in Manchester, and life isn't too much of a blight there. You will doubtless find it less beastly after the ice is broken all round. I hear you have been having snow – I wonder if there has been any more skiing for you this year. I am enjoying the warmth and live in the thinnest clothes, even at night and have skinned my neck by sitting in the sun for a morning – the light is very powerful in these latitudes. It's very pleasant not having too much work to do, and to be able to laze all day however it is rather a lonesome business, as usual, when ones mind isn't smothered with thoughts of work. I feel as if I want to go away for ever and never see Cambridge or anything else again – however I suppose I shall cheer up later.

The ports of call I find very entertaining, and was quite thrilled with such filthy disreputable places as Port Said and Aden. We get to Bombay at mid-day, and all the pleasant folk are getting off the boat. Miss F is quite a pleasant soul – if dull, but I can't cultivate any particular affection for her.

I won the sack race yesterday, amid shrieks of 'Cambridge' – how uplifted C. ought to feel at my not letting them down over such an important item!

I know it will be weeks and weeks before I hear any news, but do send me a line or so when you can. Good luck to the crucifers* and to the JOB, the start must be a trial.

Lots of love,
Sidnie

13

[*plants of the *Cruciferae* family, she was counting their chromosomes.]

Sidnie Manton (seated) with a school friend she met
up with whilst in Columbo

Letter 6

P&O S.N.Co.
S.S.Mooltan
Columbo
January 6 1929

Dear Daddy,

We reach Columbo at 5 am tomorrow and stay four hours. Mouldy isn't it? We are already a day behind time, and will be at least two by the time we reach Melbourne, as we shall get to Adelaide on a Saturday and will have to remain till Monday because nobody works on Sunday.

I've just been swimming in the minute bath – water at 85° and air at 84°. It's stuffy warm except on top deck, and the sun powerful. The sea has been calm for the last ten days and usually sunny. We are now surrounded by flying fish. The sunsets are simply marvellous, quite unlike anything I've seen before. We hit a sandbank outside Bombay and got stuck two hours on that, and another two hours manoeuvring up to the key [sic] over a few hundred yards. The bay there is extremely fine. We went on shore and I bought a sun hat with various peoples' valuable assistance, and then had a look inside the Northern Frontier express – a marvellously sumptuous train with a wonderful dining car and no corridor. The coaches are divided into rooms, all most comfortable, with fans etc and meals happen only at stations. The vibration here at the end of the boat is excessive, the middle part is quite stable.

The post is just going so I will stop – there isn't any news.

Lots of love,
Sidnie

16

Letter 7

P&O S.N.Co.
S.S.Mooltan
January 8 1929

Dear Daddy,

I hear you are having a black fog, while I am just on the equator – and very nice too – only 82° air temperature, water 84° (at 4pm). It is cooler than since some days before Bombay. However it is extremely damp and I feel more collapsed and lazy than at Naples at 93°.

I had a great time at Columbo. I met a girl I haven't seen for ten years who was at the F.E.I. [Froebel Educational Institute] and at St Pauls. She had come into Columbo specially and was there two days waiting for the boat which was over a day late. She motored us all over the show and told us all about everything. The country round is very luxuriant compared with Bombay – thick belt of coconuts all round the shore and the most brilliant flowering trees and shrubs imaginable everywhere. Heaps of rickshaws about and the smallest cattle in the biggest carts I've ever seen.

The weather continues fine and the sea calm. The boat moves a good deal now as there isn't so much cargo onboard as there was.

January 12

Yesterday we passed the Cocos Islands, five days from anywhere on the ship routes. They looked lovely surrounded by reefs and covered with palm trees and bright yellow coconuts, the shallow sea between them being bright green compared with the deep blue elsewhere.

Today is a mouldy cloudy roughish cold day. I had to put on a vest and coat for the first time since the Mediterranean, and the swimming bath water is below 80° - I like it at 85°.

The southern hemisphere summer seems a poor show so far after the tropical pleasant warmth of the northern parts of the Indian Ocean. This is a very boring ten days between Columbo and Freemantle, and the company is awful. I seldom say a word at meals – opposite and around are two atrocious flappers and an equally awful man, a retiring sea captain and wife going to start a public house in Australia, a half baked Eurasian and two awful shop keepers from Sidney. However I'm making lots of socks so that I hope I shall not have to knit for years when I come back. I play some deck tennis, but all the deck games are ruined by tournaments organised by an officious committee. Even the dancing is quite spoiled by having to avoid so many persistent and unpleasant partners.

There is scarcely any phosphorescence of the sea at night – very few flying fish, no birds or porpoises or whales or anything that there should be.

I'm very glad I didn't come via the Cape - it must mostly be like this ten days all the way by that route.

Jan 15

It has been rougher still the last two days – quite difficult to walk about at the extreme ends of the ship – however it's not nearly as bad as the storm we had in the Mediterranean. I don't mind the motion, but it is so difficult to do anything much with the ship tossing about. I continue to sleep all the afternoons between lunch and tea as well as all night – it's a good way of passing the time. However it does not feel like three and a half weeks on this boat already. The company is being fined £1000 for being two days late with the mails at Freemantle, but they don't seem to mind much. We only did 336 miles yesterday against 392 on a calm day. I am nearly reduced to the ship's library having read nearly all of our combined supply of literature. I took some very nice photographs in Port Said and Columbo, but nearly ruined the lot by washing in the ship's soft water at about 79° without a hardening bath, I more or less saved some by getting as much iced water as I could.

I wonder so much how all is going, it will be such ages before I get any reasonable news from you.

Lots of love,
Sidnie

MILL POINT AND SWAN RIVER, PERTH, WEST AUSTRALIA.   VALENTINE'S. M.3761

Perth. (Please keep)
June 6.

Had a wonderful
day going by car into
the "bush", where every
plant was different -
masses of Eucalyptus &
other evergreens in full flower
& legion species of Araucarias
etc. Cycads -
Lots of love
Sidnie

VALENTINES
REAL PHOTO SERIES

Published by the Valentine Publishing Co Pty Ltd
Queen St. Melb.

Received

Mrs Manville

18 Ennerdale Rd

Richmond

Surrey

England.

19

Letter 8

P&O S.N.Co.
S.S.Mooltan
January 19 1929

Dear Family,

Tomorrow we reach Adelaide, but it being Sunday we do nothing all day because nobody works, so won't unpack till Monday – isn't it ridiculous? Meanwhile the P&O has to pay countless overland fares, so that the Sidney passengers can catch the New Zealand boat. I may go by rail from Adelaide to Melbourne if they won't guarantee my catching the Tasmania boat on the 23rd as Prof Flynn has delayed going to Sidney from Hobart for several weeks, and I don't want to keep him any longer than necessary. He is being very useful and has booked me rooms in a Hobart hotel and is one up on the mountain, and is getting my cabin on the Tasmania boat and writes and sends telegrams etc.

Things have cheered up since we reached Australia. I had a topping day at Freemantle, was met there by a mob of newspaper photographers to start with, and then motored to Perth, three quarters of an hour run and saw the zoo – mainly interesting for the vegetation, and was taken out to lunch by the chemistry professor, and then motored over a national park of untouched 'bush' on a high hill overlooking the river and everything else. It was wonderful to be in a flora new in every species - even the grass – masses of eucalyptus and gum trees of legion species, and all sorts of smaller things and huge cycads and so on. The flowering eucalyptus of every colour – masses of hibiscus rosa (I think there is some in the temperate house) and other flowers were just marvellous. All the small flowering plants were over. The temperature too was just right – two days previous it had been 102°, not that that means much without realising the degree of humidity.

The ship disgorged cargo for ten hours and we proceeded very light in ballast and consequent less stability.

For two days rounding the SW corner of Australia we met the waves sideways for the first time – and rolled marvellously for the first time – one needed the fence to keep one in bed. I thoroughly enjoy the motion on the boat – it is so slow and big - and never gives jerks leaving your middle in mid air as the channel boats do. We have also had a choice icy south wind which aided the roll. We tried to dance with the bad roll on – great fun seeing everybody suddenly being shot onto the rail or into the deckchairs – it requires great skill to keep going at all.

For the last three days we have been followed by albatrosses – they are marvellous birds. There are several kinds, the sooty, golden billed and I think the wandering, but some over 4 to 5 feet spread I should think. One or two Mother Carey's chickens play around with the albatross. The latter come within a few yards over and at the sides of the boat and one can see every feather. I spent an afternoon hanging onto some gear at the back of the boat taking photographs of them – a difficult business as it is not easy to keep one's footing unless propped up on something.

Today I sat in the sun for the first time since the Gulf of Suez. We had it cloudy between the Cocos Islands and Australia, but it is fine again now. I have great respect for the tropical sun – it does not look or feel much different from the summer mid day sun here, but I walked round the boat deck near mid day on the southern part of the tropics without a hat for five minutes, and the after effects were most unpleasant. People are justified in being extremely fussy about the sun. I bought a most superior sun helmet at Bombay with much extra assistance for use on the Reef.

Tell Bibs that Wadham has strewn letters to me all along the S coast of Australia!

In a week I shall be establishing myself up Mount Wellington. There is a hotel fairly high up with suitable streams near and I shall encamp there to start with. I can hardly realise I am nearly there – this boat almost feels like one's natural home it seems such ages since I got on it.

21

I hope all goes well at home – I don't say much as you know what I feel without my saying it, and you can take it for granted. I wish the posts were not so slow – I shall not get an interesting letter until about March or April I suppose.

I'm extremely well and positively fat and idle. I've exhausted all my sewing and books and nearly all my knitting wool so it's just as well I'm nearly there.

Lots of Love,
Sidnie

Letter 9

Rec⁴ 4/3/99

The Astor

Affiliated with Astor Farm
Telephone 1398

Macquarie Street, Hobart

January 22ⁿᵈ

Dear Family,

 Here I am after a two day scuffle from Adelaide. The boat berthed at 1 pm and I took the 4:30 pm train to Melbourne so that I could get to the Tasmanian boat and not keep Prof Flynn waiting any more for me. However all Port Adelaide is on strike or won't work on Sundays except two men and one truck on the quay for a 21,000 ton ship! My cabin trunk came off at once and it took me two and a half hours' bribery and persuasion to get my box lifted out of the hold on to the quay. The ship was using its own cranes but had no control over its own lasgars and none over two pig headed stevedores who seemed to rule the roost. Finally when the box did appear I had missed the last local train and had a 26/- taxi (three quarters of an hour drive) and just caught the train at Adelaide, my luggage being left behind to come by the next. In a local paper the first page was covered with lurid accounts of lack of work and starving women and children at Port Adelaide.

 The train reached Melbourne at 8 am the next day and the views out of the windows were fine. The only familiar plant was the pink flowering oleander one sees in Italy and the only animal not strange was the rabbit. I enjoyed it all – except the fare £4.10.0! In Melbourne I collected information etc at shipping and railway agents and collected my confounded luggage and caught the 3 pm boat. Melbourne

23

isn't such an awful hole as the other towns as regards buildings. It is astonishing to see such a small town of such pretentions built almost entirely on the tin shanty principle with nothing tidy or finished. They would be ghastly in our climate, but the brilliant sun and the flowers and trees cover a multitude of sins and save the situation.

The boat arrived at Launceston at 8:30 am – and a more pestilential boat I never struck. It is just an example of all the local Australian boats. When the government gave them the monopoly over inland passengers they converted all two berth cabins into four berth ones, put up the prices 30% ran half the number of boats and sold the rest of the fleet. No Australian can ever share a cabin with his wife on a boat. Well my boat was about two thirds to half the size of a channel steamer – all built up high with several narrow decks in the middle and nothing much by way of a keel – (presumably because they go 30 miles up the River Tamar). We had a stiff lateral wind from the west hitting us flat sideways – and I leave you to imagine the roll. I departed in the middle of dinner – in the middle of the fish to be precise – and went to bed and remained quite well – really a triumph for me! I don't think the motion was as great as on the Mooltan in rough weather, but it is so beastly sharp and sudden instead of being slow and controlled.

Finally I came on by train, a 5 hour run. The railways in Australia seem to be built with the least possible levelling, regardless of length of line necessitated by always running like this.

Tasmania in places might even be England, if you don't look too closely at the trees and see that they are mostly the ubiquitous gums. Today I saw some willows, a lombardy poplar and a gorse bush and I think a buttercup – great

24

excitement. Everything I've seen lately has been so entirely different.

Tomorrow I go up to Springs Hotel, three quarters up Mount Wellington (4,164 ft). Professor Flynn has been most awfully kind and has arranged everything for me – got me permits to go to good spots on mountain etc and is coming up there in 2 days to show me places and tracks and pools etc. Dr F is still stewing in the Mooltan and will come on in course of time. She won't stay with me long.

Hobart is a good spot, at least the country round it is and Mount Wellington is a fine lump.

There's no more news of note –

Lots of love,
Sidnie

PS I've just had dinner – 6:15 pm is the hour here – the folk all talk the most atrocious cockney - quite extraordinary to hear it all in a mass in a semi smart hotel.

I shall go to bed in a bed tonight – astonishing thought – in fact I find it difficult to take it in that I am really nearly as far away from you as I could be as the crow flies.

The View from Mount Wellington is the finest in Australia – and I shall look upon it for weeks – pleasant thought.

Letter 10

Springs Hotel
Mount Wellington
Hobart
Jan 27 1929
[received 11/3/29]

Dear Family,

This is one of the most wonderful places in the world. No snow about now, but the view is marvellous – I don't remember when I wrote last – I hope I have not already written from this address.

Professor Flynn is a perfectly delightful person and has done endless things for me. Everybody from the town clerk to the mountain ranger is clamouring to assist. The latter has instructions from the town hall to give me every help and see that I don't get lost in a mist etc. Professor Flynn even wrote to the steward on the Bass Straits boat and told him to look after me! Two days ago he came all the way up here and spent the night to make sure I was all right.

I have turned my room into a complete lab – all the inhabitants have been in on the sly to look at it! The place is a tea shop effect which revives the folk climbing up the mountain. It is 2,366 feet up and is the highest habitation. Mount Wellington is only 4,173 feet high but you get half of Tasmania map-like at your feet from the top.

It's just as well that I've got a functional pair of legs, as I have a stiff 1½ hours' climb to the top of a watershed, and then I go down the other side of the mountain to bogs and marshes and springs giving rise to streams which form one of the rivers.

Anaspides is abundant up there – but only quarter of the beasts are mature and it is a bit like looking for a pin in a haystack to hope to find its eggs in the weeds and moss. I've got tubs and a bath quarter of a mile away containing captive beasts which I hope may lay eggs. The temperature varies widely. Three days ago I was up there in a cotton frock and was terribly boiled – and today I had about four layers of

26

wool and your leather coat and was still cold – it was blowing an icy blast from the south west. Wind is a pestilence as it ruffles the water so. The water telescope you made is a great success – and quite invaluable.

Anaspides is almost the only beast in these streams and pools – he grows to 2" long and has been there unchanged geological ages before men were even thought of. He is quite incapable of fending for himself – can be killed instantly by a half inch caddis larva – I expect that this is why *Anaspides* has died out everywhere but here where he has no competitors.

I'm hiring a cinema camera to film *Anaspides* – last week we had a suitable day – sunny and no wind to ruffle the water – but heaven knows when another such day will turn up, and it is useless to attempt it otherwise. However I hope for the best.

I'm now in front of a gorgeous wood fire – hard gum wood which burns nearly as slowly as coal and gives out huge heat and wonderful smells. I'm awfully full of fresh air and my legs feel very stretched after a long day on top of the mountain.

The reef folk are fairly gasping in a permanent Turkish bath, heat and damp – it won't be so bad in March when I get there. It's been 106° in Melbourne, but was quite cool the day I was there.

Lots of love,
Sidnie

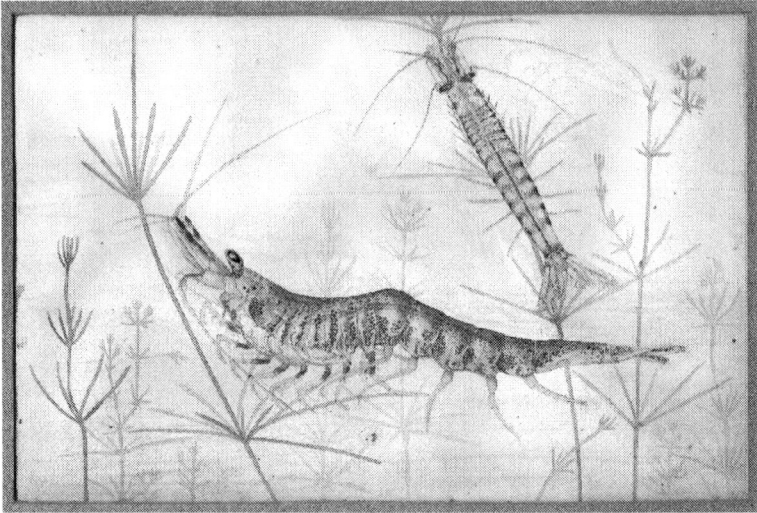

Anaspides,
water colour painting by SMM

Letter 11

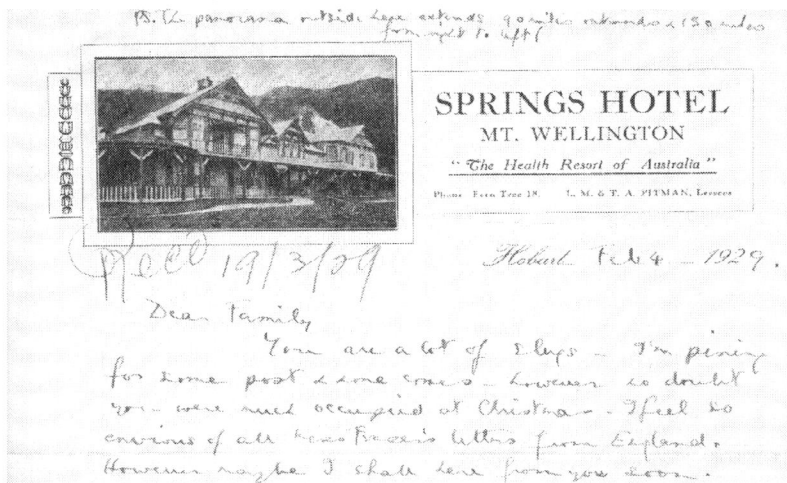

Springs Hotel
Mount Wellington
Feb 4 1929
(Rec'd 19 March)

Dear Family,

You are a lot of slugs – I'm pining for some post and none comes – however no doubt you were much occupied at Christmas. I feel so envious of all Miss Fraser's letters from England. However maybe I shall hear from you soon.

I'm still expanding much energy climbing this old mountain – to no effect, as far as embryos are concerned. I've now established running water tubs ¼ of a mile away well stocked with full sized beasts. The fishing thereof has been rather difficult owing to the weather. After two fine days it has hailed, rained, snowed, fogged, blown etc incessantly, and the beasts go into hiding instead of all being in evidence, and anyway there is a great minority of males of a good size. Yesterday was better – in fact half of it was quite fine. An economics professor from Hobart came with me to the top and I tried photographing the beasts close up. I worked the camera and he tickled the beasts into the field – it was rather fun, but the exposures were all wrong etc however I now know exactly how to do the job as soon as the sun reappears.

I had quite a following yesterday, also there came the ranger and friend, Dr Fraser and two folk from the hotel! Usually I'm alone. Last night I spent a night in Hobart in order to section some *Anaspides* at the university – I walked down – and a jolly fine walk it was too, through thickest 'bush' nearly all the way, with streams and waterfalls and giant tree ferns in the valleys sheltered from wind, and wonderful views over the sea and drowned valleys and back at Mount Wellington. I've taken quite a decent lot of photographs here – perhaps some too contrasty, but I expect printing on soft paper will make it all right. Everything is very contrasty to look at anyway.

The reef folk are pining for me to join them – it is like a perpetual Turkish bath there now, and will be till the end of March. They miss Dr and Mrs Russell (who left at the beginning of December) very much – and the loathsome pt II man from Cambridge I fancy is annoying them somewhat.

I'm now in front of a log fire of large dimensions – about three trunks 2'6" long – all hard gum wood which burns for ages and makes wonderful smells. They do one very well at this tea shop effect, their ideas on strawberries and raspberries and cream are good – more cream than fruit, and as much as ever you want.

Lots of Love,
Sidnie

PS. The panorama outside here extends 90 miles outwards and 130 miles from right to left!

Letter 12

Springs Hotel
Mount Wellington
Hobart
10 February 1929

My Dear Stubbins [her sister, a botanist],

    Just to say I've been <u>that</u> botanical – taken 17 successful close ups of the vegetation!! Flowers, trees, leafage etc – I've lugged about a tripod and black cloth and ground glass screen (which I fell down the mountain with and bust – since repaired). I don't know the names of some of the things yet. Tree Senecios galore grow here, up to 20'! I've got a fine negative of a grass tree, *Richea* sp after much exploration and gardening in the dense bush to get a photographable one – tree ferns 15' or more high are very difficult to take as you can't get away from them, all is so dense and incidentally dark. I've got fine close ups of Tea tree flowers – native lilac, heaths (which aren't heaths, at least aren't Ericaceae) in berry, saxifrages, gum trees, etc, also leaves of the myrtle – really evergreen beech, a lovely tree.

    I bet your boots the *Anaspides* lays its eggs in November – isn't it a curse however I'm making arrangements for hunting them up by locals and students next November. I've found the nearest approach to an albino variety of *Anaspides* in a certain stream! I have 4 nice negatives of *Thylacinus* [Tasmanian wolf, extinct since 1936] taken at the zoo – great thrills to see him alive. The T. devils [closely related to T wolf] were having such a scrap inside their house that I couldn't get them. However I must try again.

    The weather has pulled up its socks – instead of hail and snow we now have it 85° even up here; there must be a fug on in Hobart – it was 65° last night even!

    Dr Fraser has departed (quite a pleasant change! says she unkindly). Prof Flynn has been so useful he has now

31

gone to join his wife in Sydney and I shall see them again there where we intend to dance!

I've busted 30/- worth of cinema film on *Anaspides* – 4 minutes worth – not cheap enough as a plaything! I'm being very active and busy here – going off to the Great Lake in a week about.

I hope your job progresses nicely at Manchester.

Lots of love,
Sidnie

Letter 13

Springs Hotel
Mount Wellington
12 February 1929

Dear Family,

I am still here, but am going off to the Great Lake in a
few days – at least I hope so. There is some difficulty about
getting there as yet, but the manager of the hydro-electric
works is going to arrange something. The only inhabitants
there are connected with the power works. It will probably
be a wash out as far as *Paranaspides* is concerned. The beast
has never been found anywhere but the Great Lake, and they
have now raised the level 22' in the last eight years and the
beast is probably extinct. The country however is beautiful I
gather.

The last three days have been a wash out – buried in
cloud and very cold again, after several cloudless days at 84°.
The mist is lifting in places this evening. I've been using the
bad days by doing some coloured drawings of the two main
colour varieties of *Anaspides* – rather lurid efforts they are
too.

I've found a stream in an isolated position peopled by
an almost albino variety of *Anaspides*. At least they are
yellowy brown instead of being very dark. I shall not get any
embryos now. I'm sure that about November is the time.
However I have found ways of keeping the beasts healthy in
captivity and the mountain ranger will keep my menagerie
for me, and I shall leave a fund for bus fares for as many
students who can be persuaded to come up and hunt in
certain hopeful places.

I took dozens of photographs during the last few days
sun, and have seventeen good close ups of plants and
blossom etc. The vegetation is fascinating – it differs
extraordinarily at various heights. I am only beginning to
pick the picture to bits and recognise the various plants and
trees. There are so many species and all so new and strange
that for some time one simply takes everything as a whole. A

relation of our groundsel forms a tree 20 feet high here, a beech is evergreen with wonderful sculptured small leaves, mimosa trees grow immense and the species of gum trees are legion – likewise small flowering shrubs. Saxifrages form trees and heather climbers and so on. A gully full of tree ferns is a marvel – they grow up to 18' high and trunks a yard across, although they are usually smaller – great buttresses grow out as sharp edges when the trunks are not straight, the leaves (in a crown at the top) are each up to 9' long or more. They grow thickly cutting out all daylight. A path going through the gully - about half a mile long, is made of cut trunks of fern trees as thus

It's like walking on soft sorbo sponge. No wind gets down there, and here and there a shaft of sunlight gets in and lights up a mossy stream in which the birds of beautiful colours wash themselves. Otherwise it is absolutely silent. All birds are tame here – you can get within 2 yards of most of them. There is a wonderful blue wren – dorsally of kingfisher colours and a tail like this, literally.

These tree ferns survive even though they are covered in snow for long periods most winters.

I have not had any letters from you yet. I do so wonder how things go, and even when I do hear from you it will be six weeks old news.

Lots of love,
Sidnie

Letter 14

Springs Hotel
Tasmania
Feb 25 1929

Dear Family,

I had nearly given you up for dead and buried, after 5 weeks here and no post however a note from Bibs arrived today posted Jan 4th.

I've just had a marvellously wonderful week at the Great Lake – 3,330 feet high on the top of a mountain – 90 miles of shore and 17 miles long NS. It took a day to get there on the mail car, a stout 6 seater with a soft top and no luggage carrier, which took 11 large persons – 20 mail bags – endless luggage and parcels, newspapers etc – a revelation in what can be done. It rained most of the way, and did likewise at the lake – the wind making the water unavigable [sic] in a dingy. I was promptly adopted at the accommodation house there by two earnest fishers one 50 and t'other 40 years older than myself. They caught 6-10 lb rainbow trout and I paddled about the edges, and we lit fires in the rain – a great feat – and grilled chops and made 'billy tea' in the fine Australian style. Then along came a perfect dear of a man from the hydroelectric department with 25 miles of telephone wire – 1½ tons of cable etc and the fine weather. I went down the lake in their launch with the stuff to the north end – a day's trip with the loading and unloading. It was great fun. We had an awful job loading, as the waves swamped the dingy at the shore where the stuff was being taken on – and they got a rope mixed up with the launch's propeller, and a poor wretch had a chilly bathe in untangling it. However we got away with a good 'slop' on as they call it.

I started to feel peculiar at once, but devoted myself to feverish cutting up of food and bread for the seven men and hoped nobody noticed I wasn't eating anything – mercifully the wind dropped a bit and I was all right. The lake is fascinating – the level raised by a dam 22' in 8 years, and the gum forests are swamped – their head tops sticking out. The north end is most uncivilised. We slept in a primitive hut effect, and watched sheet and fork lightening play over the distant south end at night. I arose at 4:30 next day and went trawling from 5 – 8:30 for *Paranaspides* – reputed to be extinct. Fortunately with the aid of an aged boatman after 2 hours fruitless effort I found some. I'm vastly pleased, as no one has been able to get them for four years or so. We then came down the lake again in perfect weather, landed and cooked a wonderful lunch and reached the south end at 4 pm. The trout in the lake go up to 22 lb!!! They are not really good eating though.

Next day the hydro-electric man motored me back to Hobart by a longer route (140 miles) to see the scenery of the Derwent valley. Glorious weather – and we cooked another lunch. I got the beasts back here alive – a triumph as the low country was jolly hot and 60° is fatal to them.

I'm very busy – only a week to finish up now. My cinematograph effort of the *Anaspides* is successful so I'm going to use up a few more hundred feet of film by way of extension and padding as 100 feet only lasts 4 minutes (and costs 30/-).

Tomorrow and the next I shall leave all pretensions of work (for the first time) and am going with a girl to the Hartz mountains. We motor in her car for 2 hours and then start off with guide and packhorse there is a hut at the top where we sleep and then we return next day. I hope the clouds won't envelope us. Cloud here is the frigid limit. One sat down over Mount Wellington down to 1,400 feet for a week earlier in the month.

Everybody continues to be very kind and helpful – I never met such a place so full of really nice folk. I shall be very sorry to leave. I seem to have endless folk to see in Launceston – Melbourne and Sydney on the way north too. Prof *[Wadhorne]* late Cambridge is going to look after me in Melbourne, besides rows of other people.

As far as work is concerned I've had a successful time – although no trace of embryos as I'm at the wrong season.

However I've paved the way for the finding of embryos next November.

Excuse haste, but I never get a minute to write, it's late now and we depart soon after sunrise tomorrow, and my room is just chaotic – covered with bottles and tubes and tubs and jars and beasts all over.

I must stop and pack my rucksack, blankets etc.

Tell Bibs I've got another 12 botanical closeups.

Lots of love I hope all goes well,
Sidnie

Letter 15

Dearest Daddy,

Eureka – what ho loud cheers and hoots of joy – two letters from you dated Jan 8 and 15 have arrived. It's 10:30 pm – I've just got back after motoring 80 miles (each way), walking 28 miles going up and down 5,000 feet in the last two days. I'm dirty and in need of a new pair of leg muscles, but I hasten to reply before even removing my boots.

I hope you haven't been finding my letters heartless – I continually try and guess how things are with you – it's dreadful not knowing, and being six weeks behind with the news even when it does come. However it is a relief to have the good news of January 15th, and I only hope to goodness all goes well now. I'm terribly off the map here. I think of you all and wonder and hope – but there's no need for me to say things like that – you know it well enough. How I wish we had a telephone laid on, even for a minute. If only we were millionaires and you could be with me – all fit and well the lot of you. How Mother would delight in the 'bush' with its smells and plants and birds – the parrots are simply amazing – flocks of them as brilliant as you make them.

For my egotistic news – gosh the last two days have been great. Glorious weather – best two days for a month – got off with packhorse and a guide all right – and went up and up for eight miles through a track carved out of the solid bush. The sort of track that takes a gang of men one day to do 10 minutes worth. Giant gum trees – the biggest I've seen in the lower parts. We got up to the hut two hours before the moke [slang for donkey]. The hut is a two roomed wooden affair – full of unintentional ventilation and wooden bunks. By the time the guide arrived at 5 pm I had a fine log fire going and the billy can boiling. We had such a meal! Breakfasted at 7:30 and nothing since. Grilled chops, toast - spuds, bread and jam and gallons of tea. I'm the complete

Australian now – wise in making fires in the rain and grilling things and can dispose of unlimited amounts of billy tea and jolly good it is. At 7 pm we set out for a lake 1¾ miles up to set some lines for the 6 lb trout intended to swell the larder – as we couldn't get more than 5 chops for the lot of us by way of meat. The way the guide – who had not been up for 8 years, found the track back in the dark was a marvel – I thought we were hopelessly lost. Bush and scrub is the devil to get lost in as you can't see more than two yards. It was very cold at night but we kept warm. I cooked all that was cookable for breakfast at 6:30 this morning, and we moved off at 7:15 for the top. The Hartz range is a ridge while the Mount Wellington range has plateaux on top. We made the highest at 5,200 feet - at least I did with the guide and looked at the most wonderful view in Tasmania. To the east the Wellington range etc. and to the west fine mountains and uninhabited, unexplored and unknown land! We kept along the top of the ridge for a couple of hours with the view on either side – wonderful tarns, up to the size of several Serpentines 500 foot down and the country of the wildest. Few people ever get to the crest and look into the Unknown as we did. A hefty wind impeded our movements considerably. No snow this time of year, and no great height as mountains go, but they take a toll of life owing to cloud and blizzards.

We made the hut again for a late midday meal, and ate up nearly everything there being no trout on the lines – a monster (about 12 or more pounds having broken one line). We humped off the four hours back to Geeveston in the afternoon, passing dense groves of tree ferns low down the valley – and were entertained there to a good meal at 7 pm. We motored back from there – Geeveston by the way is entirely populated by the family of Geeves, and we saw the old boy who originally got up to the Hartz mountains and his son who cut the first track. Such it is in a young country full of undeveloped possibilities. The unexplored country we saw is going to be prospected for gold and rubidium in a few months – there being a good deal of both.

What luck we had – it's only possible to get up to the Hartz mountains in fine weather and we got it just right.

Sleep is upon me thick and fast so good night and lots of love,
Sidnie

Letter 16

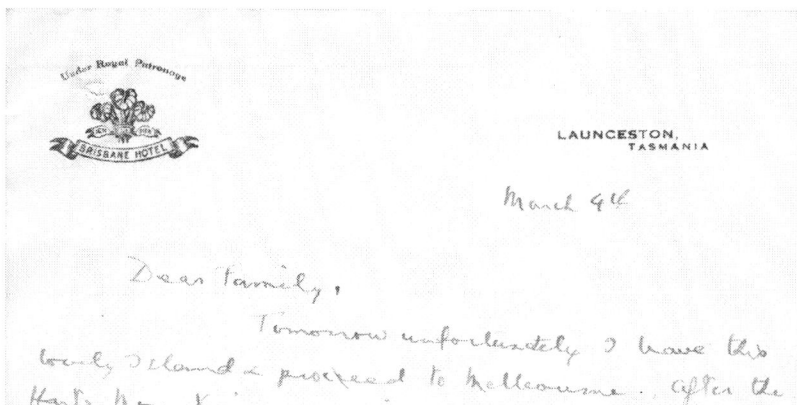

Brisbane Hotel
Launceston
Tasmania
March 4 1929

Dear Family,

Tomorrow unfortunately I leave this lovely island and proceed to Melbourne. After the Hartz Mountains excursion I had two more days on Mount Wellington and two nights in Hobart. Saturday was a fine day and I had a most enjoyable afternoon and evening picknicking [sic], bathing and dining with Mr and Mrs Gepp. Mr G being the worker of everything useful at the Great Lake, besides turning up from nowhere with a car just as I had heaps of rushing around to do in Hobart and only an hour and a quarter to do it in. They are such nice folk, it's sad that I shall probably never see them again. Here it rains in sheets – not much hope of doing much by way of seeing Mount Tasmania. I'm going now to look up an Old Cambridge Botanist, great friend of Mr Brooks, who is here with his wife with a government mycologist.

I'm having another row, with the Tasmania Railway Co. this time. The S. Australian railway stumped up £1.2.8 as the result of the row I had with them which lasted some weeks. I'm only after 3 bob [3 shillings] this time, but I object to being swindled under any circumstances.

Dad's letter acknowledging my second one has arrived.
I shall not get any more post for some weeks now – I should
reach the reef by March 22nd about. I'm going to Brisbane by
the Oriente 'Orford' – most posh – first deck cabin all to
myself on a second class ticket and no extra to pay, thence
two days by train – with a free pass, thereby saving about £17
on a return ticket, so that's all right.

Must stop – I hope all goes well –
Yours w lots of love,
Sidnie.

Letter 17

Port Melbourne
S.S. Orford
March 12 1929

Dear Family,

I've much neglected you of late – however this should get the mail if I can contrive to post it from the pier. Of all the 'fur lined' boats this takes the bun for more than oriental splendour – 20,000 tons and the star turn on the Orient Line as were the Mooltan and the Maloja on the P&O. I've a four post bed, wardrobe, chest of drawers – lots of space etc in a single cabin.

I've had a fine six days in Melbourne neatly wedged in between two heat waves – another starting today. I've lunched and dined out every day with somebody – been to huge official parties of various kinds, met heaps of people and inspected some descendants of Joe Manton [distinguished gunsmith, and probably a relation] who welcomed me with open arms. One lot owns a huge drapery store in the city and others are mostly engineers I gather. All most entertaining. I lunched with a charming elderly Mrs M whose husband, very aged, since deceased, was the grandson of Joe M. She said I was very like her son – an engineer aged 30 whom I did not see. There was yards about me in the Melbourne papers and they tracked me down from that. The Manton petrol vendors round Perth aren't anything to do with these folk.

I did so enjoy seeing Mr Wadham again – I should probably have been very bored without him to arrange everything and take me about. On Friday we motored out to an apple orchard run by an old Cambridge friend of his, and very interesting it was too to see trees perfectly grown on good soil when there are no frosts, and pests kept down scientifically i.e. American blight very effectively done in by an introduced wasp which parasitizes the aphids, and you find groups of dried aphid skins with a hole in each.

Melbourne is a jolly fine place – I wouldn't half mind exchanging for a couple of years sometime with the senior lecturer here – a woman if it could be worked. I shall find our climate mouldyer (I can't spell it) than ever when I get back. The sun is so good here.

I must stop and try and find a post box.

Lots of love – looking forward to letters from you on the Reef,
    Sidnie

T.S. MAIRANA DILSTON R. TAMAR TAS.

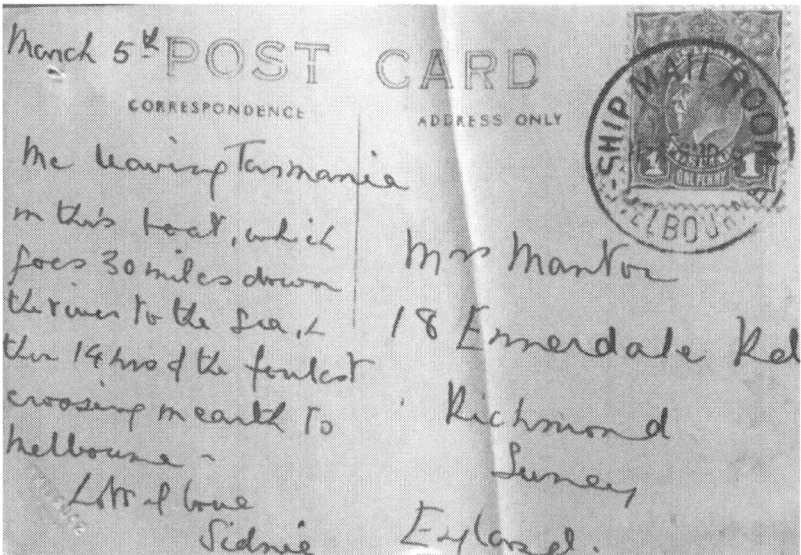

March 5th POST CARD

CORRESPONDENCE   ADDRESS ONLY

Me leaving Tasmania
on this boat, which
goes 30 miles down
the river to the sea, &
then 14 hrs of the foulest
crossing on earth To
Melbourne –
        Lots of love
                Sidnie

Mrs Manton
18 Esmerdale Rd
    Richmond
        Surrey
    England.

46

Letter 18

Orient Line
England & Australia
S.S. Orford
March 13 1929

Stubbins,

    – I forgot to mention that one box of plates and one envelope of films have already been printed, so don't have them done again - they're labelled.

    The more than oriental splendour of this boat is phenomenal!

    It was good to see Wadham again – I did not recognise him on the quay at first, as he has grown a moustache and got a new hat, and it was 9 am after 14 hours of the foulest crossing – I just wasn't properly sick, and it takes so long to recover then so I was fairly parboiled. I wish I could take life as philosophically as he does – however I am gradually coming to my senses at last.

    Life is expensive here – in spite of endless hospitality and comparatively cheap accommodation I've got through over £70 in the last seven weeks – gosh.

    I hope your job is proving bearable in spite of the climate. I can well understand folk coming here and stopping, and refusing to return to our sunlessness.

    Lots of Love Old Bean

Letter 19

Orient Line
England & Australia
S.S. Orford
March 13 1929

Dear Family,

I only had time for a very hurried note yesterday – I had a fair scuttle round to catch the boat, my beastly luggage by then having been split up into three lots in various parts of Melbourne – it would be simple enough without my vast cases of apparatus etc.

I dined t'other day with one of the Great Lake fishers and his wife – he is a dear old fellow – a publisher, and I am going to write him a few pages about the lake shrimps for a vast book on fishing he is writing. Likewise he is going to reproduce some full page coloured drawings of mine of *Paranaspides* and *Anaspides* I did them for fun in Tasmania, thinking they wouldn't be of any practical use as no scientific journal can afford colours. Mr and Mrs Critchley Parker are coming to London next winter to fix up about printers for the plates etc which will be done in Edinburgh – and will thus be of the best.

I've just written an article for a Melbourne popular natural history journal about my shrimps, I must try and snaffle a typewriter on the ship somewhere, and post it tomorrow from Sidney [sic]. The thing to do is to get up and see the sunrise as we enter Sidney harbour tomorrow. I get two days in Sidney, two in Brisbane, two in Cairns – always supposing the railway from Brisbane to Cairns will function. It has been mainly collapsed for two months owing to floods after a five year's drought and now parts of North Queensland are being washed away. My correspondence north is largely done by wire! It will take me eight days to get to Low Island from Brisbane even if all goes well! It is pretty hot now – about 94° and very damp at that. The wet season north is nearly over so that I shall only get the tail end of it, which is just as well when one is not acclimatised to tropical conditions.

This boat is truly wonderful, same tonnage as the Mooltan with twice as much passenger accommodation – beautifully furnished and a good library full of travel, biography and decent books. The boat appears empty with only 150 passengers. It's the tenth fastest liner in the world – doing 21 knots against the Mooltan's 16. I don't think deck cabins are worth having. I far prefer the other kind which are very much quieter and I prefer a port hole with a draught catch sticking out of it to a window opening onto the deck and a spout of forced draught.

I must try and grub up a typewriter so good bye – I hope all goes well - with lots of love
Sidnie.

Letter 20

Orient Line
England & Australia
S.S. Orford
Approaching Brisbane
March 17 1929

Dear Family,

I'm thus far – with twelve other passengers instead of 1,600 which they started with. However I have no use for deck cabins and first class luxuriance, I was far more comfortable 2nd class P&O. What is good on this boat is 3rd class – the saloon is better than the P&O 2nd. If I come out again ever and have to pay myself I shall go 3rd on a new Oriente [sic] boat for £45 single instead of £90 2nd or £140 1st.

I had a jolly two days in Sidney, and finished up with a dance with Professor Flynn & Co and was deposited back on the boat just before it sailed at midnight. As usual I was entertained for every meal except breakfast! This is a little world – quite by accident I met one of the elderly G. Lake fishermen, Simpson by name here – there are 1¼ million people in Sidney. Moreover he met you at the City Rifle Club and knew about your musketry instructing during the war.

The coast has been in sight all day – very variable – distant mountains, cliffs, white sandy bays etc, now mostly blotted out by deluges of rain on the coast although no rain at sea. Never have I seen such rain as the second day in Sidney - huge rivers rushing down the streets, cataracts pouring down flights of steps, I could believe any number of inches fell. By the way Low Island may get 15 inches of rain in a day at times!! However I shall have missed most of that. I get three days in Brisbane now, as we left Sidney 12 hours early and arrived one day earlier. I should far prefer to have had more time in Sidney.

I've fixed my passage home – leave Brisbane July 22nd by Dutch S. Packet – arrive Surabaya [Java] August 3rd leave

Singapore August 23rd P&O. China boat with the option of breaking my journey again at Suez and taking the next boat a fortnight later arriving at Marseille September 28th and so home overland. If I'm not broke I shall do Egypt – I've got lots of information about getting to Luxor and back and doing the Valley of the Kings and the Queens and Tutankamen's tomb in 5 days from Cairo at a not too devastatingly inclusive cost – I forget what but under £10.

I must stop and do my washing before I reach the tropical weather – it is now cooler than in Melbourne when I left, and I expected to be fried in Sidney by all accounts. However the thermometer goes up.

Lots of love,
Sidnie

Letter 21

Womens College
Brisbane
March 18 1929

What ho folks,

Here are some prints of the first photos I took, not much good – all my others are heaps better – the plates were developed on the equator ass that I was [sic] – hence the bubbling of the gelatine.

It's good and hot here, giant bamboos, palms, stags horn ferns etc all luxuriant and out of doors – masses of brilliant tropical butterflies as big as plates, all the houses on tin covered posts to keep clear of white ants – below the house one has the laundry, keeps the car and a thousand other things.

I'm being put up at the above for three nights while waiting for the train – all very nice. No fireplaces in the houses here, and all have verandas to sleep on and mosquito nets and incomplete room partitions to get a good blow out in the summer. We had a marvellous storm after my arrival yesterday – even beat the rain at Sidney which is saying a lot. I buzzed about the university today, was given free rail tickets and an allowance for 3 cwt [hundredweight] of luggage – likewise very nice. I so wish you were all here too to see this wonderful old world and all. The rail journey should take 2 days – Dr Fraser took 2 weeks owing to floods etc – so I hope for the best. I hope that all goes well – I'm looking forward to post on the Reef.

Lots of love,
Sidnie

Letter 22

Strand Hotel Cairns
March 22 1929

What ho Folks,

 Here I am in the most swagger hotel in the place, most tropical and full of gadgets for keeping cool. I <u>was</u> glad to get out of the train at 6:30 pm after 3 days and 2 nights of it – a slow, rickety, square wheeled, springless, uncomfortable seated, very smutty and insecty contraption. The windows are huge and fans are provided, but what with the insects 1) already there, 2) ones one brings in, 3) that come in at the window, I was chewed to bits – not to mention being hove out at 5:30 am to breakfast in stations etc. However I wouldn't have missed it for the world. It was the second train able to get through to Cairns for some time. It was still, sunny tropical weather, difficult to believe that an average of 1" a day rain has fallen since January 1st. The storms I hit in Brisbane had fairly caught the place – rained 2" in 10 minutes, 31" in 24 hours and blew off rooves [sic], blew in walls and windows and wrecked the power lines etc.

 From the train I saw forests of palms and gum trees or both mixed – cleared land for pineapples, sugar, paw paws etc. Further north wild and cultivated bananas, numerous huge rivers and ponds full of blue waterlilies, vast deep water gullies with luxurious vegetation, then today through real jungle dense with climbers, epiphytic ferns, orchids and everything imaginable - in places the air must have been nearly saturated, (<u>wet</u> bulb thermometer had been at 100°!!) One felt that the water could be squeezed out of the air as out of a sponge. It's a wonderful journey, only opened up to Cairns for the last 4 years. There were fine wood wagons too with 20 bullocks each bringing wood from the jungle.

 It's funny to be only 40 miles (by sea) from my destination after just three months of travelling on and off. I ate paw paw for 'tea' here, rather disappointing – really good custard apple is jolly fine, and I think passion fruit is the most delectable thing the almighty has ever produced.

This isn't really a very swish hotel, but in this land of corrugated iron and jungle and oceans of sugar cane ones standards are different. You should also see the numerous crowd of folks who travel first class too – where they get the money I can't imagine.

I carry round cool weather wherever I go – I haven't had it really hot yet and have exactly missed the heat everywhere. Nothing here yet equals Naples in a super heatwave on a really hot Italian train – bar the last twelve hours today.

There is a slight tropical shower on now – you can't hear yourself think for the noise on the roof (iron of course) or see a yard through it.

The way darkness deposits itself of a sudden like is quite uncanny. In fact I could go on for ever telling you about things here all so different from at home.

I've got three days here then by local steamer to Port Douglas and then I shall be collected, with food, by the expedition's boat. I'm now going to try and bag a bathroom and have a grand wash of myself and clothes – it is hard to say which is blacker.

I've quite lost track of when the mail goes, you may get several letters at once.

I hope you all flourish –

Lots of Love,
Sidnie

PS Aren't mosquito nets beastly things to sleep under.

March 23

Still vastly wet and cloudy, how lucky to have had it fine in the train – cooler than they've had it for months – must be well below 90° by the feel of it, excessively damp, everything indoors oozes water (and ants incidentally). All the water used in houses comes off the roof and is stored in tanks – to do the washing they never put water in the copper, always take some out only!

Letter 23

STRAND HOTEL
CAIRNS
N Q

Cairns,   March 25 1929

Dear Family,

I sail at 7 am tomorrow, and should be on Low Island before dark. It has been hot with a vengeance since I wrote. In two nights and a day of intermittent showers we had 14¾ inches of rain – the town was flooded, shops inundated etc – but they are used to it! The way it drains away is astonishing, as it only drains actively at low tide.

Yesterday – Sunday was fine, I took a train effect up to Kuranda, 1,000 ft up a valley to some vast falls on the Barron River. The carriages are a sort of open work, and you eat the engine's smoke in going through the 15 tunnels on the first 20 miles of rail – however the views are wonderful the rail being the only method of getting up to Kuranda, the steep sides of the valley being densely wooded, each tree different from the next, and the lot firmly tied together with tropical climbers. The black aboriginals all travel first class on the railway. The head of the valley is blocked by rocks and over this dashes a mighty river. The station at Kuranda is like the tropical fern house at Kew – rows of tubs and above them rows of hanging baskets growing every conceivable kind of maidenhair, filmy, staghorn and other ferns and delicate plants. From there I walked one and a half miles back to the falls – fairly hot – excessively steamy – the butterflies were marvellous – and I saw the big blue Morpho ones coming out of a clearing in some dense jungle. I went back to Kuranda, a minute village, and had a very expensive lunch at a scrubby hotel. The afternoon was spent in sleeping under a tree, and in playing with sensitive plants and watching the birds and butterflies, such things vastly please my childish mind. The sensitive plants are wonderful.

Today was hotter than ever. I walked solidly this morning for three hours along tracks through thinnish forest, passing mangrove swamps by the sea, and wonderful water below the trees full of blue waterlilies whenever a bit of sky was uncovered over the water. Palms and all sorts of queer trees are everywhere. They are quite different from the xerophytic gum tree type of vegetation I've seen in other parts of Australia. Cycads grow 20 feet high here too. Not only did I drip perspiration but my saturated garments did likewise! This afternoon I spent spread out with no clothes on in my room in a draught leaving a wet patch wherever I was. It's a spot cooler this evening and my top garment isn't very damp for once.

The noises here are strange – the jungle certainly is quiet, but the parrots and other birds at sunset make a deafening noise for 1 hour before going to roost, and then the cicadas and crickets and locusts begin – I'm sure you would hear a big cicada half a mile away – and the frogs in the swamps are as noisy as the parrots, and as varied or more so in notes. I must wash my wig - or try to, and then pack so good night.

Lots of love,
Sidnie

56

Letter 24

G.B.R.E.
Low Island, Nr Cairns
N. Queensland
March 30 1929

Well folks,

And I did mean to remember your various birthdays, and it now being the very end of March it's a bit late in the day. However there were all sorts of good intentions. I've been here 5 days – mostly spent in marvelling at this spot and in learning new animals at great speed. At the moment I'm trying to catch up with the party's seven month experience beginning with the ABC. The amount they've done and the bright and intelligent things they're at is astonishing, and a little overpowering at first when you plunge into the middle of it armed with abysmal ignorance. They work jolly hard too, I'm too much under the desire to sleep to do nearly as much as they do, but I hope to get acclimatised quickly.

Low Isle - Lighthouse and Roofs of Laboratories
and Accommodation

The island is not a real island – it is toy, made in an absent minded moment by the Almighty – it is quite round, sea, then an even steep beach of coral sand, then a ring of brilliant green bushes flat at the top four foot high – then a ring of huts and sheds and habitations with alleys cut in the bushes and the lighthouse in the middle with coconuts and other palms and trees.

We feed at 8 am, 1 pm and 6 pm – many folks get up at 6 am to do laundry or work in the lab, and they are at it all day up to any hour at night. The season is past for low tides only at night – they all worked at night then with lamps. The tides here are quite mad – low at 6 or 11 am or later anytime – never at 8 till 10 am – remains low for three tides running missing out a high tide, gets high tide 2 hours after a low – and does a sudden hiccough over 6 hours skipping then, and plunging into a spring tide – all this complicates ones calculations. The food is very well wangled – very little tinned stuff, a refrigerator provides cool drinks twice a day and keeps the butter solid etc. It has not been too hot, just nice, one wears a bathing dress or shirt and shorts well rolled up in all directions and bare feet about the camp – all is sandy and shoes would be impossible. Outside if fine I have to wear stockings as my skin isn't sun proof and some chinese boots I got in Cairns are fine for walking rather wading [sic] about the reef. It has not been very sunny so far – heaps of rain on and off – the wet season theoretically should be over but it shows little sign of departing. The coastline is visible and very fine too, and is mainly clothed with deluging clouds – it's far less wet here than on the mainland. The temperature is fine, not too hot and clothes superfluous day and night, really delightful. It has been very hot here – highest sea temperature was 37° that's about 99°F. It's only about 26-28°C now.

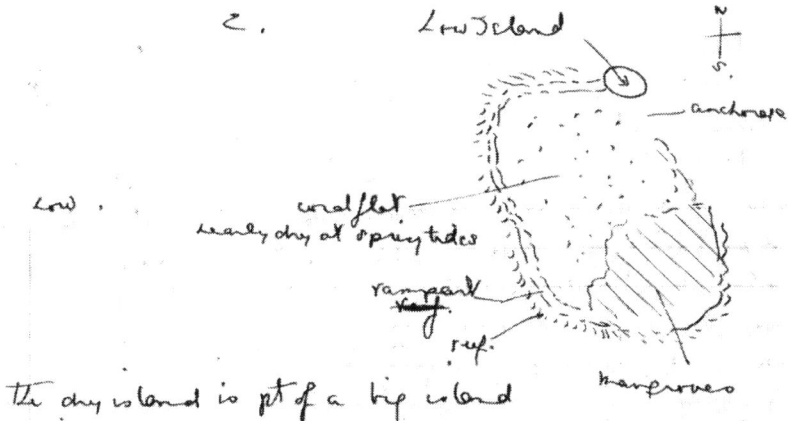

The dry island is part of a big island mainly underwater with a mangrove swamp, partly dry at one end, a fringing reef all around except for a deep anchorage at the NE. Outside the rampart round the edge, formed of dead broken coral the ground slopes at once deep to the lagoon all round. Just inside the rampart is a moat a few feet deeper than the 'flat' rich in corals.

The colours of things are marvellous, brilliant corals, clams of huge size – up to 2 feet, they are big bivalves sitting with wide open mouths the inside all frills of the richest and most brilliant tints imaginable and every one differently coloured and patterned. One has to be careful not to put a foot inside a clam: small coral fish equally brilliant abound and likewise crabs. Sea urchins are lovely – spines of multi colours up to 10" long and so on.

I am going to help the 'reef party' work, leaving the boat party and the physiologists alone. They have given me a fortnight in which to become a coral expert as far as identifying the corals found here is concerned! At spring tides I shall be out on the reef identifying and counting and mapping the distribution of reef animals in various places of different kinds – also collecting and pickling crustacea for them. During neaps I shall play about with feeding mechanisms and food of reef crustacea, and on starting some work in watching budding in corals. The latter will be fun as it fits into other work being done by Stephenson. He has succeeded in rearing small corals from larvae – the first time it's ever been done, and seeing how they grow. He wants me to help him over working out the internal embryology leading up to the larvae the year after next on material preserved here, and if I find out something about growth in large colonies here it will complete the whole life history of a coral – hitherto unknown or only inferred from the skeleton. The two universally quoted conditions for coral growth – i.e. clear water and brilliant light are a complete washout – <u>neither</u> are necessary. The symbiotic algae in the corals are amazing, during the day they make so much O2 that the sea contains over 200% oxygen !! At night the O2 in solution falls again. During the rains the sea water gets to 50% its proper salinity and the coral doesn't mind! The rate of deposition of sediment here is great, but the corals keep clean by powerful ciliary action all over the outside.

I spent the afternoon out in a boat pumping air to somebody diving after sediment pots and all sorts of gadgets in up to 4 fathoms of water. It started to pour so I did not go down myself. It takes a lot of practice to be good under water. Judging distances are so deceptive. The diving gear is simply a weighted helmet and a bathing dress with ordinary light boots.

The Diving Helmet and A.P. Orr

Everybody is very well - bar cuts and scratches which get in a mess and do not heal readily in this amphibious existence. A more cheery lot of folk I never struck, everybody gets on well with everybody else, and the Oxford and Australian folk are nice – we number 12 now.

Yesterday found me making concrete slabs with holes in them with the help of a willing aboriginal. On to the slabs go the corals and the slabs fit on to a wooden pin affair half a mile out along the reef. The same minute area of growing point can then be examined at intervals with a binocular [microscope] to see how budding happens in the soft parts.

We have a white boatman and motor boat for stores and long excursions – otherwise aboriginal labour in the form of a good cook and three boys, and one or two men occasionally. The two black children are most amusing and love bringing in the food and taking away the plates at meals.

The good wood used for huts is wonderful – mostly silky oaks, 'oaks' (ie eucalyptus), cedar etc – all hard and finely figured – you get an odd bit of wood for a packing case or something rough, and they give you cedar or something really superior.

This is a slack Sunday - only every other Sunday can be a holiday, as folk are always busy at spring tide Sundays. I shall not have much time to write usually - but I will try to write every week - or as often as the stores get sent for – post day is a great event here as you may well believe.

I hope your mouldy winter is getting over and that you are being out and about – I was pleased to get your letters and Mothers. I don't expect I have given you in the least an adequate idea of this place etc or answered questions that come to your minds. I'm very well and being careful not to tread on poison fishes or sea urchins, both of which lay you out for 7 weeks or so. I must go to bed,

Lots of love,
Sidnie

Interior of the laboratory on Low Island

Letter 25

Dear Family,

No post by this week's boat – however I expect you were busy or nothing much to say. I haven't much to say - or rather don't know whereabouts to start. Today was a typical busy day with a spring tide – I was dug up at 6:15 am to muck about with crab's gonads – a weekly expenditure of energy chasing out breeding seasons, breakfast at 8, incidentally the tide was so up that I had to swim for the crab basket tied to a slab of concrete. Then I tinkered around cleaning out coral aquaria, packed baskets of labelled bottles and tubes and hammers and chisels and nets and grub and tin openers and heavens knows what – went out to fetch the boat in a fearful craft known as the 'flattie' – a hefty kind of punt effect. Got started at 10:30 – three of us rowed across to the mangroves – had a premature lunch at about 11:30, rather than carry food, and spent till about 3:30 in smelly mangrove swamps, queer coral shingle banks, alleys of open water between and under the mangrove trees etc catching crabs and other beastly creatures. We pursue such madness every spring tide getting a general survey of animals and plants growing all over the 'island' in various types of bottom. We were up to our knees in mud at times, and the sandflies were fairly obnoxious. White herons abound all round the mangroves fishing on the flat. They are lovely beasts. Other birds come over from the mainland nine miles away for fishing at low tide and then go back again. The rest of the day was spent pickling beasts and other silly ass jobs, and we made cocoa and went to bed. In the mangrove waterways is a beastly fat sting ray, about 5 foot long we have to hastily climb up the roots of the trees until the brutes can be persuaded to shift where they occupy the whole water space.

April 7

Today was spent on the Reef intensively investigating corals – dressed in a shirt, bathing dress, stockings, boots and topee – a queer mixture. I'm just recovering from an awful sunburn on my legs, and now the red has subsided they aren't a bit browner than before – my arms are now sun proof, but goodness knows how long the rest of me will take to get immune, and it's such a painful process. Distinguishing corals is a fearful game, so many are so alike. The other animals mixed up with the corals are wonderful. *Synapta* 5 foot long all gorgeous patterns (Bibs will know what the name means), like a sea snake with tentacles at one end; perfectly ridiculously shaped fish, one like this from above

eye ⟶ ⬭ tail
fin.

patterned brilliantly like a curtain brain coral; heaps of angel fish like the zoo ones, only lots of different sorts; fish that blow themselves up like balloons when they see you and lots of little ones like streaks of rainbows an inch or two long.

The temperature is just lovely, all underclothes unnecessary and one is seldom if ever too hot, even if sitting in a puddle on the reef in the sun, as a wind usually blows. The sea water is warmer than the air now, and the thermometer is between 84° and 90° all the time. The rain has stopped the last two days and the air is drier and altogether pleasanter - one feels so floppy in very damp air.

I will write a proper letter next Sunday which is a Sunday off, being neap tides. No time for more now –

lots of love,
Sidnie

65

The Library

Letter 26

G.B.R.E.
Low Island
Nr Cairns
April 14 1929

Dear Family,

I hope you all flourish as I do and that spring is more or less upon you. Here it is glorious tropical winter, not hotter than 82° today, fairly sunny, windy and no rain for the last few days. This is my 'every other Sunday off' at least this afternoon of it was. This morning before lunch, it being a [mossy] neap tide, I went out with the folk diving to do the weekly collection of sediment pots and various gadgets from the bottom of the shallower water. I did a prodigious amount of pumping for the experts, and then went down for about 10 mins myself in about 15 feet of water. It was simply marvellous, the water previously had been murky with sediment etc brought down by the flooded Daintree River 12 miles away or so. Today it was clear, and the sun shone down, and swarms of large and small fish, striped and wonderful colours swam about one and in the coral. I find it very difficult to walk about, I can keep upright easily, but it is difficult to get a push off with a foot as you try to walk, I finally swam partly horizontally just over the corals, much to the experts' amusement who were watching me with a telescope. Doubtless I shall learn in time. It would be no use sending me down for 2 hours to collect marked corals just yet! However I can judge distance much better now. The colours of the corals are much brighter in deeper water than in the moats and exposed parts of the reef, where browns predominate with spots of brilliant colour on the polyp mouths (which may be 1 mm – 2 cm across). The diving helmet restricts ones range of vision and one wants to see much further through the water than the light permits.

I'm feeling vastly clean, having had a bath and washed my wig – there has not been time for either for ages – it having been spring tides for ten days. I'm always getting soaked in the sea intentionally or otherwise – one leg is now sunproof, but t'other is very sore over an area that got burnt after shedding sheets of skin. The atmosphere is much drier now and I no longer feel floppy as in the damp. I've been up early most days, and out in the reef every day. The other 'shore party' as I believe I've said have been making a general survey of fauna and flora, the whole place being mapped. Dr F and self are doing a detailed survey of a couple of strips one yard wide and about 200 yards long from the outer seaward slope across the rampart and moat to the 'flat'. It's a long job – we do 12 to 30 yards a day during spring tides. I'm getting quite expert at coral identification - many of which are new and of interest quite apart from the survey (which includes algae and corals only). In June some of us are going to Lizard Island (NW of here) for two weeks and we shall do rapid similar jobs for comparison with this place. The ship survey is a two handed (really three handed) job, I have a writing shelf tied on to me, likewise string and labels and write lists and tie labels on to doubtful corals to take back, and dig up things with hammer and chisel. The adding up of lists, identifying and the making of maps and graphs occupies much time - not to mention the curing of a double type collection of corals. You mentioned my companion in your letter of last mail – frankly I had seen more than enough of her before reaching Low Island, and now we share a room and work together. She is by far the least congenial member of the party to my temperament, and very slow in uptake and action over work, and being 20 years my senior it's not quite seemly for me to be always bossing the show – work or travel. However it can't be helped and we get on all right. During neap tides I work alone thankfully. Unfortunately nobody else can come to Java, being bound by free [?] tickets or lack of time or funds not to go that way, or having arranged to go other routes for particular reasons. I am undecided still whether to have a fortnight in Ceylon with Hilda Roversi an old school friend of mine who owns a car, or to have a fortnight in Egypt mostly by myself.

Nothing much has happened of note – the week's meat supply was washed overboard en route to the island last Tuesday in a rough sea, but a fish trap (in the stocks for months), was just finished and proved very effective, the first night trapping a fish 5 feet long which was quite good eating. The black boys spear coral fish too, but it takes them a long time. Normally we get little fish, as it takes too long to catch, and we do not really have much tinned stuff.

I am sending you some reports of the work etc here which may interest you – please keep them for me. I have taken a few photos – mostly bad compared with my nice Tasmanian ones, the light strength is poor owing to thick water vapour in the air, and one needs big exposures, tropical light tables are useless and so to bed,

lots of love,
Sidnie

Surveying in the 'Flattie'

Letter 27

G.B.R.E.
Low island,
Nr Cairns
Australia
April 17 1929

Dearest Daddy,

Yesterday was mail day, and your letter was ever so welcome – I was wondering if a letter should come as I had one by the last mail. I'm writing now as it is 7:45 pm and I've done for today, and this does not happen when spring tides are on. We have had a marvellous sunset – I walked round the island after 'tea', it was getting dark and the high land (<5,000 ft) on the mainland stood out fine and dark against a brilliant sunset sky in the far distance and the darkish sea between us and the mainland. At that time last night or a little earlier we were all collected on the shore and the lighthouse keepers' families and the aborigines waiting for the supplies to be rowed off the launch in various 'flatties' – stout flat bottomed craft characteristic of these parts. Everybody carries packing cases of food etc up the coral sand beach to the lab or store, and then the 'tea' gets cold while we eagerly sort the post bags. The meal is usually a silent one, everybody being immersed in letter reading with their thoughts far from the limited horizon of Low Island.

You say that there is no news, but it is a relief to hear that things are as they are – or were six weeks ago when your letter was written. I do so hope that you will continue to have some relaxation and change in the form of golf and bridge occasionally. I hope the housekeeper lady continues successfully. I've been seeing rather aged English papers since I arrived here and see that Miss Phillpotts appears in the New Year's Honours [she was Mistress of Girton College].

In two or three weeks I will try and send you some prints of photos from here, I've ordered paper from Sidney which will arrive in time. I made a mess of a lot to start with, what with developer not functioning well at high

71

temperatures, and the light not being photographically intense. I can't understand the latter – it's not more bright than in Tasmania, although it skins you, and tropical light value tables are useless.

Tonight is positively cold – the thermometer has gone down with a bang to 75°, a heavy wind blows and I've had to put on a vest since 6 pm. The tides are quite mad – in 5 days last week they moved 1½ hours – then stood still for 2 days – today was low at 12 am and again at 3 pm, and springs are beginning after 3 days neaps.

I've now got over my bad sunburns and am venturing forth without stockings, the snag is one's good cultivated brown hide peels off in vast sheets and you have to begin again. I'm quite acclimatised now and this autumn weather is truly perfect, literally not too cold and I never get boiled or even sticky to any extent even doing strenuous jobs such as rowing, or carrying tubs of water and corals up and down the shore etc. I must stop now and make up two huge stone jars of 10% formalin. Maybe I shall have time to go on with this later.

April 22

Two marvellous days, yesterday and today – sunny – blazing sun for the first time (usually there is a haze about) and no wind. The latter was marvellous as one can then really see through the water. I took a pile of photographs of corals etc in the water yesterday and today, and they are really excellent, the best taken here, as I've never seen better. It was jolly hot out standing in the sun from 12 till 4:30 pm on the reef, but I don't notice heat now – I hardly notice if my one and only layer of clothes is dry or wet with perspiration. My legs and arms are the darkest brown I've seen in any of our family, but my hands aren't burnt, at least not in comparison. Last night I was sitting in the moonlight outside the lab – one could read by it, laboriously washing dozens of negatives: quite a pleasant occupation, as the honey birds fly about and look like shooting stars as they pass through the beams of light from the lighthouse. Yesterday and today I had a real good swim – for the first time - the water is over 80° - just fine.

Our fish trap continues to provide food – of not quite such a disgusting variety – we had 5 fish to 30 lb yesterday, and very good they were, far better than the 28 lb monsters. How the latter get into the trap is wonderful - it is unbaited, and inside one finds huge fish wider than the entrance and curled up as it is not long enough for them!

The heat the last two days has a queer effect on appearances. All islands, cliffs etc which are really ……appear…..and finally the islands look aerial…..when the air gets warmed up enough. It's quite uncanny.

Soon I become head cook and bottle washer – at least housekeeper here, as the Yonges and two others go to Thursday Island, four others to an island north of Cooktown, leaving me to cope for the family left behind, it's Mrs Yonge's job really. You can imagine me doling out stores etc to the aboriginal 'cook', and cooking things etc myself.

Lots of love,
Sidnie

73

Low Isle at Low Tide

Letter 28

GBRE
Low Island
Nr Cairns
April 17 [her sister Irène's birthday]

Dear Stubbins,

Just to wish you many happy returns of the day 6 weeks late! As I didn't remember to write so that you got the post by the 17th I am doing it the other way round! It is 8 pm here, so that it will morning in Manchester – what ho – and you must be toddling along for your 10 o'clock lecture, while my day's work is done.

I enclose your Genetical Soc notice – that ought to larn yer about not giving them a changed address! I warned you as to the effect!

I hope your job proves not too bad and that the folk are as nice as they promised to be. If only you were here – I have to work with the F woman, and she is such a mug. We are doing a detailed survey of algae and corals yard by yard along certain strips, and you and I could do it so much more expeditiously. As it is I do all the identifying of both and three quarters or more of the work involved. However it just can't be helped as it is a two handed job and there is no one else. I am even feeling lukewarm about Java, I would far prefer to go alone, or with you or Nic, the latter would be really great. However nothing of that sort happens, does it.

I wish you could rise to a little correspondence occasionally, I did so appreciate the letter and a half I have had from you in the last 4 months.

Post is a great thing on an island like this where most things remain the same after you have first got used to the place and its ways and acclimatised to the atmospherics.

I'm doing mainly donkey and team work here, *Squilla* [a crustacean, genus of mantis shrimps] is nearly impossible to catch and not breeding at that, and the only crustacean available for feeding mechanisms are crabs and I hate them and their habits are not significant anyway.

Everybody here is very nice - I see lots of the Stephensons who are dears, and Miss Marshall and Mr Orr from Millport are very nice. Two mad and jolly souls - Michael and John from Oxford liven things up wonderfully. It is a great picnic in many ways - only not so picnicy as one might expect as there is such an atmosphere of work about, even if we are vastly frivolous over it at times. Michael nags Anne perpetually to everybody's joy. Maurice and Mattie (Yonge) are just off to Thursday Island, leaving me to housekeep with the aboriginal cook!

I must stop.

Lots of love,
Sidnie

Letter 29

Great Barrier Reef Expedition
Low Island
Nr Cairns NQ
[April 29, crossed out] May 3 1929

(To KPM Agents, Bris, [crossed out])
Dear Family,

I'm running short of paper – and we've exhausted the Australian supply of Agfa film packs, which is worse, as they're the only sort that will stand up to this climate. Tuesday, as usual was the eventful day here, I received two letters from Daddy, evidently the one due the week before having been delayed. The camp is now reduced to four whites – so my housekeeping is simple, except that not one egg arrived with the stores, a blemish on possibilities for breakfast and puddings – eggs have never failed before. The aboriginal cook is a moody creature, but so far I haven't put her out.

May 1st was an event also – the Stephensons and John and Michael – (two very efficient youthful products from Oxford) went off to 'Three Isles' 300 miles north. It is a true desert island, rather like this one, so they took food and water for themselves and two boat men. I saw them off – we arose by starlight at 5:45 - having loaded the boat the night before. At 6:10 as I pushed off their dingy it was barely light, and at 6:25 when they really started with motor going and sail up the sun popped up suddenly into a marvellously lighted sky and clouds, and they soon sailed out of sight. The boat was absolutely full with gear and persons and rolled like anything in a following wind – poor beggars. I was very envious – however I am going next month to Lizzard [sic] Island, and there we may have to sleep in the boat, as sandflies etc may prohibit a camp – it will be the last word sleeping on an anchored cockle shell of a boat. Meanwhile I look after endless doings – wind the chronometers, take 5 thermometer readings at 9 am – coax the hydrograph, barograph and

77

thermograph, row out to the tide gauge and do an acrobatic climb up 12 feet of poles etc to make time marks or put new papers in it, – watch the aquarium circulatory apparatus three times a day, etc etc etc. It has been neap tides the last few days – and I've had such fun drawing a map of 22 sq yards of coral area and putting all the corals in in different colours – a job fitting into Stephenson's category of 'elegant pastimes' – I get quite a lot of such jobs in neap tides – watching coral growth for budding details and drawing bits at three week intervals under a binocular microscope is another such job.

May 3

Providence – apart from the eggs - has really come up to scratch – four hours after the 'Luana' (our boat) sailed taking with her our dingy and only anchor, another perfectly good dingy, containing an anchor, drifted out of the blue and appeared in the lagoon coming in over the rampart at high tide!! Heaven knows where it came from!

Here are a few prints – rather bad – next week I will send some really beauteous ones of beasts under water, and a panorama in twelve bits from the top of the lighthouse, but I want to keep them till the other folks come back so that they can see them. This hand printing paper is beastly, but it is the only kind that works here. I've taken masses of negatives good bad and indifferent, but there is so little time to print them, and I'm doing a treble series of prints of the corals etc in situ.

Today we played French cricket with great gusto and energy after lunch as A.P. (Mr Orr) needed exercise after prolonged estimations of oxygen, it was 82° but we didn't feel in the least hot rushing about over the sand and fallen coconuts etc. The tide is quite mad – two days ago we expected decent spring tides again, but nothing happens beyond the tide going out half way and remaining stationary for 24 hours and other useless idiosyncrasies – so to bed for now.

Tide still misbehaving itself – hence more free time – an erratic boat arrived with our post yesterday, so I've done more printing (with new paper arriving). I came off with two birthday cakes yesterday!! On the sly, with the aid of Mrs Lighthousekeeper, Sheena and the aboriginal cook made a cake with no eggs – I never expected a cake under the circumstances – then the unexpected boat arrived with post, potatoes and <u>eggs</u> at 5 pm. The eggs were hidden from my storekeeper eyes and a proper cake appeared for tea at 6 pm! The one without eggs is very good – a cross between cake and toffee and fruit! Most indigestible perhaps. Tonight I'm going to do more printing and have an onslaught on the cockroaches which abound in the store – cockroaches of vast size. (likewise spiders 4-5" across, also numerous).

May 7
The boat should come today – so I must stop this. I've done more printing to amuse you – but I don't think I will send my superior coral photographs just yet – as they are useful here. Please urge Bibs <u>not</u> to lose the prints in Manchester if you send them on to her. Time flies amazingly here, I can't realise that I've been here 6 weeks already.

Lots of love to everybody – I hope the weather is by now decent and that nobody is having any more 'flu',
Sidnie.

Letter 30

GREAT BARRIER REEF EXPEDITION.

Sunday May 12th

Dear Family

Time flies – as usual – a boat did not

Sunday May 12 1929

Dear Family,

     Time flies as usual – a boat did not bring our stores and post till Wednesday and your letter was very welcome as usual – by 'your' of course I mean Daddy's letter as he is my only correspondent. What an institution the 1½ pence post is – when the boat comes I read about doings at home and can quite fancy myself there instead of half way round the world. I wonder if the blue tits are now really tame in the Gardens – talking of birds – I have missed the expected myriads on the reef – the last of the pigeons flew a few days before I arrived – they had pigeon pie frequently, you go out and knock a few down with a stick! A sea eagle six to seven foot span lives in the mangrove trees – otherwise we have only herons, terns and snipe like birds.

     This week has been wonderful – if rather too busy. Spring tides on – one of the two lowest lots in the year. The other lot are next month when I go off to Lizzard [sic] Island north of Cooktown. The night low tides were very poor and the day ones marvellous – (one foot between night high and low water – 8 feet between day high and low) in the summer the good tides were at night only. For five days I was [hole in paper] detailed surveying for half the day in a bathing dress and up to my neck in water. I was among marvellous coral under 1-3 or more feet of water – the sort one sees in the diving helmet as a rule, and the fish everywhere were great. This deepish water coral is terribly brittle, and one constantly 'goes through' all of a sudden-like, dropping a few inches to a few feet and getting very bruised and scratched in the process. Keeping upright at all is often difficult and I often went sploshing over, tipped by the current or by a foot 'going through' and my notebook would get soaked etc all most trying, but great fun. On one traverse I got out to a coral coated (rock) rising steeply from 5 foot of water. I had a high old time getting corals off its sides with hammer and chisel when I couldn't identify them with the water telescope. There are deep sandy pools between areas of coral which one swims across + line of string, measuring frame, telescope etc etc.

The camp has survived my rule and I fished out all sorts of forgotten or expensive delicacies from the store, such as tinned cream and mushrooms and strawberries. The 'Luana' has been expected for three days but still no signs. There is a fierce south east trade blowing, so she may be stuck at Cooktown not caring to embark on a rough twelve hour (at least) trip back here. I hope it won't be so windy when we go to Lizzard Island, as it is a good two days sail up there in fine weather and more in rough. They will be ill poor beggars in this weather.

At new moon all sorts of jobs beset me in the absence of other people – some animals do, some don't, (and some do in other localities) spawn at new moon. I had the aquarium (containing seven running seawater concrete tanks) full and boards covered by various sea urchins standing on their heads. From 10 pm till midnight mainly is the spawning time and I was busy examining microscopically eggs and sperm of various beasts. One wretched sea urchin known as 'tripe hound' otherwise Tripneustes [a genus of sea urchins] began at new moon and has continued for three nights – to my disgust, I have to get a dozen a day until they stop. It is most exciting seeing the tripe hounds spawn in tanks – the eggs come out as five fountains and the sperm as a cloud at great speed. Miss F is a perfect ulidge and quite useless except to

81

carry out a few buckets and other impedimenta to and from the reef. She doesn't mind running around barefoot and getting wet (up to her middle only), but never sees what wants doing, can't identify anything or much coral, can't 'get a move on' when necessary, never 'gets ready' or clears up impedimenta, and doesn't lend a hand on a busy day when after tea she sees me deal with the spawning animals, give round bed linen - make the pudding for the next day, write up and analyse the traverse records, give out 'stores' to the cook, order the next day's meals, give the aboriginals their tobacco allowance, unpack innumerable cases of stores and put contents in the store etc. It's not that she isn't willing, but she's just incapable or rather doesn't find out how to help. I try not to take the upper hand too markedly, but it's not easy as she is senior. (I wouldn't half make her hop about and be useful if she was my junior assistant!). Nic or Bibs would be ideal here as one needs to be alert of mind, athletic, able to swim and use a hammer efficiently etc. Today has been gloriously idle – I 'did' twelve crabs to see gonad maturity this morning, and otherwise I've been immersed in frivolous literature, and went for a mere walk on the reef this afternoon at low tide with no object in view. Why we live in the filthy climate we do is the outside edge – it is so delightful here – what could be more pleasant than some of our jobs, such as rowing out to the tide gauge, seeing wonderful fish etc in the water and then fiddling around on the poles getting a good view of everything; or paddling around and washing 'curing' corals in the sea, all in weather not in the least too hot, and feeling the warm air blowing around inside one's loose and scanty clothing.

Some time I hope to go up the Daintree River when the 'sediment pot hunters' go there next. It's a three hour run there, a real tropical river full of crocodiles etc and banked by forest. Incidentally our water comes from there when we run out of rain water – nasty water it is too I believe – all polluted with crocodiles etc. Next low tides I shall continue our detailed survey in the diving helmet from a boat - how possible it will be remains to be seen. I shall write on a slate but it will not be easy to manipulate things as well as oneself – oneself is difficult enough – I shall do it and all and have F to pump air – it's no good sending her down and she can't even manipulate herself let alone identify more than three of the twenty kinds of *Favia* or nineteen kinds of *Madrepora* coral.

I have been reading Wood Jones 'Corals and Atolls'. It's about the Coco Islands I passed in the Mooltan, and a lot applies to this island – you might like to get it from the library. He also criticises S. Gardiner's work on the Maldives too.

I'm washing some more decent negatives of coral etc but not again has the weather and tide coincided to make underwater photography possible.

I'm looking forward to the Luana's return, as although it is just glorious here, congenial companions add a lot, and I never tire of the amusing company of Anne and Allan Stephenson and John and Michael. The Yonges won't be back for two weeks yet.

And so to bed, with lots of love to everybody of course.

Many thanks for the paper,
Sidnie

First I have to ring round jam, bread etc with Vaseline and other anti-ant contraptions – ants here are a plague.

May 14
Still no boat, so I may as well continue. It's now 5 pm and we are anxiously awaiting darkness to get a reply by morse flashes from the mainland from a message we sent last night by flash asking for telegrams to be sent to Cooktown etc. enquiring as to Luana's wherabouts. She should have been here last Friday and now it's Tuesday – however a stiff S.E. trade continues to blow and she may not have ventured back against it. Even telegrams are slow – from Port Douglas

opposite, the wires go south to Townsville, and then away inland over the tableland and east again to Cooktown. All our meat will be going bad at Port Douglas, as the Luana should have collected stores today – I can feed the flock on food of sorts for ages out of tins, and we have fresh fruit for a week yet so all is well as far as we are concerned. We flash messages from the top of the lighthouse. Our numbers have increased, a few more folk being dropped by a lighthouse boat the other day.

May 15

Last night was showery and misty and we couldn't make contact by flashing to the mainland – today there is no sun so we can't heliograph either. A wind and sea covered with white horses continues and we are a little agitated about the Luana. At midday Mr Orr and two aboriginals set out most precariously in a minute dingy, sail and outboard motor to try and reach Port Douglas – it took 1 hour to get the engine started in the sharp showers – I gave my oilskin to one of the boys, and gave them a supply of tinned food, water and tin opener, and they started out on the 9 mile crossing to the mainland with the top of the boat <u>very</u> near the water surface behind. We didn't like to see them go a bit. All the afternoon we watched them with glasses and telescopes – they actually left at 2:30 pm – were soon blown far north out of their course and by 5:30 could still be seen about 3 miles north of Port Douglas near the coast with wind dead against them. The engine died on them once, during the afternoon, and we thought it had collapsed altogether at 4:30 and that they were rowing – a wave on the engine does it in, and it was a marvel it lasted so long. We knew they were safe when it got dusk as they could run ashore anywhere and walk if necessary. It was a nasty sight seeing three large people in a minute boat scarcely big enough to hold them, being tossed about in a windy sea. All was well however, and at 8:30 pm a shower stopped and we saw Port Douglas lighthouse and morse lamp – slowly the letters came and we pieced together the words –

it was a very tense moment – a telegram from the Luana came first – a great relief to hear they were sheltering off the coast opposite Three Isles and not stuck in Three Isles eating oysters and drinking rain. Then we enquired about our relief party – the morse conversation I enclosed [see next page]. So all the fuss was for nothing, but we felt so cut off with no boat and no flashing and no heliographing previously, and unless we did get in contact with the shore we couldn't do anything for the Luana if wanted.

Lots of love,
Sidnie

The post will go tomorrow in the 'Daintree' doubtless.

Message received by morse lamp from Port Douglas Lighthouse.

'Luana Luana Luana wind bound off Cape Bedford three of party returning by 'Merinda' tomorrow proceeding to Low Island by 'Daintree'. That is all'.

'Has the dingy reached Port Douglas?'

'Yes. Just arrived all wet.'

'Tell them to get wet inside'

'Mr Orr has already had three. Did you get the message ok?'

'Yes thanks'.

'Labour forty three etc' and followed local election results.

Cheerio_____

Letter 31

Low Island
Sunday May 19 1929

Dear Family,

Here I'm beginning again – the last letter having just gone to the post. It has been a heavenly day – dead calm – spring low tide – warm and sunny, and I've loafed the whole day – and one couldn't find a more heavenly spot to loaf in than this. What with a winter tropical sun and a sunproof hide, I walked about the reef and boiled myself in a bathing dress – collected a dozen corals and parked them for a future experiment – I can never boil myself too much in the sun here or anywhere else so far, provided I've got a sun helmet on – I just love being fried. I lunched at 2:30 pm and washed my hair, dried it in about 5 minutes on the beach and went to see a corner of the island where I've not been before. Then I went in the dingy with Mr Orr and the outboard motor, I sat on the very front, and we went for a two hour spree – all round the outside of the island over the deeper reef – seeing huge corals, in boulders, sprays, brackets, cushions etc of many colours through the clear water – sandy bits intervene, across which fine fat fish up to 8 lb dash about from one coral clump to another. I saw two small blue sharks about 5 foot long but we didn't see any of the giant rays that are often there. I suppose we spent one hour going round the whole island – by island I mean the whole show – not the tiny sand cay on which we live. The tide was then well up, so we crossed over the covered 'flat' in the middle of the island and had great fun pottering about in and out and through alleys among the mangroves. The rising tide brings lots more fish – and others pop up and down from their sand holes as the boat goes over them. The sun was setting and everything was glorious – the coast opposite is magnificent – mountains up to 5,000', four ranges in sight, one behind the other, islands off the coast and bays etc.

I shook off the shadow of F for nearly the whole day – which always pleases me – I shall be doing more mapping of coral areas the next few days and her presence – thank goodness - is not required in any way.

The week after next – all being well, I shall go off to Lizard Island. It is a small mountain in the middle of the lagoon between the reefs and the mainland sixty miles north of Cooktown. It is granite – rises 1,000 feet up and is the nearest get-at-able island to the real outer Pacific edge of the Barrier Reef which has as yet never been visited scientifically – it is only three miles from Lizard Island.

The folk had a great time at Three Isles and the place is vastly interesting in comparison with this. Owing to the risk of wasting a precious week by Luana getting stuck again with bad weather, the Luana isn't going to Lizard Island. The 'Tivoli' a similar but more powerful boat had already been hired for the job – the two boats going up together. Now Tivoli going alone made them decide to take three of the same people again, leaving Fraser and me behind. I was too fed up for words at that decision and said they could have my Worts Fund Grant of £50 (just heard about it – that makes £350 in grants!) in order to get a bigger boat. Now three of us (F, Michael and I) are subscribing and probably the expedition will also pay a bit, so it won't be so much for me, and we hope to get the coastal traffic boat to take us up and dump us and bring us back ten days later. The expedition money is very short – hence my offer rather than not go at all. F calmly said she thought my cash well expended to take folk to the place (i.e. herself!) she having offered £10 only! If only F had never been here I fancy I should have gone in both stints, as one person could easily be squeezed into Luana or on Tivoli, but not two and she being senior and being here on the island longer naturally comes first, and so we both get done in the eye.

May 20

Now please Daddy detach your thoughts from here and consider a few other matters. I have decided that the time has come for me to get a car. I could then come home at least one weekend in three during the term. It would be useful in the vacs to take you and mother further afield – to the river etc in warm weather, and anyway mother likes car drives. Incidentally it would wipe out my large taxi account in Cambridge and I should not have to bike out at night in the filthiest of winter wind and wet. I could find other reasons but these suffice. It now remains to get the thing – and whether new or second hand, and what make. I'm told I can run a baby Austin for £50 a year – that's ok, but a Morris Cowley would be a nicer bus if it doesn't cost too much to run - I don't know anything about the Morris Minor – haven't even seen one. I think a closed car is desirable. I don't know a bit about getting new or second hand – second hand <u>without</u> a constitutional disease would be all right if it could be found. Then – the most reputable car place in Cambridge is King and Harpers Garage - Sydney Street. They like to sell you a new or second hand car – teach you to drive - and keep an eye on the engine and do repairs at a special rate etc if you do all these things – It seems quite a good arrangement, judging from reports about them, as if a second hand car sold to you by them goes wrong - then I believe it is their funeral - not yours. I don't know the details in the least. As to garaging I can do it at college if a space is free for £3 a year – at home a spot will have to be found. My ignorance on cars is quite sublime as you are aware. Now if I am getting a car I may as well do so as soon as I return. If you feel inclined, and have the time to make inquiries into the matter it would be very nice, as you are much more skilled than I am at buying things.

Today is a beastly day as regards weather - howling trade wind again and much cooler - however I suppose you would consider it hot but I don't. I was out mapping most of the day, getting very wet and scratched. It's wonderful how we get used to few and large meals - I lunched at 11:45 and food didn't cross my mind until tea at 6 pm. I'm tremendously fit and flourishing here, I don't know when I've flourished so much before.

I had a long letter from Jean Young by the last mail - it was full of this sort of thing "I suppose you've heard about Isabel from Bibs" and many illusions to happenings and folk all supposed to have reached my knowledge via Bibs, and Jean goes no further - most tantalising as Bibs never writes!

Lots of love,
Sidnie

PS Origin of Species arrived thanks - and newspaper.

Letter 32

Low Island
May 24 1929

Dear Family,

May and June spring tides are the best in the year - hence the excitement.

I've had such a marvellous day that I must tell you all about it, as there is nothing on this evening before brewing cocoa at 9 pm and going to bed. I started with donkey jobs like cleaning corals and their tubs (corals are cleaned by leaving in tubs of sea water until the flesh decays, washing daily in the sea, and bleaching in the sun), etc then at 11 am I set out in the flattie with diving helmet - 2 square yard frame with weights at the corners - pail full of hammer, chisel, slates, pencils, opal glass sheets, big water telescope (now patched all over with plasticine and sticking plaster, as it has rusted through), F and black boy, 2 anchors and air pump. Yesterday I fixed a rope at low tide to an iron stake 4 ft long 140 yards out on the rich coral rock area, jumped out into space from the coral edge with anchor and rope in hand and swam out with it dropping it in position - I quite forgot that booted and gaitered and carrying the anchor swimming would not be so easy, and I only just kept my nose out! Today we found the place and I went down, bucket and frame in hand and pencils tied about me. You may be able to decipher the diagrams - I doubt it. However once down there I floundered about and managed to find the upper edge of the coral zone where the traverse had been left.

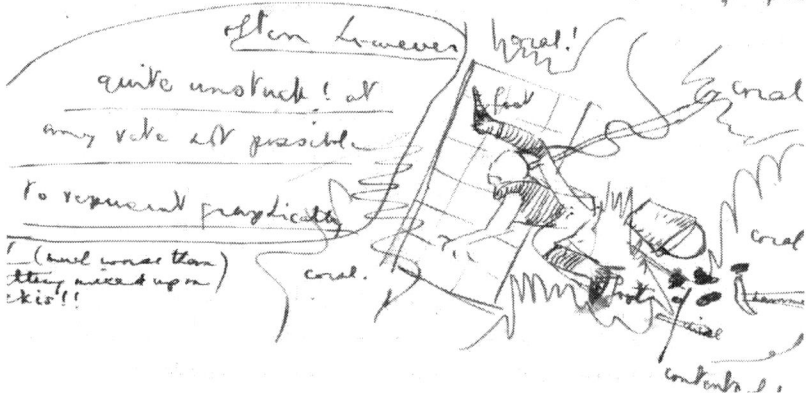

I had to recognise the corals, as marking the place was impos. Then I staggered back to where I started and hauled along the frame and planted it over the line – lurching accidentally into the most spinous bush of coral I've yet met. Swarms of fish of every hue came around to see the fun, I got out a piece of opal glass to write down the contents of the first square yard – my pencil tied to my belt I just could not find (you can't look down at your middle in a helmet) finally I saw it floating under my chin in the water surface inside the helmet! I had slates also but the writing rubs off at the slightest touch – a great disadvantage. So I progressed, digging up things at intervals and putting them in the pail, and occasionally losing my balance or getting swept by a current and getting too tied up for words. I had great difficulty in manipulating the frame once, and just as I was getting put - slowly and surely my feet left the bottom and I became suspended in space – I cursed and swore inside the helmet – quite powerless – as that idiot F hauled me up thinking I had given a signal. I gesticulated violently with my arms when near the surface, and was let down again and had all the trouble below over again. I did 15 square yards and finished the traverse – loud cheers. In we came, sorted out the goods – had a huge lunch at 12:30 and I and Dr Stevenson hiked out on the reef – in a dry bathing dress. I had a boat and was collecting and listing corals and animals and algae in an isolated rocky area a little way off the island – up to my middle in waves mostly, and the rocks all around finally going down very deep. Never have I seen such animals and corals! I got heaps (at least 10) really superior catches, mostly rather weighty and needing much hammering to shift – all most exciting – I got one sea urchin about 15" across all colours of the rainbow with fat striped spines and streaks of green and slender needle like spines. Subsequently I got spiked – and a nastier beast I never knew – the spines are poisonous a bit, and hurt like blazes – I got the end of a spine left in my finger – so I cut a large hole and extracted it and messed around with my finger which will be all right. I pickled beasts and had a huge tea – having previously boiled myself in the sun after so much wetting. I thrive exceedingly on an amphibious existence – so to cocoa.

May 26
Another lazy Sunday pleasantly spent – morning spent with a book under a palm tree facing the sea and away from everybody – however I wasn't long undisturbed, first a goat (there are three on the island who try to eat our washing and who have to climb trees to get their green food!) then sand

flies, but not many, and then Stephen's practicing terrific
vocal efforts in preparation for his next corroboree
[a ceremonial meeting of Aboriginal Australians].

May 27
Had a real field day diving in another place continuing
the first traverse of detailed surveying. It was much more
interesting and exciting than the last – deeper water, but the
sun shone down, boulders and rocks everywhere like a range
of mountains all covered or partly covered with corals – it
was very difficult going, I gently dropped off a precipice and
landed in a scraggy gully three yards deeper, to rise again
steeply. Manipulating the frame was not at all easy. The
corals too were much more interesting zoologically than
hitherto – one can't see very far, and with the huge boulders
and blue impenetrable gaps and holes from which emerge all
sorts of fish, and queer light effects it was rather eerie at
times. I only stayed down about 1 hour and did 14 square
yards. F kept me short of air the whole time and I was
puffing like a grampus [a killer whale or dolphin] and
continued for some time afterwards when I came up. Also the
sea is beastly cold now – only 75°. I could have easily come
up and complained about the air supply, but I didn't bother. I
certainly shall another time if it occurs again, as the after
effects are not pleasant. F then couldn't pull the helmet up
into the back of the boat – ass – so I had to get out of it and
come up with soaking hair and pull it up myself.
The Yonges arrived back today, and have had a
perfectly marvellous time at Thursday Island, Murray Island
and parts of the north end of the reef, all amongst pearl
fishing islands and fleet. The non scientific wives here do
jolly well, far better than such as me. Anne Stephenson has
been on heaps of trips all over the show – lucky dog, as there
are so many occasions when she can go in virtue of being
Allan's wife on boats with no accommodation at all, when
they can't take such as me. There has been endless talk and
telegraphing and rushing over to Port Douglas over the

Lizard Island trip – even my 1) offering £50 towards a boat, 2) offering to go by ordinary steamer to Cook Town, get a black guide and walk 25 miles through the bush to the mission station at Cape Bedford, there to be picked up by the Tivoli and conveyed by her the last 7 hours by sea to Lizard Island and vice versa on the way down, both appeared hopeless up to today; but now I hope another boat is materialising to take Fraser and I up there, one day later than the Tivoli, and bring the lot of us down, mainly paid for by the expedition. I hope it will work, as it will be my only excursion. Also they badly want me there to do mapping of coral areas for comparison with here.

I am fitting nicely into a round hole in the reef party's work – I'm trying to do this – as another show is simmering for the dim and distant future for four people, three fixed ones being Anne and Allan Stephenson and Spender, the geographer – I should like the fourth to be myself! These are dreams – there is to be a decent boat and island similar to this and Three Isles are to be investigated –

I must stop and clean up for tea – lots of love to everybody. The life history of mangrove trees – species *rhizophysus* I-VIII, are for Bibs, good prints can be made later. I'm awfully fit and flourishing, brown and fat and not working too hard in the least, going to bed early and doing lots of other virtuous things.

Lots of love,
Sidnie

Letter 33

Dear Family,

   Daddy's letter as usual was very welcome, also Mummy's of the week before which I omitted to answer. Bibs as usual is a deplorable letter writer – her last being written in early January and now it is June (tomorrow). If she reads this she can take note that she is also a scurvey knave. My last Tasmanian letter home has been acknowledged and weeks before that I wrote asking her to get a Norwegian rucksack sent out to me here. If she delayed very many weeks in doing this it won't arrive before I leave, as parcel post is incredibly slow, as she never replies to letters it leaves me very much in the dark, I am now anxiously awaiting a letter or pc from her saying if my films etc posted in Melbourne have arrived, but I expect that is too much to hope for.

   Time here flies. I have as usual, seen the glorious rapid sunset during tea. From my side of the table I look out through the door, and in the middle of this frame stands a very fine cocoa palm – behind it is a light screen of trees in a row and then the grey silhouette of the mainland (the direction is Mount Harris, over the [boulder zone] region of the panorama from the lighthouse) and Snapper Island, and behind all is a flaming sky of great brilliance. I never get tired of watching the colours fade. Sun sets at 6 pm and at 6:30 it is quite dark.

   We had such a feast for tea today, it was Mattie's birthday, and we had a homemade iced cake and cream with fruit salad, and a meal composed of nothing (except cream) out of a tin – also some Edinburgh shortbread and some chocolates. The chocolates were fine – we had just been admiring a sumptuous coloured advertisement of chocolates – the nearest approach we ever get to such things here. This all sounds very greedy, but we do appreciate a change in our good plain diet here.

Winter is fairly upon us – it gets cold in the evenings now – at 73-4° we are found wrapped up in sweaters and drinking hot cocoa – what on earth shall I do in a Cambridge winter with my lab at about 56° I don't know.

On Tuesday I depart to Lizard Island, and my letters may cease for a couple of posts. It's a ridiculous show as to expense. Anne, Allan and Michael and the goods depart at 6 am tomorrow, Friday, on Tivoli. Fraser and I go by 'Merinda' – the coast mail boat (also minute, but powerful) bringing a 'flattie' and the diving helmet. We sleep at Cooktown and go on the next day to Lizard Island, the others meanwhile having established a camp. 'Merinda' will bring the whole crowd down on June 13th – 'Merinda's' cost is £70, the exped paying half – a ridiculous sum, but there simply are no boats on this miserable coast and no competition, you have to beg and bribe for a boat of any kind. We may not use the helmet, it depends on sharks – when you meet a shark diving the correct technique when and if he starts to eat you, is to put your thumbs in his eyes and he goes off with all speed – according to the Torres Straits pearl divers! Tivoli we have all the time to get about the reef in etc but she might get stuck as did 'Luana' if a fierce south east Trade blew, so the assurance of getting back by Merinda and not wasting time is a good thing.

Then I sleep one night again here (probably under a bush, or on the orange cases in the store as a visitor is having my bed), and go off again on Luana for the weekend up the Daintree River with three other folk. That is a pleasure stunt as far as I'm concerned, as I'm only going to keep Shiena company and make the party respectable – the other two being Mr Orr, a humorous Scot and Mr Moorhouse a passable Australian. The Daintree River contains crocodiles, and penetrates jungle – what fun – we sleep on the boat of course and don't bathe!

I'm not sending more photos now although I've simply piles – I did 74 prints last night and 56 the night before, they are of beasts and I want them here.

June 2

Tomorrow I'm off for Lizard Island – cheers no end! My luggage consists of a rucksack, an open box of diving helmet etc and a flattie and paddles! Very nice mixture I'm sure. Yesterday (Sunday) was a great day. We all went off to Snapper Island for the day – a heavenly tropical island one mile long and 5 miles away (on the panorama looking into the sun over the "boulder zone"). Luana took the crowd and grub and I went off with John in the dingy and sailed across! It took 2 hours nearly, as there was very little wind and a fair swell. I endeavoured to learn the elements of sailing and coped with the boat alone for half the journey, it was great. Wouldn't have suited Bibs she would have been very ill. For half an hour we wallowed in rough water just off the long coast of Snapper, and I couldn't have stuck that indefinitely, but I didn't have to – so that was ok. We promptly bathed, diving off the Luana into deep water four yards from a steep shingle beach. Lunched early, having collected many baskets of wild paw-paws for dessert. There are five knobs on the island going up to 350 feet and nearly down to the sea in between. One is dense proper tropical forest, and the others with less dense 'bush' and 5 foot grass, I climbed to the top of four knobs getting wonderful views. We saw a baby shark 4 foot long basking in the sun, and a 5 foot turtle in the clear water below a nearly sheer precipice. The day was hot, but not too so – climbing – quite steep rough going, was fine, with boots and our usual scanty clothing – it was good to stretch ones legs after 2½ months without a walk. Wild bananas flourish, but were not in fruit then. Tonight I may go out with a lamp on the reef to see the corals expanded, only very few show their anemone like faces during the day. Well, I return from Lizard Island on Thursday week, and on Friday go off to the Daintree river - (sorry I seem to have said all this before). Life you see is rather divine.

Lots of love to everybody,
Yours
Sidnie

Letter 34

Dear Family,

A hiatus of a post was unavoidable, as I was on a true uninhabited desert island [Lizard Is] miles from anywhere and only visited once in a blue moon by a Japanese lugger for water – incidentally the most wonderful experience all round of my life. I can't tell it all at length now – it must wait – I've cultivated vagus nerves like an ox and have been out in rough seas, like the roughest 'channel' I've seen, in a 40 foot or an 80 foot boat, starting breakfast-less at 5:30 am etc, with waves dashing all over the boat, daylight visible (from another vessel) below the keel as far back as the foremast as we pitched. At times we had to slow down the engines on account of the wild seas. I thoroughly enjoyed it all, and missed one meal only. We started off in fine style, two days steam up to Lizard Island, sleeping at Cooktown. Cooktown is a marvellous place, as dead as a doornail owing to the inland mines being worked out – overgrown by grass and tropic trees and dead shops and hotels and a monument to Captain Cook who landed there in 1770. Wonderful situation – saw sunset over surrounding mountains. First three days at Lizard Island were perfect – it is a granite lump – 1176 feet high and 1½ x ¾ mile with heaps of almost white sandy beaches and fringing reefs. We spent 3 days on the outer barrier – marvellous quite undescribed structure, all so-called descriptions being of inner reefs of quite a different kind. A typical day was this – arose at 6:15 am, I tidied the 12 x 14 tent and cleaned corals etc while Anne and Michael cooked breakfast – Allan and Dr F washed themselves in natural Pandanus Palm 'bathroom' and tent respectively. Ready by 9 am on Tivoli and chugged out 1½ hours 12 miles to the outer barrier, did terrific manoeuvres in and out of the boulder zone [dead coral boulders sticking out of the sea thrown up onto the reef flats during storms] as close as possible in barriers' inner side, and then we took to the flattie the last half mile or so – me with pail, hammer, chisel, 'chicken run' and numerous things tied about for mapping, Anne and Michael doing a general survey of bits - Fraser merely messing about and Allan painting (he is a first rate artist) or surveying. Coral is quite past description - low tide being 2ft better than normal. The reef crest dries at low water and you can stand within 12 yards of the pacific edge with house high breakers at the edge, but the broken water never reaches you, as there is 300 fathoms of water 1 mile from the edge so it must go down steeply. Also as the wave curls you may get a prismatic doubly refracted image of the corals on the face of the barrier, somehow like this:

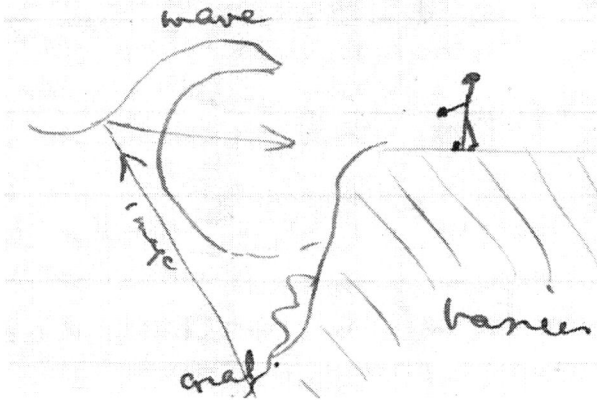

Worked like mad till we returned to Tivoli for lunch at 4:30, a long meal-less interval from 7 am breakfast, but all is so exciting and marvellous that thoughts of food never arose. I climbed, or rather was slung, up the masthead to photograph the barrier, and we chugged home again, getting soaked with spray and having to hold tight to a seat or one of the boxes of kerosene, (we started with 300 gallons). Got back to the camp just after sunset, cooked a huge super meal – Michael being an expert in stews – four vast spoonfuls to start with and three more to come! Evening spent in dealing with specimens brought back and writing up and wearily to bed to sleep like 5 logs in a 12 x 14 foot space. After three days the weather cracked and it blew so hard that we couldn't approach any reef at all in the Tivoli, so we more or less pottered for three more days around Lizard Island fringing reefs – and doing a little discrete diving in places. Diving at the outer barrier, to our disgust, was too much of a risk with so many big fish about. Giant clams abound – I had one awful moment when I found I had one foot within an inch of the gaping mouth of a clam nearer 4 foot long than 3! You could easily sit inside one. Views from the tent were great – a sunset – pink sky gold tipped clouds – vivid emerald sea with blue horizon, and <u>pink</u> sand, owing to wet reflection of sky, terns diving for fish a few yards off dropping like stones into the water and a green reflection on their under feathers making them look like kingfishers – and so we were rescued by Merinda arriving in a gale and wind. All our gear we packed in Tivoli who took 5 days to get back here. Merinda got us back in two days, being two hours late over the last five hour stretch, and it was some sea, getting calm in comparison near Low Island as the Trades are never so violent here as further north. At L.I. once on shore we saw our comparative 'flat calm sea' in these parts to be the wildest greyest tempestuous affair I've seen since I've been here. We hit about the worst weather ever going here other than cyclones. Seeing a grey scene round Low Island making it look like an English scene forcibly made me realise the ordinary excessive brilliance here.

In two days we had a flat calm yesterday (Sunday) and John endeavoured to teach me more about sailing, but there was scarcely any wind at all.

I'm fearfully fit and flourishing, never flourished so much before – never been so long without a cold etc which I've not had since I left home – not overdoing it at all – had heaps of compensating laziness on the voyage back after the busy time on the outer barrier – so set your hearts at rest.

My Ox-like vagus nerves have decided me to give up Egypt – take the next P&0 back from Penang sailing September 7th and pot about the East Indies in little boats, visiting Celebes, (four days in Makassar etc) Bali (three days) Java (ten days) islands off Java I hope – few days, Sumatra (six days) getting a boat from Belwan-Deli (Sumatra) to Penang, having travelled overland from Padang across the wonderful Padang Highlands by car and rail to Belwan-Deli, arriving home by same boat at Marseilles. Gosh it sounds ok.

I leave here in three weeks – take a loop inland, one day's train and four hrs car to accept an invitation to stay at a cattle station on the table land belonging to the relations of the Mrs Manton that I met in Melbourne – then four hours car and pick up the railway further south. Heavens this is a good life. No time for more – as usual I have kept my coral photos – but send a few oddments for your amusement – sorry this is illegible – I must go and fetch corals for gonad samples – foul job –

Lots of love,
S

PS You wouldn't own me here, I walked into the best hotel in Cooktown, barefoot, wearing oilskin and SW hat, and shirt and shorts that would stand up of their own accord with dirt and salt – my colour would pass for a half-caste any day!

aPS We found a bottle containing Japanese postcard dated 1910 for currents!

aPPS On the cliff at Lizard I. was inscribed a Japanese luggers name and then 'He Ben Hir' obviously put up by the aboriginal crew

Letter 35

Sunday June 23 1929

Dear Family,

I hope you all flourish as I do. Daddy's letters by every mail are a truly welcome spot on the week. I heard from Bibs too – loud cheers – I was vastly pleased. Rucksac has just arrived too for which many thanks.

My news is scanty this week, the Daintree River stunt was postponed owing to weather – the rough weather we struck up north must have been truly rough, as in Cairns and Townsville where it was nothing like as violent, all the shipping was tied up and pegged down in fear of a cyclone. However it is not the right time of the year for cyclones and nothing materialised.

We now chatter with the cold and your leather coat is very welcome. It seldom gets much over 72° indoors now, and a beastly wind howls outside, for two days the thermometer outside stuck at 70°. Very inferior. It has poured with rain for two days, and I've been keeping out of the sea the last few days as one leg insists upon decaying in places and simply won't heal up – however it's nearly better now I hope.

I'm up to my eyes in a pile of maps which won't get done for months and months so I'm not bothering about them – on the principle that if you have two committee meetings at the same time you play golf instead of either.

We have just made level sections of my traverses with theodolites and soundings – I was working in about 24' of water to end up with – I had no idea it was so deep. The sections are truly handsome – nobody has ever made a section of a reef edge before let alone examine its fauna with anything but a dredge.

I may have to scrap my visit to the inland cattle station, as I can't get away early enough - the last lot of tides being bad and rendered useless by stormy weather. If the people can motor me miles and miles to Cardwell so that I can catch the Brisbane train then all will be well, but otherwise it is off as there is only one train a week from Cairns inland and the days won't fit for the return journey.

I'm sending a few more pictures - some odds and ends of mine of Snapper Island, Cooktown etc. some of Mrs Yonge's and some of somebody else's from Pixie Reef. You ought to be able to identify Snapper Island now on the panorama from the lighthouse.

I hope my remarks about cars a few weeks back are being taken seriously.

It is a horrid thought that I have but a fortnight more on Low Island – the time has simply evaporated and I have no desire to move at all – although I shall be very pleased to see you all in September. A semi uncivilised life with few conventions is so far preferable to our complex more or less artificial conditions.

We are a heterogeneous collection of folk, if you like, but the veneer is scraped off everybody and you know them as they really are. We are all equal - either married or otherwise or of either sex, and there is no fuss or bother about anything. However I suppose a community of this kind would only work on a small scale.

I've got several letters to write this week so will stop.

Lots of love to everybody,
Sidnie

from cave on
shore at Snapper
Island

Letter 36

"Luana"
Daintree River
N.Q.
Australia
June 30 Sunday 1929

Dear Family,

Thanks as usual for news – I'm awfully sorry about the Copland's news – how simply dreadful for them. What a mouldy show this life is for some people.

My letters I'm sure are most inferior – I simply splutter out an abridged edition of my doings and nothing more – however time is limited and other things can be taken for granted more easily.

Today has been one heavenly sitting of complete idleness, I've basked in the sun and done nothing – leaving the men to do the cooking and washing up even – but I must begin at the beginning -

Three days ago the weather cleared and became the good old tropical winter reaching 82° (in the shade of course) instead of the arctic beastliness of the last fortnight. Promptly my time was swallowed up with domesticity instead of (or rather as well as) reef work – what with the skipper of Luana having a fever or a bilious attack, Mrs Yonge being in bed with a temperature and a throat as she had in Cambridge once, and Shiena being collapsed with a huge budding abscess or boil or something on her leg; so that what with putting antiphlogistine poultices on Shiena and fussing about over food and washing and stores etc I didn't do much else. All went well until Mattie insisted on getting up and wanted to do a little surgery on Shiena's leg – which she was mercifully dissuaded from doing (I wouldn't be doctored on by Mattie at any price, although she is a friend of mine). However we bundled both Shiena and Mattie off to Port Douglas, where there is a hospital although only about 2 houses one pub and one shop – the hospital catering for untold hundreds of miles around – I hope they flourish. Then

106

on a marvellous oily sea we worked at a level section from the shore seawards on the windward side of the island, a unique opportunity re weather. Beacons had been erected, and we did the first few hundred feet by a steel tape on the ground, a ruled staff being held in places and read off on the theodolite on the shore – me being up to my middle in water manipulating the tape and staff. Then we continued from the boat – and an awful job too reeling out steel tape and collecting same, and keeping boat on the line and reading water levels on the staff. We then continued by soundings and finally did the position readings by a sextant, instead of a tape, over deep water. I also made lists of coral species along the section up to 3 fathoms when I couldn't see down any more. The results are very amusing, as there is a belt of corals on the 'breaker zone' like 'Outer Barrier' corals and unlike anything seen anywhere else on Low Island – then there is a huge long plateau two fathoms deep and a precipice rapidly going to 15 fathoms which is deeper than any sounding between us and the mainland. All most entertaining.

We also took some flashlight photos of corals at night – as most have their tentacles in by day.

Now I'm getting to the expedish upon which we started this morning. The mouth of the river is guarded by complex sandbanks, and then it meanders about. I suppose about half a mile wide, with dense mangrove forests and tributaries on either side. I didn't see the alligators unfortunately, but lots of vivid kingfishers, herons and sea eagles flap round. The river narrows to 2 x Thames size and mangroves 30 feet high give place to dense tropical rain forest on the banks. Beyond lie ridges covered with forest and towering upwards is Mount Thornton 5,000ft and eight miles away on one side, and lower mountains on the other side. I needn't describe tropical rain forest, but it is good to see it in the flesh – mostly we hugged one bank or another seeing vast climbers - palms, cycads, giant epiphytic ferns – fine ones and stag horns etc growing among the dense tree and bush growth. Curiously devoid of flowers in any number, and all the greens are the same, broken only by the brown trunks, and vast buttress roots and aerial roots coming down from branches 20-30 feet high. A great sight for the first time and wonderful surroundings. The river water is just like R. Kipling's 'green greasy Limpopo River' I'm sure – can't see the bottom ½ fathom off! Not a sign of habitation for miles, a small settlement flourishes ten miles up but we stuck on a sandbank one mile short. Not a ship at sea or a soul in the river did we meet all day until at 5 pm a canoe softly paddled past us containing 5 blacks, one paddling and two standing up with raised fish spears, but they hadn't caught anything then. And to see and smell the rainforest etc in an equitable climate was marvellous – I wasn't a bit too hot in a well rolled up and very loose shirt, although most of the men were only half covered. We abandoned Mr Orr and Nicholls in the dingy and out board motor and piles of gear 9 miles up the river, and they went on to do a 24 hour series of water samples – oxygen and Ph [sic] estimations etc. We then dropped down near the mouth and abandoned Moorehouse for another 24 hour series of water sampling up a foul sandfly infested creek among the mangroves and squelchy mud and anchored close by: the remaining 3 of us stopping on board, where we cooked a 4 lb King Fish for 'tea' (the fish we caught at sea on a trailing line with a hook and piece of white rag on the end.) The sunset was great – all red and purple and gold reflected in the water with the mangrove forests black as ink, and the purple mountains beyond on either side – the seaward view encompassing the coast round Port Douglas instead of the open horizon. Now the night is starlit and moonless, a planet giving a reflected line of light on the water – but the stars here are not a patch on our N hemisphere ones and the Southern Cross is a comparatively poor affair. However the Great Bear and Orion put in a furtive appearance here, upside down on the horizon, reminding me that after all I'm not so far away.

Tomorrow I'm going off on my own on foot - booted and gaitered to play about the less dense forest (if I can find any) – I want to see the orchids at close quarters. This is a purely pleasure party for three days for me! I may have time to add to this or I may not – I hope we shall reach Port Douglas before the mail goes out on Tuesday.

I'm enclosing a few prints – some of Anne and Michael's negatives from Lizard Island etc and two crocodiles of mine from Lizard island – both underexposed. I hope I'm managing to convey glimmerings of the wonders of these parts and our work on Low Island. The Stephensons are leaving in three days – they are pining to come home via the D. E. Indies with me. If funds can be scratched up the Stephensons, Michael Spender and self and perhaps or perhaps not two others will run another expedition to these parts. We aim at two years hence – we know just what we want, where we want to go, and how we want to do it, but of course nothing will be breathed about it in public until it is hatched.

Everybody is green with envy at my route home literally I'm the only person who has enough beans to rub together to go a decent route home – everybody else is busted and going free passages and Blue Funnel etc – even the Yonges don't expect to arrive home solvent – silly isn't it – while I have a glorious holiday back and have a surplus of £150 - £200 on the year's activities. Talk about charmed footsteps!

Letter 37

Dear Family,

It is long past midnight, but I must just send a line by tomorrow's mail to show that I am alive. I arrived back at Low Island at 10 pm or so after 4 days at sea in a stout 20 ton cargo boat about 40 foot by 12 foot. We had horrible, rough, cold weather – just plain beastly – last night for example we were anchored twenty miles from land in five fathoms of water near one of the outer Barrier Reefs – spring tides on, so at high water the Pacific swell came slop over the barrier two miles off – a wind howled, reaching a 'moderate gale' of 45 mph at times. You can imagine the motion of a small anchored boat in that sea and wind! No accommodation on the boat – some of us slept in the hold, foul place where you get about on all fours: and others on deck. John, Michael and I constructed beds on the hatch over the hold, we rolled up in two blankets each, lashed a ground sheet over the three of us and also a couple of life lines across our chests, as when we had a really good roll there was a risk of the outside man slipping off the hatch, - missing the scuppers altogether, and falling into the sea! That's no exaggeration. We erected a wind break out of a sail and kerosene boxes in front of our heads, so we were warm and comfortable in spite of the motion and the spray coming all over us. We spent the low tides of oilskin days on three different reefs, very interesting too. We were eight plus four crew. Weather was bad all the time, but I wasn't ill, only one person was. Pounding about on a wet reef up to your neck in cold weather is just too horrid, especially as it is equally impossible to keep dry in the 'Daintree' owing to shipping seas all the time, there being no shelter, (except in the hold, smelly with bilge water). However it was a great experience.

This sketch shows 3 people strapped on top of the hatch of the boat - SMM in the middle - and three sleeping in the hold, identifiable by their initials – CMY's bed is labelled "not to be used for lamps" – and someone appears to snore!

Before leaving for this trip and after returning from the Daintree river trip in Luana I had much more domesticity than I cared for here. We collected Shiena from Port Douglas Hospital where a deep abscess in her leg had been opened and she was in bed for a few days. Mattie Yonge also returned – rather worse than when she left, and I had her for a day with a temperature and a throat so bad that she wouldn't eat or drink anything. I didn't like it at all and mercifully Dr Yonge sent her back to P.D. Hospital. Then Mr Orr had caught a chill working for 24 hours in the dingy up the Daintree River through a misty cold night, and I had him in bed for two days – however he was a fine sort of invalid who mopped up all the hot sloppy food I gave him and recovered. I also sent Nicholls to bed for half a day with the same symptoms as Mr Orr but he soon revived. Then Stephen, one of the black boys, thought he was having flu, but a stout dose of epsoms soon brought him to his senses. I'm fearfully fit and regretting the fact that I have but three more days here.

I'm writing now as I'm really a bit upset by a horrid bust up that occurred tonight. We arrived home tired and hungry as you may imagine and expected that the Australian in charge of camp and blacks would bring out the flattie to the anchored 'Daintree'. No boat came, so John, Michael and I took the first load of gear in the Daintree's dingy ashore, found Vigeon on the shore, and asked why on earth he hadn't come to meet the boat as we had three small boat loads of gear etc to shift that night, he replied 'Catch me going out a night like this in the flattie', we unloaded the dingy with difficulty in the dark and rough sea and we naturally expected Vigeon to play the game and row the boat out for the next lot – he refused to go, so Michael took the boat out again – Michael being dead tired, and that lazy devil Vigeon having had four days holiday and then not doing his paid job. I was black with rage and fairly let fire at Vigeon. Then John and I launched the flattie, me up to my waist in water, and John rowed out and I baled, and we fetched the last load – it was quite a long row too, while Vigeon did nothing. Later after a meal Vigeon, who deserved to be thrashed, demanded an apology from John (who had told him to boil his head), and on not getting it attacked him in the mens' hut and then was an all fired row which was brought before Yonge. Yonge is a dear, but has not a scrap of stout leadership in him. He merely feebly tried to pacify the raving Vigeon and ticked off John for losing his temper momentarily. Vigeon's neglect of his duty goes unmentioned, and the resulting row is as much my fault as John's and I'm not at all looking forward to having to speak to Yonge about it tomorrow. It's all confoundedly unfortunate, I never meant to put my foot in it.

I enclose some photos – from the Daintree River and from some rainforest in which I scrambled for some hours.

I must try and go to sleep so goodnight.

Lots of love,
Sidnie

Letter 38

Dear Daddy,

The Low Isles Mail left yesterday and it contains no letter from me – the first such occurrence. However as I am now travelling with the mail it makes no odds – and I will start a perambulatory letter.

I should have left L.I. on Friday (and now it is Wednesday) intention being to do a few car stunts on the mainland. However when the time came to barge off alone, I simply couldn't do it, and Luana went to port without me. I finally left yesterday – 6 days before my boat sails – we arose at 4:30 am – got to P. Douglas at 6:45 am after a tempestuous 1¾ hour crossing. Most people then went on a pleasure party up to Mossman by train to see a sugar mill and eat a luncheon. My polite clothes have gone to Cairns so I couldn't join the sugar mill stunt, and John and Michael refused to wear ties and trousers at any price. The three of us had an extremely happy day walking for miles along a glorious beach with old fringing coral reefs exposed by the tide and fine trees at the top of the beach. It was warm and sunny and altogether perfect, and we lunched by a rivulet mouth with violent coloured 'kingfishers' circling and playing round us. But all good things come to an untimely end and I was whisked off on 'Daintree' at 4 pm and conveyed to Cairns during 6½ hours of choppy weather. Again I took up a strategic central position – ate sandwiches and drank tea – (the latter v difficult owing to motion) while seasick passengers groaned on either side – and it wasn't at all rough – not what I call rough for these parts. At 10:30 pm I was to be found enjoying fish and chips and omelettes of vast size at a café in Cairns – still in my uncivilised clothes. (Cairns hotels can't provide late meals at any price). Today again I saw the sun rise and now sit in the mail train at 8 am under the cloak of civilisation. My L.I. manners I hope will soon wear off. At breakfast I found myself spiking the butter from

114

afar off with my knife – and I must not forget myself and try to scratch a hole in the floor (instead of sand) with my foot in order to dispose of cigarette ends. In three days of horrid Queensland trains I reach Brisbane, and then come all the way back again by sea – it's like going from London to Scotland via Naples, but one does not think that sort of thing odd at all here.

L. Isles is very depleted now. The Stephensons and Dr F left a fortnight ago – the latter I shall find again at Brisbane, and one or two others have gone. Michael and I have had an orgy of photography the last week, photographing various experiments of other peoples', necessitating photographing the same corals all day at intervals. We have also blazed off some colour plates with mixed results – some excellent – we had to develop all colour plates early in the morning to get the water cool enough (cooled by hanging it up in a canvas bag dripping all night). During the recent cold snap we had a pestilential cold night with a minimum temperature of 61°F!

July 19

Still in the train – however the Brisbane Townsville mail for two days and two nights is far less tiring than 10 hours of the Cairns Townsville train – which takes the bun for first class discomfort – in all senses of the word - although the tropical scenery is finest along this stretch. I had three hours in Townsville, leaving at 9 pm, and was met by the taxi driver who came on the 'Tivoli' stunt. He motored me all over the place – took me to Mr Butler's house (B being owner of Tivoli) his family being there but not Butler who was away at sea. Then I was taken to coffee at the poshest café in Townsville – too fancy for words – and so seen safely on to the train, and very nice too and all. Butler and Mrs B and 'Jim' have just inherited £12,000, but they go on just the same as ever, Jim with his taxi and Butler with the Tivoli although they contemplate a holiday in England.

I'm a few hours off Brisbane now - and the sun has warmed up at last. Last night and this morning was poisonously cold – the bush was white with frost!!! A very unusual state and the whole train was excited about it. I put on twice as much clothing as I would do at home and was still cold – a Cambridge winter prospect fills me with gloom. Never have I flourished so exceedingly as here. I haven't had a trace of an ache or pain or a cold or anything since I left home, just fine. What a pity we can't live permanently an active out door existence in a climate that requires no clothes. (My ideal is low humidity, average temperature 83°, and diurnal range of about 10°).

I will write again before the Nieuw Holland sails but will post this at once to catch the Sidney mail. I'm sending some more prints home – they probably won't mean much until I arrive to tell you what they are all about, but some may be amusing. The animal ones are nearly all underwater – the coral ones I shall keep for the present.

Well I will stop now – I shall miss Daddy's weekly letter very much now I'm on the move again. I notice Daddy is writing twice more to L.I. , these letters will be sent on to Colombo or Penang – it's funny to think that by the time I get to Penang I'm half way home with only three weeks to go! Naturally posts from me will now be spasmodic as circumstances allow. Please ask Bibs if she remembered to collect the goods from Eleka Gardens. Rucksack arrived OK- I don't think I mentioned it.

Lots of love to everybody,
Sidnie

PS These Queensland so called towns take the bun - purely bungaloid in structure, with big verandas and large rooves [sic] to collect rain, all elevated on piles because of white ants and annual rains, made of weather beaten sun baked shabby timber and that ubiquitous product – corrugated iron – some buildings are entirely made of the

116

latter, or of metal derived from kerosene tins – I could give a whole lecture on the uses of the kerosene tin and the wooden case which carries two 8 gall tins! No pretensions about architecture or style – no gardens, no made pavements, all open and weed grown, sunburned and unkempt. In fact the kerosene tin and the local 'store' made of iron and stocking tinned foods of universal monotony are the key notes to the life of Australia on the mainland. Give me the islands and reefs and occasional excursions to uninhabited parts of the mainland, but I want none of the settlements.

Lots of love,
Sidnie.

Letter 39

Dear Family,

Here I am all complete, sailing tomorrow, and living in the lap of luxury, comparatively, at the Women's College here. I have had two days here, vastly busy, spent enormous amounts of money on nothing in particular, such as essential oddments, a mighty settling of photographic material and other bills, and a few charts of the coastal waters and coral sea. I've had two hot baths !!!! Strange to say the mahogany hue of my legs has not entirely washed off – in fact is little altered by a bath. I deposited Dr Fraser in hospital yesterday and at this moment she is parting with her appendix. Thank heaven she didn't die on me or anything when in the Dutch East Indies. I've got enough quinine to last me for the trip, but the mosquitoes won't be too bad this time of the year. I've had endless information about the islands direct from folk who have been there and otherwise from shipping and tourist offices. You needn't worry about my doing anything rash or silly or getting ill or anything as I shall be quite all right. A sun proof hide to start with will be an asset. I feel it in my bones that I shall spend a dickens of a lot of money, especially if I motor across Sumatra – however when I'm spending a lot anyway a bit more or less doesn't matter, provided you have the cash.

I had to address a mothers' meeting yesterday – at least not quite that, but a female gathering at the Lyceum club. I didn't turn a hair at having to speak – completely unprepared for about half an hour about the expedition – but it was slap in the middle of my busy Saturday morning – a perfect curse.

I'm leaving Penang on September 7th by the P&O S.S. 'Kashmir', I haven't enquired if it goes direct back or whether I tranship at Columbo or Aden to an Australian boat. Anyway I get to Marseilles on September 28th, or should do.

Could you write me at Marseilles to the boat telling me the times of trains direct to Boulogne or Calais from Marseilles Ville station, then I can decide whether to take the P&O express or not. If I have to spend a night in the town in order to get the ordinary train I might think it worthwhile to take the P&O train and save a day perhaps. You had better find out if it is the 'Kashmir' or not, and address me as a second class passenger thereon, and then I shall not have to wait hours for the letter.

I will stop as I am very busy with letters and packing.

Lots of love,
Sidnie

Envelope for previous letter
(last to be posted from Australia)

a/c S.S. Nieuw Holland.

July 22nd

Outside Moreton Bay.

Dear Family,

Here I am – feeling rather dazed by this excessive plunge into civilisation. The boat is like a palace – my cabin vast and the best on the boat other than the two de luxe ones. What a difference to my last night at sea on the 'Daintree'! I've been a perfect glutton all day, sampling the marvellous creations of the Chinese cooks and gobbling up custard apples left me by my hostess [Miss Boge]. It's great to eat something not out of a tin or composed in part of those two tired standbys 'Rex-Pye'and 'Red-y-mele'.

1929 Advert

I hope I never see either for a long time! The crew is Chinese, the passengers horrid – too highly civilised and empty headed for words – Australian and American – not much to chose between them. Doubtless my outlook is greatly warped, as life would be so perfect if the Stephensons and John and Michael were here too instead of me only and an unused wasted ticket laying about owing to Dr F's appendix.

I'm longing to get into the heat. Brisbane is far too chilly now – I had four blankets and a coat and bedspread on at night and was still cold in Brisbane, the weather being equivalent to a warm English summer. I'm like a hothouse plant at the moment. I saw in the 'Brisbane Courier' that the district railway trains had ceased to function over Kew Bridge owing to rain – what a little world it is!

July 24

We are now among the reefs I know so well, but unfortunately pass Low Island at 4 am tomorrow. Otherwise the captain was going to take the ship out of her course and round L. I. so that I could take some photographs of it and bid it a fond farewell. I seem to be the honoured passenger on this trip. I had tea with the captain today, and am welcome on the bridge to look at the charts and talk navigation at any time. The passengers are a bore – somebody is always extracting information from me about reefs or the ships position or something.

Yesterday we passed an 8,000 ton ship stranded on a reef – it had been there for four years and is red with rust. It got there by careless navigation. They moved off the folk onto the neighbouring sand cay [a sandy island on a coral reef] and lighthouse. The next day the ship could have been got off the reef but the crew refused to work overtime even at double wages! Thus the boat was abandoned and remains there, apparently intact. What a country!

I'm busy with my usual ship's occupations – reading and sock manufacture and sleeping. I haven't had much exercise yet as they have only just put up the deck tennis net, and I have no use for deck quoits or 'bull board' and other futile games. Nobody on board, except the captain, has the faintest glimmerings of how to dance, so I don't patronise that form of exercise much either.

July 26

Had two marvellous days full of interest, and I've spent most of the time on the bridge getting a good view. I bade farewell to Low Island at 4 am and saw the ghost of Snapper Island pass in the dark. I got up properly at 6:30 am, and all day we passed close to a fine coastline, with reefs galore to starboard and lots of coral islands of 'Low Isle' type only less or more developed – all perfectly fascinating – we passed close up to Lizard Island and other old friends and it was fine to have a comparative birds eye view of it all. We diverted to go close round the Flinders Islands, fine rocky piles, for my especial benefit. Today we passed the barren cannibal inhabited northern end of Queensland, rounded Cape York and spent the morning in the Torres Straits – wonderful place, Thursday, Wednesday and Hammond Islands on one side with their fringing reefs and pearl fishers and some perfectly vast reefs on the north of the narrow rock bespattered channel.

So I reluctantly said farewell to the Pacific and the coral islands, and now we are far from land on the way to Timor. Getting warmer. Before I forget – would Bibs be angelic and get lots of brown paper so that I can make a picture book as soon as I get back before going to Cambridge about on Oct 9th or so?

July 30

Nearly at Makassar and now in the Salayer Straits. Yesterday was another glorious day. We scuttled along the shores of Timor for half the day, sometimes within 150 yards of the shore. It is a wondrous island – mountains 1,100 metres rising steeply out of the sea and a complete elementary geography lesson in weathering and subsidence – fine weathered deeply dissected valleys, wave cut beach in most places, and relics of other similar beaches at higher levels – drowned valleys, embayed shores, fringing reefs, and thick tropical vegetation – coconuts behind the reefs where present and a few cultivated patches of coconuts, bananas and vivid green rice fields with Kampongs of native huts among the palms. Near the shore is a sort of road and a few brilliant white and thatched residences of the Portuguese governors. Blacks were spearing fish on the reefs etc. Seeing the brilliance of a rice field and the queer native dwellings were most impressive. Then we wandered NW between other mountainous islands, usually far away with an enchantment lent by the tropical haze and queer lighting of a partly hazy and cloudy sky. Today is jolly hot – I spent the afternoon hair washing and packing etc in my cabin with all the fans on and all my clothes off. Very pleasant. I get off this boat tomorrow. I should think that the reputation these boats have of being the finest in the world is well justified. Nobody on board has any complaint of any kind or sort. It is not the strong splendour of the Oriente [sic], but perfect in every way of comfort, decoration etc. and excellently run. It couldn't be better. The captain gave a dinner last night and the ship provided champagne all round ! I've got a chit for 15/- to blue in the barbers shop having won the deck tennis tournament! I forgot to tell you about the flying fish – go about in 100s like swallows in a flock – well the rest can wait. This is a marvellous bit of the world.

Lots of Love,
Sidnie

Letter 41

Dear Family,

I left the last letter on the Nieuw Holland this morning to go on its way, so will start another now. Sunrise as we entered Makassar Harbour was a never to be forgotten sight. Half the eastern sky vivid and half pitch black clouds over the mountains, native dwellings all about the shore, islands out to sea all round, and wonderful native sailing boats all over the place. The Captain introduced me to a Dutch lady – the harbour master's wife, and she motored me all around Makassar and among the native villages. The latter are marvellous to look at, even if too smelly for words, all made of bamboo and sitting in and under dense groves of coconuts or bananas. The colours everywhere are fine and the sarongs worn by the Malays are perfectly beautiful. Makassar is full of Malays and Chinese with a fair sprinkling of Dutch. It is very hot at the moment (2 pm) even on my stone balcony outside my bedroom. There is only one Hotel here, spacious and cool but not up to much.

I forget whether I told you of my matured plans. If I have you needn't read the next bit. I leave here on August 3 for Bali, arriving on August 4th, I have three days there in the 'Paradise of the D.E.I.' and go on to Sourabaya on the 7th . I spend from August 8th – 21st in Java, I expect to have a few days in Batavia, and the zoological station folk are going to take me to see some coral islands in the bay of Batavia, which I believe are very like the 'Low Island' type. I've got a heap of introductions to folk in Java from Prof Goddard of Brisbane. On August 21st I sail for Padang on the west coast of Sumatra arriving 23rd. Then my extravagance begins and I hope to go by a Government car over the Padang highlands via Brastagi to Medam, an item of £25 (for the car) unless I fall in with a party. It is the most marvellous route from all reports. So by boat from Belwan Deli to Penang. I'm the

125

only member of the expedition who has any cash at all, and they are all green with envy at my route home. Even the Yonges won't get home solvent. My luck is truly surpassing belief. I'm not a bit lonely, there is so much to see and think about, but it would be fine to have you all here. Most of my luggage has gone on to Penang – spent the whole blessed afternoon fussing over my luggage - however all is well and they have found my three packing cases in the hold. I have sent five packages on to Penang and have a small case and rucksack with me – half the bulk of my goods now is photographic – what with 20 film packs (tinned) 8 dozen plates, developing tanks, stacks of tabloid developer and a whisky bottle of chrome alum hypo and a few pots. Plates aren't as satisfactory as films in heat – they pinhole and peel .

I find myself in a very advantageous position. Owing to my suntan and fearfully decayed topee [pith helmet] I am not taken for a tourist, (unless I have a camera), and can go about in an inconspicuous manner unmolested by the natives. I suppose they think I am a Dutch inhabitant. Mosquitoes don't appear to be too bad, although they are present. I seem to be provided with a bamboo switch inside my mosquito curtains for swatting mosquitoes. I'm consuming a daily dose of quinine so won't get malaria even if I do get bitten.

I have fallen in quite well with three decent Americans from the boat and the four of us are going shares for a three day car stunt in Bali, likewise a half day trip to some falls and stalactites and limestone mountains 30 miles off Macassar. As we are all desirous of economy it ought to work well. In Java I shall patronise the railway as that is good and very cheap while you can pay absolutely anything by road.

August 2

Had two indescribably wonderful days. Yesterday we started by car at 7 am and went out to a place where there is a huge bi-weekly market. Hundreds of Malays and Chinese thronged to the place from neighbouring villages etc and we

126

walked about and took photographs for two hours till about
10 am. The Yanks have the proverbial forwardness and
chivvied the natives about to get close up photos – while I
profited by the opportunity and have a fine lot of negatives of
all kinds of scoundrels buying and selling goods. The Yanks
were great centres of attraction with their ridiculous clothes –
vast plus fours and idiotic felt hats nearly 1 yard across,
while self in 1 ordinary topee and shorts evoked no sensation
at all – partly because my shins are the same colour as the
paler Malays. Then we left the market under its bamboo and
banana trees and went on to the mountains 30 miles away,
stopping to look at the native kampongs as we passed – the
Yanks getting cinematograph cameras to work in all
occasions. The waterfalls were not impressive, but the
country marvellous, huge limestone rectangular cliffs this
sort of thing

several hundred feet high - trees on top and stalactites from
all undercut edges. We walked up a gully half a mile, along a
stream, self perfectly cool and full of beans, while the Yanks
were slimy and hot and got blistered by the slightest scrap of
sun and got correspondingly tired. We went through some
caves (full of stalactites) and saw the river arising from the
base of a cliff in a cave, forming two nice lakes on leaving
the source.

So back to Makassar – lunch at 3:30 and off to tea with
Mrs Harbourmaster. Then today we started at 7 am and two
Chinamen rowed us about for three hours while I looked at
the coral through the clear water and we chased numerous
native craft for photographing. This afternoon we took

127

another car and explored native life and villages around Makassar.

Utilising the Yanks has been a great success, both for saving expense and for getting about to places. However, personally I shall have seen enough of them by the time I leave Bali in four days. Taken as a joke they are all right – in fact they are quite decent folk. Papa Koenig is 79 and decidedly senile and quite amusing, son Koenig about 35 is rather bumptious and modern but quite harmless and extremely considerate for other people (speaks 3 foreign languages fluently), - third party is too funny for words – looks like a tramp – age quite unknown, earns his living by travelling and giving lectures about it afterwards, has no teeth (not even artificial) and his ignorance is marvellous. Talks Arabic to the natives, some are somewhat Arabic in race and hoot with mirth and talk away to him with great gusto. He and son Koenig have but one object in their travels – and that is photography – they don't know anything about it much but take so many exposures that something is bound to turn out all right. I have used up 5 dry negatives in 3 days here, but that is nothing in comparison to their activities.

I will send all my Celebes negatives to you registered when I find some time and a P. Office.

S.S. 'Melchior Treube' 3000 tons
August 4

Reaching Bali this afternoon and will leave this letter on the boat. Sailing south from Makassar last evening we hit a side wind, and I promptly went to bed and had no dinner – too silly, as there was scarcely any motion compared with what I've put up with in really small boats. It is a most amusing boat, a sprinkling of Dutchmen and many rich Malays travelling first class, Malays second class and a solid mass of coloured third class folk.

I have the greatest contempt for European clothes in the tropics – they are perfectly idiotic. In Makassar I was hot and

128

unenergetic at temperatures lower than or the same as on Low Island and humidity <u>much</u> lower, whereas on Low Island dressed sensibly we were working at times much harder than any of the aborigines ever worked and we thrived on it. If only one of the expedition folk were with me I should always go bare legged, but I have not the face to go about alone in shorts except out of the towns. I should like to have gone to the interior of Celebes. Three hundred miles inland is perfectly marvellous I gather – there is a population of 3 million in the island [now known as Sulawesi, population 19.5 million in 2019], and last year seven thousand native boats unloaded and sold their cargos of copra etc at Makassar bringing it from other parts of Celebes etc. The native cargo boats are small, built on the same plans as the English and Dutch 17-18 C sailing boats with high sterns and low bows and large fixed lee boards and made of hewn planks and painted brilliantly.

Bibs would have a good time here if she did not mind the heat, as she could talk Dutch to everybody – however I suppose that in 5 minutes she would be talking Malay to the natives – it is an easy language I am told. I use about 2 Malay words out of a phrase book! There's nothing particular to say except that I am having the most astonishingly marvellous time. I hope you all flourish and are having a summer holiday somewhere.

Lots of love,
Sidnie

Bibs
Please would you see if Wallace Heatons will do any printing at reduced rates – I shall have 2-300 negatives 2¼ x 3¼ and the Baby Sybil [name of camera] size and I may not have time to do them myself before going to Cambridge. Also would you extract prices for large numbers of contact lantern plates – both bound up finished, and for the positives only.

Letter 42

Hotel Ngemplak
comfortable and well furnished rooms
private baths, (h&c), fans and telephones
Rice Table Tues Thurs Sat and Sun
Concert every night except Friday)
Soerabaia

August 8 1929

Dear Family,

Just arrived in this horrid place and found 2 post cards and 2 letters from Daddy and one from Bibs waiting for me - loud cheers. So glad you've been having a good time away. This is a disgusting European town full of heat and cringing begging natives. I travelled from Bali here on the S.S. 'Vander Lijn' 2,000 tons – otherwise known as the 'Pig Express'. Cargo was four passengers, 1500 Bali pigs each in a round (tubular) basket, stacked in piles, and 300 bullocks, not to mention smells and flies <u>innumerable</u> and of <u>every</u> kind belonging to the four legged ones.

Pigs go to Singapore. All this is incidental. I had four heavenly days in Bali – truly named the earthly paradise and Garden of Eden etc. It quite surpasses any description or imagination – folk in the boat who had travelled the world for 30 years in 50 countries said it was the most wonderful country they had seen. It has only been open to tourists for three years and can accommodate 20 visitors a week so is quite unspoiled. From 6 am – 12 pm I was seeing wonders – glorious mountains, valley and hilly scenery, marvellous terraced rice fields and palms – wonderful villages –

magnificent carved stone and wood temples everywhere – people charming, exceedingly beautiful, half naked and highly civilised – carvers, weavers, metal workers.

I can only tell you about it by aid of pictures - I used 14 doz negatives! The three Yanks and I motored about all day, jumping out of the car and wandering around every other minute almost – we went into humble dwellings, high caste establishments and palaces, fascinating markets, native dances, and native music depicting 2,000 year old tales performed under the village banyan tree in the shadow of the temple gate, wondrous gamelan [Indonesian percussion band] orchestra of silver gongs; saw a funeral ceremony in a house, a most joyous and solemn affair embalming the corpse, paying it offerings, gong music, processions etc, and we appeared welcome to honour the proceedings attended by 150 or more Balinese; another corpse, mummified for 2 years, was being put in its coffin – a huge hollow carved wooden cow preparatory to its cremation – cow and all, to gamelan music; 9 pm - midnight "shadow dance" – elaborate shadows of figures on a screen, man telling the story in Sanscrit which nobody understands and then retelling it in Malay with clown shadows for the people to understand. I was entertained by a princess and dressed up in gorgeous silk woven sarongs with metal silver and gold thread woven in – all conversation by signs – saw Hindu pagodas (unique) in plenty – old (1200 years) Buddist tombs and temples etc and 1000 other marvels. I have seen so much and have so many glorious memories that I could go home today without a murmur – however there is Java and Sumatra to come.

I'm spending pots of money, but it's worth every brass halfpenny I could borrow or steel [sic] if it came to that. Twelve guilders a day for a hotel (1 guilder = 1/8 [1 shilling and 8 pence]) and endless travelling expenses so far. However in Java I hope to get hotels at 5 guilders.

I think I must go to USA for long vac and do some popular lecturing on the Barrier Reef with coloured slides of corals under water etc at 150-500 dollars a lecture and send you and Mother to Bali – even going straight there and having only a <u>few</u> days in the island would be worth it. This is not altogether a joke – the American travel-popular-lecturer (one of the party) is enthusiastic that I should do it, and has given me the ends of necessary strings, and introductions etc.

Saturday August 10
If anybody makes a practice of always falling on their feet it's me! Yesterday I had planned to leave by train for Sourakarta – however by an incredibly circuitous route Mr Ostrander (the American travel lecturer) and I became known to the manager of the car touring company – result was a 7 seater car and driver gratis for two days so that we could go to Tosari and then walk or ride to the famous Bromo Volcano! Naturally I jumped at it – having cut Tosari out of my itinerary on account of expense, yet feeling I might always regret it. We started at 7 am – reached a pub at 6,000 feet at 11 am – heavenly scenery – walked 7 hours there and back with a guide for 1 guilder – at least I did – leaving Old Ostrander gasping by the wayside half way up. The crater is 15 miles round – a "sand sea" fills it and cones lie in the crater one being the famous Bromo – got up its cone and looked down a fierce funnel disgorging smoke and gurgles – a veritable downpour of smuts descended on us and we beat a choking retreat – it is a dust-sand volcano, no lava as on the volcano in Bali (which I forgot to mention). Hotel at Tosari was excellent for 6 guilders – arrived back here at 12 am today to catch the banks – was entertained to lunch by the owner of the car who has made me a detailed itinerary for Java and Sumatra with endless tips as to details – cheap hotels, travelling etc and is coming round this evening with more details for Sumatra. He frankly said that when he meets rich folk he makes what he can out of them and when folks haven't pots of money he likes to help them – he is Australian. Tomorrow I start for Djokjakarta [sic] by train at

5:40 am! Ostrander goes off to Borneo so I continue on my own.

Run out of paper and time – my days are so full, and nights busy with developing and writing diary – the latter is a prodigious task often as I do so much! I've two packs to develop tonight – I did 6 packs and 2 dozen plates in the 'Pig Express' night !

Vastly interested in the house proposition, but can't give any opinions shortly on paper.

Lots of love,
Sidnie

Letter 43

HOTEL „BOROBOEDOER"
MAGELANG
Tel. No. 25
Beheerder G. L. N. BRITT.
Gep. KAPT. INF.

Boroboedoer, August 13th 1929

Hotel Boroboedoer
Magelang
Aug 13 1929

Dear Family,

It is 7 am and I have just seen the sunrise from the top of the Borobudur Temple! Marvellous edifice 1,100 years old situated on top of a hill and surrounded by mountains – yesterday I thought I was overlooking a vast plain to the east – dotted with sugar and rice fields etc. However at sunrise I find a colossal volcano 20 miles away or less of great height standing in the plain to the east, perfectly regular in shape, and smoking at the top from a sharp peak and a glorious sunrise behind it – the plain being filled with clouds, a few pimples of hills and heads of coconut palms sticking up through it! Two other volcanoes stood up likewise from nowhere in other directions. As soon as the sun cleared the top of the volcano it and the others just disappeared in the haze formed by the rising clouds, and although sunny, only the near mountain ranges were left visible.

The temple is vast – 2 miles of wonderful wall carvings – picture stories of the lives of Buddha, over 500 figures of Buddha apparent from frescoes – the temple has no interior, it is an edifice of galleries and balustrades, and the pilgrim walked round the galleries learning wisdom from the carvings until he reached the top and beheld the wonderful view, then he went away a better man.

I return to Djokjakarta today – see more temples – and leave for Garoet tomorrow. This hotel is a shanty at the side of the temple miles from anywhere – I slept in a room open on two sides - with the temple in the moonlight in view – fireflies and mountains opposite, two white cats on the

134

doorstep – distant sounds of a gamelang native bell orchestra and numerous cicadas about – geckos rushed about the walls and ceilings catching flies.

August 14 Djokjakarta

Spent a marvellous day yesterday seeing endless Brahmic temples – I did no developing last night and now have 5 blasted packs waiting to be developed. However it is silly to economise films, as I'm seeing far too much to remember it all without assistance of that kind, or rather the hitch lies in mixing things up in one's memories.

People think me quite mad – I'm busting with energy and rush about from before sunrise all day not minding midday heat in the least. Most folk sleep from 12 till 4 pm. I suppose there is real heat in the middle of continents, but I have yet to meet it. The nights in Naples summer are far worse than anything I've met in the tropics.

Must stop and catch a train to Garoet – an all day journey up to some volcanoes – I'm getting by rail from one end of Java to the other for 33 guilders! Cheap. Also I'm getting across Sumatra for 60 guilders instead of £25 by booking the front seat on the government buses run for the natives!

Lots of Love,
Sidnie

Letter 44

HOTEL VILLA DOLCE - GAROET (Java)

Warme en Koude
— :— Baden —:—

L. H. W. INGENHOES
WAALS REISCODE. BENTLEY CODE.
Telegram adres
VILLADOLCE GAROET
TELEFOON No. 1 INT. LGC.

Luxe Appartementen
Electrische Verlichting

Het rianst gelegen vacantieoord van de Preanger.

Bandoeag, Java
Aug 17 1929

Dearly Beloveds,

I'm still having a marvellous time. I expect my letters are all catching each other up as I'm moving with the post – however there won't be many more now – one from Batavia and one from the equator in Sumatra I expect.

I got here last night – a mossy great town in beautiful surroundings. I motored up to 4,000 feet for the views of the valley this morning – most extravagant but I had two strenuous days at Garoet - a place belonging to Paradise along with Bali. Yesterday I walked 26 km between 7 am and 12 - through wonderful rice country looking its best – you must get bored by my perpetual bleating about upland rice terraces, but they are marvellously beautiful – a brilliant green which does not occur in Europe either in paint or naturally; streams, waterfalls, flooded fields etc and glorious bamboos, mountains all around and so on – I went to a lake (Lake Bagendit) – full of fishers in canoes made of hollow trunks, and simply casting big square nets. The last 3 km were a bit of an effort, but it wasn't too fearfully hot as I was up about 2,000 feet. The day before I started from Garoet (a lovely village) before 6 am in a car to the foot of the Papandajan volcano – lovely drive up a valley towards the huge peak of Mt Thkorai. Then I got a guide for 1 guilder who carried some food and drink, having stoutly refused ponies or sedan chairs, started up for the crater, ones two feet being far quicker, cheaper and pleasanter than other methods of transport. Route was fine – steep path through marvellous shady dense forest – tree ferns 30 feet high, but no lawyer vines or wire like climbers tying the whole together as in the Queensland rainforests. Crater itself truly astounding. In 1812 the mountain blew its top off and left a crater open on one side with 3 huge vertical walls of rock towering hundreds of feet on the other sides. In the crater the arrangement could not have been done better at the Earls Court Exhibition – here a pond of boiling spluttering mud with a fountain playing in it, next deep holes with growling boiling mud surging about at the bottom in an explosive manner – then a small hole (1-2 yards) deliberately spitting out pats of larva and jets of H_2S, the larva forming a rounded cone over a small area, just as the subsiding ones do in Vesuvius – further on a spout giving off clouds of steam and H_2S – then a huge mound of pure sulphur – riddled with holes and caves all formed of sulphur crystals, forming stalactites etc in the caves emitting much steam and SO_2, and in places the yellow sulphur crystals being transformed to the glutinous syrup coloured form we used to make in the lab – then imagine a fierce tropical sun lighting the crystalline sulphur and the white steam, it's asking too much of the imagination I fear – these springs of hot water forming a fair-sized mountain stream running down the mountain. So back to the foot of the mountain by 12 am and to Garoet by car.

Travelling here I may say is as easy as falling off a house [horse?!] although I can't speak one of the six current languages (Dutch, Malay, (the official tongue) or the four native tongues) and although trains and stations are hopelessly badly marked - a boy from the hotel seizes ones luggage and deposits it and you in the right train, another boy has ones goods long before the train stops and puts you in another train or at a hotel or on the right route to a hotel etc and the hotel managers are English speaking Dutchmen. Four times I've been the only European on a train – the natives are vastly respectful and will do anything for 10-20 cents and amazing difference to Bombay and Colombo natives who are the last word.

I must soon catch a train (2:20) for Buitenzorg arriving at 7:30 pm – I spend Sunday there and then on to Batavia. I'm getting fearfully excited about my bus tour through Sumatra – 880 km! for £5.

Excuse this messy paper – it's contaminated with my anti mosquito oily mixture – which is very efficient –

1 pt of paraffin
1 pt oil of lemon grass with citronella and preservative.
1 pt coconut oil

The post cards came off menu cards on the N. Holland – two are really good, but don't show midday sun.

Lots of love,
Sidnie

PS sorry, some of my letters weren't properly stamped, hotel Malay ideas on stamps seem to vary.

Envelope for the following letter

Letter 45

Batavia
August 21 1929

Dearest Folks,

About 5 more weeks and I shall be home! I sail for Padang this afternoon having had a right regal three days here. I arrived on Sunday night – to find that Dr Dolsman, the director of the Marine Station had met every train except the one I came by etc – to bring me to stay with him – early on Monday I started off with Dr Vervey for a two days' trip in the lab's boat on the Bay of Batavia to see the coral islands and reefs – I hit a full moon exactly here so had good tides – what luck! Dr Vervey (Dutch) is a very good zoologist and a very nice person and we got on fine, and swam about over reefs with our noses in water telescopes – they have a very good breed as thus

about the size of a pail inverted, with side handles, so that you hold on with your hands and swim with your legs when you get out of your depth. It was mightily hot and even my hardened hide was slightly reddened. We spent the night on an island with two charming Dutch folk who keep a beautiful sea aquarium and a chicken farm, and moved off to another reef at 6 am. The reefs were most interesting, different from the GBR in many ways. So we came back to Batavia at 12 am and I then was whisked off to the Dolsmans for lunch and to stay the night with them. They motored me round the town after tea and out along the shore for miles and miles in the moonlight, getting back after 11. I was irresistibly dropping to sleep by then. I spent a day at Buitenzorg and was frankly bored. The Botanic Gardens were disappointing they grow flowerless trees and climbers, water lilies and victoria regias and hundreds of orchids in the trunks of frangipani trees, about ¼ % being in flower. When one has seen 1) real tropical forest, 2) private gardens ablaze with colour, 3) realises how cheap and abundant labour is, I consider it a poor show to make no attempt to grow anything that flowers – either bush, small plant or the glorious creepers that do grow here. Also I hit a horrid bad, vast and expensive hotel as the nice one was full. However one can't have things perfect always. I must go out and cope with shipping offices and a bank – a very slow business in these parts. This may be my last letter, it may not be worth posting in Sumatra as letters will probably go no faster than I do.

Lots of love,
Sidnie

Letter 46

*a/b S.S. Melchior Treub
near Padang.
August 22nd*

Near Padang
August 22 1929

Dear Family,

I left Tandjong Priok (the port near Batavia) yesterday by this beastly boat. We passed Krakatoa at night of course. The sea is calm and we role [sic] about like a cork. I should think there is no ballast in the hold. It is difficult to walk about and glasses etc upset on tables. This time I don't mind the motion a bit except that it kept me awake all night. I get to Padang tomorrow. I've got another row on – with the KPM over £3.10.00 I had to pay in Batavia owing to an error of procedure on the part of their agents in Brisbane. I seem good at quarrelling with rail and shipping companies. The Tasmanian railways paid up the 3/- in the course of time – I don't expect I mentioned it!

Fort de Kock – Sumatra August 23

The end of another perfect day, and at the moment an ardent 'Mohammed something or other' is spreading the most glorious handweaving all over the verandah before my greedy eyes – if I bought all I wanted to buy I should spend simply heaps. Well, I saw a heavenly sunrise over Sumatra from the sea, and arrived at Emmahaven at 7 o'clock – a heavenly spot – caught a train at 7:30 for here – a distance of 70 miles taking 6 hours – a marvellous journey climbing 3,000 feet. The first hour was through a fine valley, endless combinations of palms, rice fields, waterfalls, and mountains beyond, and a wonderful smell after a night's thunderstorm

142

when passing through forest. Then we climbed a gradient of 70/1000 going about 4-6 miles per hour and words entirely fail to express the glorious beauty of the country – up a place in topography and water, like the Ganges of Gando, but superimposed tropical vegetation – fine trees – forests and climbers where they could hang on to the slope, bamboo and palms bending over the cataracts, tree ferns in thousands – giant *Selaginellas* and *Lycopods*, epiphytic ferns more glorious than I ever imagined they could be – white wisps of cloud hanging in hollows in the mountains. Then we reached a plateau – not snow covered, but full of rice and maize fields and three huge mountains rising up with their heads in the clouds. Here it is marvellously cool – it felt like going from summer to midwinter moving from sea level up here – yet it is really quite warm as gossamer clothes only are needed.

After lunch I went for a super heavenly walk – mainly along the edge of a huge canyon – rice cultivated on the bottom, the path going through palm and bamboo forest and by wonderful native dwellings with roofs like-

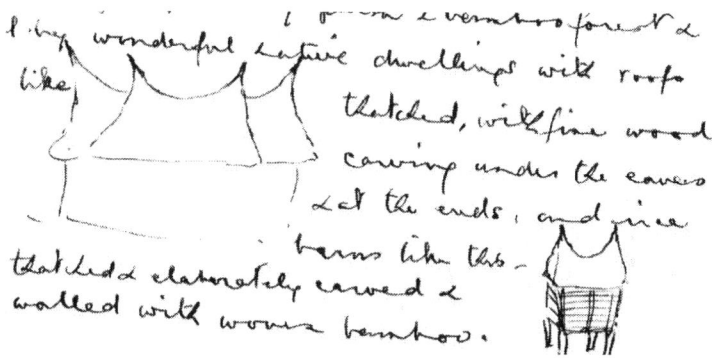

thatched, with fine wood carving under the eaves and at the ends, and rice barns like this, thatched and elaborately carved and walled with woven bamboo.

Sumatra apparently is only visited by the very rich. I was the only European on the train, and 20-30 folk from the boat were coming here. I have a book ticket for the whole overland journey and it caused quite a sensation in the train.

143

They eventually found a Malay official who could speak English and he said they had never seen a ticket like that before!! The plutocrats all go by cars. Nothing is better than a train going 4 miles per hour through marvellous country, far better than any fast car. It has just been raining a bit – it rains every day usually here, whereas in Java, Bali etc it has not rained for 4 months. Everything is greener and squishier in consequence.

This is positively my last letter. Tomorrow I spend the morning in the biggest native market in Sumatra and another walk in the afternoon – next day probably a car excursion, then three days by buses to coastal Sumatra and 4 days in various places round Lake Toba. Then off to a remote Batak village staying in a Government Rest House for 2 days and so to Penang. Today is Friday and 5 weeks on Sunday I shall be home!

Lots of Love,
Sidnie

Envelope for her Last Letter Home

THE
DIARIES

GREAT BARRIER REEF EXPEDITION 1928-1929

Diaries of Sidnie Manton who sailed out alone to join the Expedition, stopping in Tasmania on the way to search for *Anaspides*

<u>1928</u>
<u>Dec 20</u>
Left Victoria at 1:40 by the first boat train and got a good 'fur lined' place on a glazed in deck, while the P&O train people arriving late got no seats at all. Left Boulogne at 6:20 pm on a direct train and arrived at Marseilles at 11:10 am on <u>Dec 21</u> having spent a good night. Took a cab to the boat and arrived on board 2 hours before the P&O train folk, who came three quarters of an hour late for lunch. Spent the rest of the day on the ship.

<u>Dec 22</u>
Left Marseilles at 7 am, sea only just bearable in the afternoon, but calmer in the evening. The numerous black servants etc on the boat wearing pyjamas and red turbans etc in any weather are rather remarkable. Had a perfect farce of a lifeboat drill at 4:30 pm on A deck.

65 miles

<u>Dec 23</u>
Warmer and sunny and weather calm. Passed Corsica the night before and saw nothing of it. Passed Stromboli at 5 pm just as it was dark. The Islands round Stromboli were in sight the whole afternoon. Passed the Straits of Messina at 8 pm – only 1.7 mls in the narrowest pt. The lights of Reggio and Messina were lovely, no sight of Etna however.

377 miles

Dec 24

Played eight sets of deck tennis and had great fun. By 5 pm the sea was very rough, went to bed and had dinner then and survived nicely. The creaking of the ship was extraordinary, likewise its quivering when struck by a wave. No sun and a great wind.

364 miles

Dec 25

Saw the hideous results of the officers' women's table decorations. Sea calmer, and warmer air, but no sun. Spent a very cheery evening starting with a so-called concert after a very prolonged dinner at which the steward was more inefficient than ever. Mr Dicker performed with great gusto for mad song singing etc. The first class were far too sober and serious to be frivolous and enjoy themselves, but provided a band on this deck to which we danced till 12 pm. Rather cool but quite possible when dancing, but the roll of the ship got progressively worse. The 'Colonel' got really worked up over the 'one string fiddle' man.

324 miles

Dec 26

Should have reached Port Said at 6 am, but owing to the storm we didn't get there till 12:30. Most interesting approach over a calm misty sea. A crocodile pontoon was attached to the boat for landing. Walked about P. Said for one and a half hours – great for seeing an 'eastern' looking town for the first time, even if it is very dirty. Lovely mimosa trees in the streets, the bazaar was most exciting with stalls of live turkeys, pots, oranges, etc. Quantities of people trying to sell all sorts of rubbish. Bought a sun helmet at Simon Artz according to the colonel's advice. However we met him outside the shop and he insisted in taking it back in preference to the goods of Bombay!!

Port Said: The Simon Arzt Store

The boats of pedlars around the ship were fascinating. I was much wanting to get a Syrian blue carpet for £5-7 for my room. Left P. Said at 4:30 after a very enjoyable day. Entered the Suez Canal at sunset, wonderful lights of sunset down the Canal, and starlight etc over Port Said. The night was brilliant with a full moon at about the zenith at 11 pm. The desert was well lit up. The ship's search light scanned the canal in front, 3 camels were fascinated by the ship's lights and galloped along keeping level for several miles. Could not go to bed till late - danced till 10:30 seeing the moonlight on the desert.

Dec 27
Arose early as the ship passed the Bitter Lake at around 5 am. Scenery to Suez wonderful. The light of the boat gave a fine view of distant Arabian mountains, and fine stratified weathered ridges W of Suez. Sand for miles with a wonderful oasis to the W. Relicts of war barbed wire entanglements visible in the desert.
Passed Arabs and camels and works of canal widening. Reached the Gulf of Suez after breakfast in which we passed

151

all day. Scenery
here just great,
mountains and cliffs
on either side,
tremendously
weathered, usually
with no beach as
lowlands at their feet of a reddish colour. Sunset behind the
W. higher ridges just marvellous. No speck of vegetation –
everything weathered and dry and vast, one ridge behind
another. Very impressive as nothing like it seen before. I am
warm for the first time and no coats needed. Should have
seen Mount Sinai at 5:30.

Dec 28
First fine warm day and a cotton frock possible. Not by any
means very hot. The Red Sea calm, but not oily and no trace
of land except a few scattered islands. Spent two hours going
over the ship's engines, most interesting and not very hot –
only 110° in the boiler room. The propeller shaft was 26'
below water line and the propeller 19 ft across rotating 81.5 x
a minute. The twin screw makes turning in the ship's length
possible. The oil is heated to 140° before being sprayed into
the burners. The main engines have to be started by a
separate engine.

392 miles

Dec 29
No sight of land, a light breeze and pleasantly warm. The
Red Sea porpoises are more slender and far better jumpers
than the English sp. Played more tennis, not too hot, and
continued to teach my grey headed flock to dance. The
Colonel getting reasonably decent at last and catching up
Thomas.

388 miles

152

Dec 30 Sunday

Distant misty mountains, one ridge behind an other and islands visible. Scenery fine all day, with close view of Arabian ridges and mountains. Passed /Penim/ at mid day and reached Aden at 8 pm. Col. Polley took me ashore and we saw the place and motored around the rock to the tanks which were illuminated. All perfectly fascinating if hot with an all pervading scent of camel and Arab. The road tunnels through the rock in places and all is bare and dry the people living on distilled water for all purposes. Camel carts everywhere – passed an Arab wedding in a side street. Native habitations just awful – one square room in each house where they all live, no furniture worth mentioning, and lit by an oil lamp on the floor. Local hotels just awful. Met the Muirheads and co and returned to the ship about midnight. Native /screaming/ perpetual.

Dec 31

Left Aden at 3:30 am having taken on much oil and stores. Fancy dress dance in the evening and Col. Polley performed most efficiently and vastly enjoyed it – likewise Thomas. To bed very late.

136 miles

Jan 1 1929

Land in sight in dim distance all day on Arabian coast. Weather cooler, but thin clothes comfortable.

371 miles

Jan 2

Less calm, windy, but warm, spent a lazy day after the exertions of previous days. The theatrical party gave a very good show in the evening.

379 miles

Jan 3

Nothing of note, except pleasant chatter with Polley.

<u>Jan 4</u>
Arrived in Bombay at 5 pm – having spent 2 hrs on a sand bank, and 2 hrs getting up to the key with 3 tugs pushing and 2 pulling. Went a drive ashore with Polley who helped get my hat, dined very pleasantly in the frontier express and left Bombay at 9:30 very depressed. The bay itself is delightful, first sight of scavengers with gulls.

<u>Jan 5</u>
Land in sight faintly all the time. Flying fish in shoals. Very warm and slack. Missed Polley very much in the evening.

222 miles

<u>Jan 6 Sunday.</u>
Warmer – sea 84° and air 85°, very stuffy inside. Swam as a sardine in the bath and just contrived to dive in it. More flying fish. Flatly refused to function on sports committee.

390 miles

<u>Jan 7</u>
Reached Columbo at 6 am – breakfasted at 7 and left the boat at 8. To my surprise I found Hilda at the quay, having spent the whole weekend in Columbo as the Mooltan is a day behind time. We rejoiced heartily and she motored us to Mount Lavinia and all over the place, finally exploring the native shops – great fun, the carts drawn by very diminutive cattle and the rickshaws were so new. The vegetation was quite luxuriant, with dense groves of coconuts everywhere. The road labourers etc. were all S. Indian Tamils with very black skins, the Singalese being browner. The native dwellings and shops and suburbs were very attractive and doubtless dirty. The gardens of the larger houses quite formal, but brilliant with flowering trees and shrubs – the 'flamboyant' trees along the roadsides were just beginning to come out in places as a sheet of bright red flowers. Saw Mr *[-]* the marine biologist and his beautiful black and white and coloured drawings of local sea fish and lizards – also heard the origin of F. Cowpers giant *Varanus* [a Monitor Lizard] – a protected animal in Ceylon, which was stolen, dried and

154

kept for 2 years before sending to Cambridge! Left Columbo at 1 pm and the island was visible all day with a belt of coconuts close to the sea.

346 miles

Jan 8
Remarkably cool – air 82° water 84°. Wonderful coloured sea and flying fish in the distance. Fine sunsets as usual. Crossed the equator at night. Heat [damp].

Jan 9
Warmer and [damper] – feeling more collapsed than at Naples at 93°. Getting very bored with the absence of pleasant company, the second class being fuller than ever and like a monkey house with another tournament on.

384 miles

Jan10
Warm – good bathing and tennis.

383 miles

Jan11
Cloudy – less warm – passed the Cocos Islands at 5 pm – rather fine sight – numerous large and small low islands covered with coco palms intersected by shallow green seas and deep blue seas beyond the fringing reefs on which the surf was breaking.

360 miles

Jan12
Cool – vest and coat needed. Very bored.

363 miles

Jan13 Sunday.
Cloudy, rough and cool and got a touch of sunstroke on the top desk after a few minutes without a hat.

359 miles

Jan14
Cloudy, rough and cool – very bored.

336 miles

Jan15
 More sun but rougher still.   342 miles

<u>Jan16</u>
Reached Freemantle at 6 am and had a ridiculous medical inspection and left the boat at 10 am. Mobbed by newspaper reporters in spite of efforts to escape.

MISS S. M. MANTON, Ph.D.

Who, with Dr. Fraser, was a passenger on the Mooltan, which arrived at Fremantle on Wednesday last.

Fine warm sunny day – temperature just right – although 2 days previous it was 102° when the Russells passed through on the Orient boat. Motored to Perth (40 mins) fascinating ride. Tin huts and buildings astonishingly hideous, but the flora and the strong sun camouflage a multitude of sins. Beautiful flowering Eucalyptus along the streets, palms and flowering bushes and creepers everywhere – not a single familiar plant. At Perth crossed the ferry and went to the zoo – a wild pelican was swimming about in the estuary and many divers and queer 'cormorants'. The zoo from a floristic aspect was fascinating. Animals few and dull. Lunched with Prof and Mrs Willsmore – Dakin going to a reception. Mrs W. then motored us over the National Park with the highest hill over looking the town and river. It consists mainly of untouched bush – masses of gum trees (and *Arucaria* planted [Norfolk Island Pine]) and *Cycads* in huge finely growing bushes etc. The flowers of the red and pink eucalyptus and of the magenta creeper are wondrous – likewise hibiscus, rose etc etc. The scent of the bush and the sight of the flora with no single familiar plant and the sandy reddish soil and wonderful views made a great impression. And so back to the boat sailing at 5 pm.

Jan 17
Cool again with a frigid southerly blast. The waves hit us sideways – for the first time and we rolled excessively. First sight of albatross following the boat – sooty, wandering and yellow-billed, and a few Mother Carey's Chickens. Truly a wonderful flight – entirely effortless (apparently) – steering near the water with spread tail and <u>feet</u>, and resting on the water and flying within a few feet of the boat. Spent much time photographing them from a precarious foothold on the moving deck.

Jan 18
Rounded the point (SW) and in the 'Bite' – warmer sun and a good roll. Albatross following. Danced till 12.

369 miles

Jan 19
Warmer and calmer. Sunny. More numerous Albatrosses.

Jan 20 Sunday
Reached Adelaide at 1 pm – decided to go by rail 4:30 pm. However all Port Adelaide were on strike except two men and a barrow who worked on the quay. Nobody else works on Sundays, although the local paper was full of lurid accounts of lack of work and starving women and children at Port Adelaide. Took two hours of bribery and persuasion to get my box slung out of the hold. The ship used its own cranes but had no control over the lasgars or over 2 pig headed stevedores. When I did get it I had to shift it myself and take a car (26/-) with the box precariously tied to the step. Just caught the train after three quarters of an hour race, my luggage came by the next. Very jolly views all the way. At first climbed a long bluff behind A. and then the bush was luxuriant and thick. Gradually the gums became less dense and the bush opened out and was interspersed with pasture and grain land. The only familiar plant was the pink 'Italian' Oleander; and the birds were all strange and the only familiar beast was the rabbit. Fine sunset at 7:40. Comfortable 1st sleeper.

Jan 21
Reached Melbourne at 8:15 am – breakfasted on the station and went on the tracks of GPO and various shipping and railway agents. Fine warm day, not too hot. Melbourne certainly less tin shanty and unfinished than most places. Good fruit about.
Collected luggage by 1:15 train and took 'Nairana' at 3 pm (59 William Street Office) this boat a typical example of the boats of the country since given the monopoly of the

Australian passenger traffic. All two berth cabins now for four, barely fitted, bad service, ½ - ¾ size of channel boat and all on top and not much below waterline. Rolled atrociously, but by going to bed I survived.

Jan 22
Woke in the Tasman doing the 30 miles up the river to Launceston which we made by 8 am. Thence by train to Hobart arr. 2:30 pm. Lunching at Parratah (2/6). Railtrack – as on the mainland, very twisted, the line not being levelled and straight as at home. Part of the scenery might well be England if you didn't look at the gum trees too closely. A few willows, gorse and poplars made one quite excited, after so much strange and new country. The scenery S of Parratah greatly improves, with much highland in the distance, fine views [rivers] and near hills and woods and fields. Mount Wellington a fine sight.
Found Prof. Flynn [father of film star Erol Flynn]– a perfect dear, who has done endless useful things for me including writing to the Steward on the Nairana to look after me! Slept in a bed (!) at the Astor Hotel (15/-) or rather didn't sleep – it was so unutterably stable and solid.

Jan 23
Arranged through the Gov. Tourist Bureau for a 2 horse cab to take me and goods up to Springs having done various negotiations in Hobart. All main shopping streets in Australia seem to be Elizabeth Streets, and Collins Sts with banks and offices! 2 hr drive up perfectly marvellous – the giant fern trees about 2 x the size of our largest forest trees in height, heaps of flowering shrubs and ever increasing grandeur and scope of view. At first very warm, but cooler up 2,300' at Springs – lunched, and then climbed to the top 4,160' – a great experience. Firstly the old joy of a good mountain path going up and up – then the view surpasses all description (or photography). Sea, islands, rivers, estuaries, promontories, mountains, towns and fields, a literal map at one's feet, and

at the top, this on three sides with more mountains to the W. Then the wonder of the bush at close quarters – nearly everything when squeezed is strongly aromatic, eucalyptus scented or smelling strongly of cats. Giant gums of huge height with absolutely straight trunks – all gleaming greyish white in the sun – only the tops being leafy – smaller gums with brilliant foliage covered with bloom and new leaves bright red, flowering bushes in profusion – mainly pale colours, the upper leaves of some bushes being brilliant red spikes as of flowers. Not many herbaceous flowers, but many fine large blueheads and big solitary white composites. As one climbs upwards the bush gradually shrinks in height and thins out, finally ending as flowering bushes amongst the [oor] near the top. Curious organ pipe outcrops of weathered rocks about and near the flat topped dome. In the middle heights the tree ferns and others are a true revelation, mixed with the gums in gullies and at the sides of the path, which might be one in a skillfully grown botanic garden. So back to Springs and fitted up my lab in the bedroom, banished a second bed and acquired a table. Dinner, and then watched a bewitching sunset – the clouds below which I had previously looked down on in parts had gone a wonderful red and orange colour hung about the mistiness and bewitching purples enveloped the mountain as parts of the distant land was gradually hidden from view. A silence one could cut with a knife reigned. None of the numerous green chattering woodpeckers or the noisy cicadas, grasshoppers or flies – no moving black lizards etc. and so to bed, just five weeks after I left London – what a five weeks of experiences.
What a little world – here I was known as soon as I arrived – it having been noised in the local papers, and 12,000 miles away I find the same theatre shows and dance tunes.

Jan 24
Another gloriously fine day – Prof Flynn phoned after breakfast, and being busy I was to see the Ranger. I found Mr King an admirable fellow and after lunch we set out along the

'old top track' past the 'ice houses' (where snow used to be packed into ice and carted to Hobart) and through the 'gap' and over the 'ploughed fields', a heap of boulders too rough for vegetation and across the watershed to the 'plains'. A stiff 1½ hr climb over rough ground – boots essential. 'Diamond Springs' at the gap were nearly dry and empty of life, but the plains contained *Anaspides* abundantly in some of the pools. A great thrill to see this living antique alive, olive green sunning himself lazily in the warm shallow water – and to think that he has lived there as now since before *Homo sapiens* was thought of. He rules the roost and has no natural enemies there and can't defend himself at all.

On we went – stumbling over the native 'artichoke' and boulders, the bush trees being absent except the 'island' of trees in the middle of the 'plain'. Higher peaks of rock raised themselves on three sides, and all were studded with flowers, mainly bushes, and a beautiful purple (mauve) herbaceous plant. The water was sparkling clear, and the marshy pools gradually gave place to a rivulet draining further pools. Weeds abound and *Anaspides* sits persistently on and in them. The rivulet then reached the main stream of the North West Bay river which arises as a vigorous stream. No wind stirred the water surface and the bleak stunted flattish top of the mountain was warm and delightful. Mr King kept up a continuous conversation – quite an interesting fellow – and we finally wandered homeward having spent a truly marvellous day seeing a region and a marvellous beast after travelling half way round the world. On leaving my guide I found Prof Flynn waiting at the Springs having come up for the night to see if I was fixed – charming person. We tea-ed at 6:30 and then walked to the 'Sphinx' through the moonlit bush, filling the time with pleasant talk – and so to bed at 10:30.

Jan 25
Another fine day. Fixed Mr King's tub quarter of a mile off at the stream, and accompanied Prof Flynn down to Fern

Tree Bower as he walked the 9 miles to Hobart. I like him more and more – and he's so quiet over his work and all. Afternoon again with King to the 'plain' less sunny but warmer, and *Anaspides* mostly in hiding – however we fished a dozen or so and brought them back triumphantly and installed them in the tub. I picked out the path this time as the town clerk had sent voluminous instructions for my safety, as the clouds make the route treacherous – wearily to bed.

Jan 26
Spent the time watching *Anaspides* – seven millimetres – 1¾inches. [7mm is little more than 3/8"] Day poor and cloudy, certain rain, especially in the morning, and cloud effects below and above us were marvellous.

Jan 27 Sunday
Another poor day, cool, damp – cloud on tops all day. Dr F came up at 11:30-4:15

Jan 28
Poor day – spent it watching *Anaspides* in my room. Wonderful cloud effects below and level with us, and strange lighting over the Derwent valley etc.

Jan 29
Poor day – cold, windy, rainy. Watched *Anaspides*.

Jan 30
Dr F came up at 11:30 and we went off directly to the 'plains' and fished for *Anaspides* – cool and windy.

Jan 31
Worked in my room – examining guts for *[freparines/preparines?]* etc. Very cold indeed – wet and windy.

Feb 1

Wet in patches to start with – started out for Hobart walking, reached the University in two hours – weather improving, walk wondrous – especially walking through thick bush directly after a shower in full sun – scents most pungent and pleasant. Took the Fern Tree and Gentle Annie Falls route, past the reservoirs – path all the way, nearly to the [tams]. Embedded and sectioned my *Saccharote* fed *Anaspides*. Spent the night at Astor. Prof Flynn kindness itself.

Feb 2

Stained sections – no trace of *sac.* colour – awful blow. Brilliant sunny day – of course as I had left the mountain. Shopped – bought boots, hired cinema camera etc and returned in the ranger's car – a 2 seater Morris, which accommodated Mr and Mrs King and self in front, and in the dickey, luggage and rucksack – sack of chaff for the cow and friend of Mr Moor on top of the lot! Spent rest of day cleaning out tubs of beasts.

Feb 3 Sunday

Fine day – Eureka! Set out + three cameras for the plains. In tow ranger and Mr Moor, Prof Bridger, Dr F, Miss Hindmarsh and Miss Broadhurst! I worked the camera, at a range of half a yard and Prof Bridger tickled the beasts into the field – great fun. He stayed and shared the lunch, very pleasant man, economics, was at Oriel, Oxford during the war. It clouded in the afternoon and in the moment I pulled up the camera the clouds broke! However we departed and went off to the 'pinnacle' and so home. Delightful day. (Hindmarsh and Broadhurst went back at once). Mr King and Moor made tea in a billy can – very strong! Heavenly view extending 90 miles distant and 130 miles across. Developed films – all dud!

163

Feb 4

Duller day – knowing now [the] exposure and conditions of photographing *Anaspides* I decided to do it all down here. Fixed up running water tubs, and went again to the plains – heavily packed and alone. Fairly warm, but little sun. Got a good catch of beasts for the second tub, many little ones to pickle, and 'scenery' for the mock photographs to be taken in a bedroom basin! i.e. liverworts, moss, weed, fern and plants for the edge. Returned heavily packed + carried iron rods of camera stand – mist came down and I was quite tired and thought I should never reach the Springs without an ambulance. Picking every single step over rough ground is so very tiring, apart from the inclination up or down.

Feb 5

Thick low cloud at breakfast, apparently hopeless. Fixed up second running water tub. Beasts in first bath (galvanised iron) giving up the ghost rapidly. Those kept in bedroom from the first still healthy. Clouds vanished by 11 am leaving brilliant sun with distant haze and no wind!! At once set to over photography – carried cans and basins and cameras and scenery 100 yards from the hotel and set to. Many unforeseen snags –

1) heating up of water in the sun to about 65°-70° leading to the mortality of a fine large pair,

2) bits from grasses etc blown on to surface of water, and weed, although washed clouding the small volume of water. Finally successful at range of 17", depth of water 2", exposure 1/10 at 4.5 or equivalent, and vast expenditure of patience in getting the beasts still in position – horizontally as depth of focus small. Hastened to pack up - filming cinema being unfeasible, and rushed down to fir tree to meet Mrs Manning for tea. Very pleasant soul, who took us to the wishing well after tea picnic below the fern trees at 'The Silver Falls'. Fine *Anaspides* in pool with light brown colouration and transparent legs! Pool was much lighter in

164

colour and light weed and protected from wind, therefore light.

Feb 6
Glorious still sunny day – at once to the 'plains' and nearly burst climbing up in the heat + cinema apparatus. Most curious effect at top – low lands under mist up to about 1,500 – 1,800 ft and the top of this appeared as the horizon, much too high up – the sea merging absolutely imperceptibly into the cloud. Top of cloud presented a perfectly firm sharp line – inland broken by the tops of the Hartz Mountains. Dr F departed.

Feb 7
Another marvellous day – to the top again in a serious, but fruitless hunt for embryos. Recognising more of the flora – tree senecios, 'lilac', 'tea tree sps', heath berries etc. Took several successful close ups of the vegetation. Shared my bread and cheese with *Anaspides*! who much appreciated the attention. Home very weary.

Feb 8
To Hobart – gloriously warm (84°) walking to Huon road and getting a lift – embedded beast and made preliminary arrangements for getting to the Great Lake – level raised 22' in 8 years. Manager of Hydro Electric Department getting me a lift. Saw Zoo – fine to see the wallabies really rushing about giving gigantic leaps – much more than I had even dreamed of – likewise living *Thylacines*, T.devil, huge wombats etc. Back by the Huon bus to Fern Tree and walked up 'Fernglade'. Truly amazing glut of fern trees – up to 18' high, cutting out most of the light, and path being made of soft trunks of fern trees. No sound, utterly still and green and wonderful, with huge gum tree trunks lying across the gully in places.

Feb 9
Another stewing hot day – to Fernyglade plus cameras – a veritable fairyland indeed – or a jump into the permocarboniferous – then along to Crispins Well for the albino *Anaspides* – baby ones in the stream by the thousand over a stretch of 4 yds x 1! More photography in the still sunny afternoon and developing at night. Another perfect if tiring day.

Feb 10 Sunday
Hot but a thick haze which did not clear. Lazy day for once painting *Anaspides*. Many mortalities overnight in the heat.

Feb 11
Feeling ill, and thick fog prevails – mouldy show altogether – spent day drawing.

Feb 12
Fog and cold persist – feeling like nothing on earth, did a little drawing and went to bed. Whole hotel got agitated with kind attentions.

Feb 13
Feeling well, thank heaven, weather finer – morning spent in photography and drawing - drawing for rest of day.

Feb 14
Went hunting *Astacopsis* [Tasmanian Giant Freshwater Crayfish] – got stuck in impenetrable bush on terrific slopes.

Feb 15
Went with Miss Mallarky and Miss Broadhurst to Kingston and Browns River after *Astacopsis*. Saw the local school and beautiful garden. Afternoon to the Greens and saw endless foreign and native plants.

Feb 16
Atrocious weather, rain and mist. Photographed plants in my room. To Hobart in Miss H H Green's car.

Feb 17 Sunday
Awful day – wrote up *Anaspides*.

Feb 18
To Great Lake by 8 am post: a stout 6 seater car officially for the mails – consisting of about 20 bags – the car had a soft top and no rear luggage carrier – we took 11 bulky persons – mails on the step, lots and lots of luggage – a revelation in capacity! Three hours to Bothwell where lunched and proceeded on by the Miena van for another 3½ hours. Bothwell – off the map so to speak, well two shops and few houses and deliveries of goods done by boys on horseback. Pessissera - large war memorial with 29 names on it – such is this united world. The route on from Bothwell was very interesting – bad track – through extensive sheep runs, passing droves of sheep and bullocks looked after by horse backed riders and dogs – really like the wild and woolly west. Gates across the track in places, finally at 4.30 we arrived a the accommodation hut at the S. end of the lake, the latter being mainly invisible in the cloud and rain and its surface whipped into a mass of waves by the wind. Gum forests abound, many *Banksia* in flower etc. Pleasant evening at the hut, everybody making themselves very pleasant and useful. Mr Parkes having his 30th year at the lake thinks he can find *Paranaspides* – if the wind goes down and the lake becomes navigable.

Feb 19
Hopeless day – wind and rain and mist. Went out with Parker and Simpson – wonderful lunch. Made a fire in the rain and grilled steak and boiled billies etc. Found many *Planarians* [flat worm] and 3 *Pheatricus spinosus*. Great fun.

Feb 20

Hopeless day – stormy, took same company plus Barwick in the Ford lorry and went over appalling tracks, getting out and pushing etc through the bush to Swan Bay protected from wind. Fine lunch on chops etc by a huge fire, again in the rain – good catch of *Pheatricus* (100) under stones at the edge of present water – pretty rapid rate of recolonising new lake area. Two trout caught 3+3½ lb. So home in the van in the wet.

Feb 21

Mr Jepp of the hydroelectric department had arrived overnight – bringing 23 miles of telephone wire plus 3½ ton reels of cable for the north end of the lake and the fine weather! However the wind still blew, and we spent the whole morning getting the dinghy across the few yards to the launch with the load, about seven journeys! Rowing was impossible, and they had a rope from the boat to the launch and shore, inshore the waves broke into the dinghy filling it completely. However after 4 of them were soaked, and one spent a tempestuous swim disentangling a rope from the propeller we set forth at 1:30. There was a good 'slop' on, and the sight of the launch was enough to make one ill almost – firmly determined not to be ill, and cut up bread and food for the seven men hoping nobody noticed me getting greener every minute. Fortunately the wind dropped a bit and we had a fine journey – passing swamped gum forests, the white dead tops projecting – the Western Tiers away to the right, and the shores indented by bays, scarcely visible unless close to the shore. The lake is at 3,330' and the watershed round it up to 7 miles away and 500 feet higher, the area getting a prodigious rainfall, the width of the lake varies – 7 to 9 miles and less. Dumped half the wire, less difficulty as the waves had subsided. Finally we reached the north end at sunset, and took in goods etc. Shores here much more wooded and attractive at the water's edge, compared with flat plains near the lake to the south. Met aged boatman George Pennyman –

who said the trout were feeding on *Paranaspides*! Great
thrills of excitement. Late tea at the accommodation house
which we filled completely. Then to talk to George about
shrimps etc. Mr Jepp extremely nice and did everything
wonderfully rising to the occasion.

So to bed, in a chorus of frog croaks surrounded by open
watered bush and numerous white flag like flowers growing
1 yard high in the damp rocky soil. Outside sheet and fork
lightening lit up the south end of the lake – wonderful sight at
night across the water.

Feb 22

Arose at 4:30 – to go fishing, and that noble man Mr Jebb got
up mainly to see me safely into George's dingy!! Fished
unsuccessfully till 7 am over new bottom, catching ferns,
trees etc. Then hoots of joy over the beast coming up with
weed from a bit of inshore old bottom originally 2' deep and
now under 25' of water. Returned to breakfast at 9.30 with
30 small and one large shrimps. Set off in the launch directly,
and the weather cleared again, after the cloudy sunrise – it
was barely light when we started fishing. Wind dropped and
we got thoroughly sunburnt. Dumped wire etc and got off
near the 'bee hives' and cooked a billy etc and fed lustily –
after I had a dry 'piggy back' to get to the shore. Reached
Miena at 3 pm having had a wonderful 2 days, and with such
nice folk. Watched the beasts etc for the rest of the day and
to bed early !!! …..

Feb 23

Arose early to finish beasts and pack and bid TBS farewell.
Went back with Mr Jepp and two others in the Hydro-car.
He took me via New Norfolk and the Derwent Valley.
Perfect day and fine varied scenery – flourishing [hop] fields
in the valley – and jolly fine lunch and billy at the salmon
ponds hatchery. Picked up Mrs Jepp and was motored up to
Springs by about 6 pm – and so to the end of another perfect

day. We passed two bullock wagons – 8 beasts to each – taking the yearly stores up to the shepherds.

Feb 24 Sunday
Fine and warm – spent inspecting, tubs, beasts – drawing and photography. Mr King caught a few *Astacopsis* – cheers. Plenty of *Temnocephala* [parasite] on them.

Feb 25
Finished drawings of *Anaspides* and bottled pickled etc.

Feb 26
Off to the Hartz Mts, breakfasted at 7:30, and so to Geeveston with Miss Broadhurst in her car. Fine day and a glorious ride of 40 miles across the lower slopes of Mount Wellington, Huron Valley etc fine scenery all the way. Mr R Greenes drew very nice maps of the route and of the range for us. Picked up our guide, Mr Pepper and packhorse and started on the 8 mile climb to the hut, leaving Pepper far behind.

A glorious track cut mainly out of the solid bush, the sort of track that takes a gang of men one day to cut 10 minutes worth. Track at first through luxuriant valleys full of giant gums and dense undergrowth, climbing heaths etc. covering the myrtle (*Northofagus*) and *Sassafras* trunks and tree ferns towering above the undergrowth in the damp stream fed parts. In 4 miles we emerged on the flat Commandie plains originally denuded by fire and now fairly open. Thence on through dark ferny cuttings, wet and muddy underfoot, somewhat downhill and then climbing up again, leaving the red buttressed gum trunks behind. Graco trees up to 20 feet high now became evident, a wonderful sight. Finally half a mile from the hut after passing fine waterfalls we climbed out of the bush to the bleak mountain slopes – gay with heatherwood bushes in full flower – a site never to be forgotten. From the hut, itself in a hollow fed by a stream and surrounded by bush, we looked across the Heron Valley to the Mount Wellington range with a wee white cloud as usual sitting over the Springs corner, or so it seemed, Mount Nelson – sea and Rooney Island in full view, with the Hartz peaks and pinnacles behind us. Pepper arrived at 5 pm and we soon had a fine log fire and good meal cooked - and jolly fine it tasted although only bread and chops and billy tea. After tea we set out to Lake Esperance to set trout lines in the hopes of swelling the larder, we could only raise five chops for three of us for the two days before starting. How Pepper found the way back in the dark - moon not yet up - across rough unmarked country was a marvel. It was only one and a half miles, but I might have wandered all night trying to find the tree hidden hut. So to bed, 2 in a bunk, a blanket each and eiderdown on top after toasting our toes by the dying fire. A cold night.

Feb 27
Pepper arose early, to find no fish on the lines, and I had a fire and breakfast cooked - i.e. all we had left cookable, by 7 am. Set out at eight or before for the top of the Hartz 4,260

feet high fine rough walk with a steep clamber over rocks and tufts for the last few hundred feet. Green tussocks in full flower near the top. Passed three more tarns en route, and reached the large Hartz lake at the foot of the Hartz peak. The tip of the peak was in light cloud and we got no view from it, however lower down the panorama in both directions was fine – rugged Arthurs Ranges on the skyline, (no snow yet) forest clad valleys, fine rocky foreground of the Hartz range and beautiful tarns below us. So down from the peak and walked right along the north-south ridge for two hours up-and-down over the other peaks when possible - finally left the range and climbed down to Lake Perry and so back to the hut for alleged midday meal at which we cleaned up everything most satisfactory. So back to Geeveston, teamed with the Geeves at 6:30 - washed up and home to the Springs by 10 pm.

Feb 28
Exposed 100 ft film on *Anaspides* and on the top of Mt W.

March 1
Packed – to the [Greenes] to take some photographs, and to the Astor in Miss Broadhurst's car. Saw the first film at Harringtons - a washout – not good as I had been led to suppose.

Mar 2
Sectioned *Paranaspides* etc at the University, and out with the Gepps at 2:30. Fine afternoon and we motored to Kingston along a heavenly road going in and out round the coast showing ever-changing views of the shoreline, sea and Derwent estuary. Had tea at Sandy Bay and then bathed - awfully good, and so up Mount Nelson where we saw the sights through the telescope, the out going Otranto which had called for the apples etc. View very fine, as all is so much nearer apparently than from the Springs. Home to Tea at 8 pm with the Gepps, washed up, and dried my hair and out

172

again to see the "Australia" the new warship lit up - motored around "the domain" and so back to the Astor at 10:30 – the end of another perfect day.

Mar 3 Sunday
To the University - then 11 am tea with Mr and Mrs Baldwin and so off at 2:30 to Launceston arriving at 8:15 pm to the Brisbane Hotel.

Mar 4
Poor day, wettish - dug up Mr Dowson. Had tea with them, very nice house and situation, overlooking the Tasman and distant hills. However - very disappointing to be fixed in Launceston when they had expected Hobart.

Mar 5
Fine - went over the two converted prisons which will form Dr Dowson's lab - and very nice too they will be. Fine wood as usual in evidence forming floors, ceilings and partitions etc. All eucalyptes of sorts. Left by the Naiana, having been up to see the Gorge and very fine it is too.

Mar 6
Filthy crossing, arrived in a collapsed state, just not having been violently ill, always a mistake. Very good to see Sam Wadham on the quay but I hardly recognised him, plus a moustache and a new hat – too presentable for words. Endless things to talk about of course. SMW motored me to the "Greycourt" and then on over the university. Met Dr Buchanan, Prof Agar etc. Lunched sumptuously at the Wattle with SMW, Dr Buchanan and Miss Rall. - Then motored out to Ringwood collecting old Mr Searle to look for a koonuga, which we did not find but I caught a tadpole this size!!!!! [here she drew one 6"long] only I pair of legs too. Extraordinary pools of brown muddy water - no weed, about 80° or more, full of insect larvae, *Parachaereps* and *[-]*. Took home eight beasts in a small tube corked, vibrated and

kept warm and they were <u>alive</u> on return - too astonishing. To the theatre with SMW.

Mar 7
Morning spent shopping, fixing kicluts, seeing Searle, and so to lunch with SMW – tea-ed at the zoo labs – interviewed Argos reporter, dined with SMW and Dr Sweet, most interesting and attractive person, running all sorts of women's shows here and all over the world since she gave up zoology for wider interests - so to a University reception and home.

Mar 8
Went to Red Hill with Sam and Miss Woodward to the Browns. Very interesting drive, spoiled partly by weather - lunched en route. Jeff Brown [-Xrs man] took us all round the apple orchards - very interesting too - finely grown trees - good soil - no frosts and fine crops - American blight controlled by an imported hymenopteran parasite - so effective that we could find no living aphids – only groups of dried ones with a hole in each. Very nice cheery folk – had tea and drove back just in time for dinner bringing "John Arthur". Did my three weeks accumulated washing!

Mar 9
To the National museum with Miss Kaff to meet [Krawshey] the curator - saw all the lower regions and crustacean collections, giant *Pheatoicopsis* - finely preserved mammals of Australia in spirits, a fascinating ethnological collection of stuff. We handled it all for ages - spears, rope and cord work, message sticks and countless treasures. So to lunch and to the public library - a very fine building containing a vast central hall seating 240 with huge empty spaces and galleries all round for books. Was then collected by Sam to go with John Arthur to the Test Match - quite fun going with two such ardent cricketers. Rushed off and dined with Dr Buchanan at

the Lyceum – the posh ladies club here, and so to Dr Sweet's party, there were 300 other guests.

Mar 10 Sunday
Gloriously sunny, not too hot – spend morning at the Botanic Gardens – and very nice too – wonderful layouts and trees and palms etc but not many flowers. Lunched with the Agars - Mrs A. very nice, and to tea with the Critchley Parkers. Met Sam for dinner in the city and so to the cathedral - fine music and choir as at Kings [College, Cambridge]. Evenings spent over tea and learning of SMW's philosophy of life at Queens.

Mar 11
Bade a sad farewell to SMW. Walking round the university pond - then to Alphington with Miss Keff for Lepidenus Road and lunched at the Lyceum with Dr Maclemon meeting also Mrs Woodruff very nice person whom I should like to see again. Tea at Zoo department – and dinner at the Critchley Parkers, having met Mrs Manton, a descendent of Joe Manton [a London gunsmith in the early 19 century, so a distant relation of Sidnie's], on the phone.

Mar 12
Last day in Melbourne – boohoo – packed, and met Miss Webb and Mrs Manton at the public library cafe for elevenses. Mrs M is perfectly charming - widow of the grandson of Joe M. Her son (married at age 30) being very like me - so she said! So off to the boat, having a dickens of a skate around after my baggage parked in various places. Sailed at 5 pm on the "Orford" - the finest [lined] boat I've ever stuck - me in a super posh single deck cabin on a second P & O billet. Incidentally the third class is magnificent.

Mar 13
Wrote articles for Melbourne Naturalist and CP's book - slight roll which I didn't like a bit - being unused to it, I lay

down for two hours before dinner - fancy that after dancing in any old roll on the Mooltan.

Mar 14
I rose at 6:30 for the "pyjama parade" to see the sunrise on entering Sidney [sic] Harbour - and very fine it was too - berthed at 8:30. Prof Flynn met me on the boat - I nearly missed him. Had a fine day, not too hot, sunny. Saw the Sidney Museum crowd, and heard their impressions of the Reef folk – most entertaining to hear their side of it, as the two parties did not hit it off and I had only the Englishman's version. So to the University, wonderfully fine modern buildings of NSW sandstone, fine glass windows in hall and library, magnificent cedar panelling and wooden interiors of rooms etc. Back to a sandwich, bun: billy lunch at the Museum - great fun. Prof F put me on the boat to the Zoo where I was whisked round by the head keeper, ferried back across the huge harbour – a fine site, and so out to dinner with Flynn and we thoroughly enjoyed ourselves – so to the boat early.

Mar 15
Fixed up tickets in shopping in deluges of rain – never have I seen such torrents flowing down the streets as cataracts going down steps etc Dug up Miss Malarkey at the training college and to lunch with TBS. Tea with Prof Deakin and Flynn – Deakin's gas being worse than ever - I wish Sidney joy of him. So to the boat – collected by TBS and car and to a dance in the suburbs somewhere with the Flynns. Great fun as they really could dance, caught the boat by seven minutes and sailed at midnight. Watched the harbour lights and the suburbs – ferries and boats in a moonless night until we passed the "Heads" at 1 am. and so to bed.

Mar 16
Fine day on board, coast line in sight and varied, partly blotted out by coastal rain - distant mountains, cliffs - white

176

sandy beaches etc. Polished off masses of writing, finishing the Victorian Naturalist and Critchley Parker's articles. N.B. never have another deck cabin - too many snags - when hard up travel third in a new Oriente Boat - it's magnificent. Glorious sunset over the land, with a tropical storm in approach to the north along the coast.

Mar 17
Sunny day, entered Moreton Bay at 8 am arriving in Brisbane at 2 pm up to the quay. Very interesting journey up the bay and river. Was met by two students, and eventually got through the customs at 3 pm and to the Women's College just before a phenomenally violent storm - I've seen nothing like its violence before. It was only the tail end of the storm which hit Rockhampton, rained 2 inches in 10 minutes – 31 inches in 24 hours and blew away roofs, blew in windows and walls and laid out the electric supply lines. All houses round Brisbane are built on tin capped legs on account of white ants. Underneath the house one keeps the car, does the laundry etc - quite invaluable. Balconies go all round the houses, and the students pull their beds and mosquito nets out on to them at night.

Mar 18
To the University to see Prof Richards, and incidentally the botanic garden full of luxuriant tropical plants growing out of doors, poinciana (Flamboyant) in flower. It and Jacaranda similar leaf but blue flowers and more fluffy and less "layered", they grow everywhere and very handsome they are too. Miss Baye returning from a weekend away fetched me and drove me up a ridge 8 miles off, views very fine over Brisbane which is scattered over a wide area, river winding and distant mountains on both sides. So to Prof Goddard (zoology) and to lunch at Lyceum – Brisbane, unlike Sydney Museum, thoroughly appreciate the work being done in Low Island. So to buy linoleum for the college and back to tea - meeting again at 10 pm in town with some students for

177

supper, having disposed of a large custard apple between us while waiting for Miss Baye's car.

Mar 19
Pottered around helping Miss Baye, met curator of museum and Mr Marks saw amazing aboriginal stuff, and finely coloured corals set up as a coral pool etc - coral are bleached with H_2O_2 and painted with Windsor and Newton paints. Flourishing big and little *Ceratodus* [lung fish] – the little ones (8") having been caught for the first time. Evening spent talking about Cambridge to students.

Mar 20
Lunched with Miss Baye, Mr and Mrs Marks and Mrs Richards and off by the 1:45 pm train. Passed the curious "Glasshouse Mountains" already seen from the "Orford". Passed forests of gums and palms or mixed. Darkness came suddenly and so to bed as they converted the carriage about 7:30 pm.

Mar 21
Arose at six and breakfasted at Rockhampton at 6:30 am. Glorious day, still and sunny, difficult to believe that an average of 1 inch rain a day has fallen since January 1st. Passed fascinating country, luxurious grass below the trees where the undergrowth has been burned. Luxuriant clearings of pineapple and paw paw and the beginning of cane. A few wild wallabies were near the line, but few animals other than insects were visible. Rivers and deep cut watercourses very magnificent with palm covered banks. Slept better than previous night, very insecty, smuttty, rickety and bed undulating and hard.

Mar 22
Arose at 5 am and breakfast at 5:30 at Townsville. Changed trains, had two hours to spare, walked up some rocky high land by the town's reservoir and had a wonderful view with

sea or flood water in three directions, mountains with the sun rising behind them, the town and gorgeous tropical vegetation. So on by a less vibratory but more uncomfortably seated train. Weather still fine - cane increasing until it appears as limitless fields only bounded by distant mountain slopes arising at sides of the flat valley through which the train runs. The coastal high land disappears near Cardwell and the line runs near to the sea. Rivers are very large and plentiful likewise swamps and pools full of blue waterlilies. Real jungle lies on either side of the line in places, choked with climbers and epiphytic ferns – reaching the treetops – orchids are said to be abundant but not visible from the train. Wonderful butterflies and other insects and brilliant birds - all drier parts dotted with termites nests and other mud nests in the trees.

The atmosphere was extraordinarily damp – wet bulb thermometer had been at 100%! One felt the water could almost be squeezed out of the air as out of a sponge. Reached Cairns at 6:10 pm and very glad to leave the train after three days of it, although the journey was just fascinating. So to the Strand Hotel and bath got in just as tropical deluge began, which lasted all night.

Mar 23
Everything enveloped in saturated clouds and rain - how lucky to have had it decent on the journey. Poured on and off all day and all night - 6 inches between 9 and 4 pm. Spent the day devouring books - moisture of the air was astonishing - all one's clothes on and off were saturated.

Mar 24 Sunday
Little better to start with - however the rain stopped and I caught 9:30 train for Kuanda - a queer contraption - all open doors and windows and Aboriginals travelling first class. A fine two hour journey, at first over the lowlands just above sea level clothed with seas of bright green cane - everything in Cairns is measured in terms of cane - metaphorically, then

179

on the slopes through paw paw, banana and pineapple plantations. The line starts its thousand foot climb looping up a side valley before entering the Baron River Valley at a fairly high level. Fine views everywhere of the steep and almost precipitous sided valleys densely covered with trees and interspersed with waterfalls – rocky bluffs at the top, plains and sea round Cairns and distant hills all round. Very suggestive of Norway or Switzerland, only it's more densely wooded with dark tropical trees, each different from the next, and the lot tightly tied up with climbers. 15 tunnels carry the line up 20 miles to the Baron Falls passing Stoney Creek Falls and many small ones on the way.

Left the train at Kuranda on a platform resembling the tropical fern house at Kew. Baskets of filmy and maidenhair and other ferns and plants of endless species hanging side-by-side – Huge Stags Horn ferns and tubs below touching one another of ferns and luscious plants. Walked back a mile or so to the Baron Falls and halfway down the path opposite them – a truly magnificent series of falls of immense size with a cloud of vapour arising from it. However more "new" and wonderful was the walk there and back between 11:30 and 1:30 under a full tropical sun and incredibly steamy atmosphere after the excessive rain of the day before. Like 10 Kew hothouses – but I felt quite frisky – mainly buoyed up by the interest I expect. The butterflies too were marvellous, and I saw the huge blue Morphos emerging from a jungle filled gully. Birds as brilliant as the butterflies.

So to lunch at a hotel and for a walk and a sleep on a log under a tree before catching the 4:15 railcar (motor) back. The trees quite beat me here, again there is *Poinciana* carrier and *Jacaranda* and Banyan and Cascara with its long bean pods and a legion of new forms, luxurious without being xerophytic as are the blue gum regions of Australia which I had previously seen. Termites, ants and wasp nests abound. The rail motor down was great scheme, stopped for taking photos, saw rainbows around the falls in the slanting light, and no smoke in the tunnels.

So to a bath and food amid the deafening noise of parrots outside for three quarters of an hour after sunset – cicadas and crickets then carried on the noise and finally a band outside profiting by the fine tropical evening.

Mar 25
Fine day, morning spent walking round Cairns – back along rail line and off by cart tracks through light forest on sandy soil to edge of mangrove swamps. Fine palms with spirally arising leaves up trunk, 20 feet. Cycads – marvellous butterflies – and terrific heat – all my clothes dripped perspiration – so inland to denser forest – largely swamped in places and filled with blue waterlilies where water is permanent – lovely scenes everywhere with magnificent big leaved tropical trees reflected in the still water pierced by reeds etc below them and a few huge black, red and blue butterflies with bodies like small sausages. So to lunch – afternoon spent stretched out minus clothes in great heat. Rapid and fine sunset over Cairns Bay.

Mar 26
Arose at 5:30 am and sailed by the local motor boat at 7 am – from 9 to 9:30 the roll was almost unbearable, I cheered up for the rest of the time. Reached Port Douglas by 10:30 just before heavy rain began. The coast, close against which we sailed was most attractive - high land going directly into the sea, except for the flats of Cairns and Port Douglas. All forest clad with beaches or mangrove swamps near the sea. Was met by shoeless untidy members of the B.R.E., and spent day at Port Douglas getting in the week's food, regenerating boat tackle and repairs - reached Low Island at dusk – Great thrills, seeing it and the mangrove swamps looming ahead – late tea in the lab and so to bed in a luxurious apartment shared with EF.

Mar 27
Explored island in daylight and settled plans of work etc with
Yonge and Stephenson – got straight and was taken out at
low afternoon tide to the reef with Stephenson – climate on
the island wonderfully cool compared with Cairns, shorts and
shirts certainly the only pleasant garments. The reef was
marvellous – especially the giant brilliant coloured clams and
anemones on first acquaintance – small green *Squilla* [mantis
shrimp] numerous crabs abound, *Synapta* [sea cucumber
family] a yard or two long, blue *Linkia* [starfish] etc–
mangrove swamp - great fern with the viviparous seedlings
etc.

Mar 28
Looked at living *Cryptochirus* [coral pit crab] from
Symphyllia [brain coral] in afternoon went on general survey
with Ann and Michael, and learnt fauna.

Mar 29
Looked at anatomy of *Cryptochirus*, went out with Dr F after
Holothurians [sea cucumbers] etc.

Mar 30
Made concrete slabs with "Paul" the aboriginal - went out
with Stephenson and Dr F and on alone to get *Pocillopora*
[cauliflower coral] colonies. Learnt corals.

Mar 31 Sunday
Out with divers after sediment pots - examined *Pocillopora*.
Out diving most of afternoon pumping for Nicholls, fixed
Pocillopora with wine.

Apr 1
Drew *Pocillopora*, parked coral in tub etc. Very neap tide.

Apr 2
Drew *Pocillopora.* Did gonads of *Diadema* [long spined sea urchin].

Apr 3

Apr 4
Surveyed all day on flat beyond oyster pen after crabs.

Apr 5
Surveyed in the mangroves on south west side.

Apr 6
Surveyed all day in mangroves. Saw white herons etc. Crab gonads.

Apr 7 Sunday
Good tide therefore surveyed.

Apr 8
Surveyed detailed strip.

Apr 9
Surveyed detailed strip.

Apr 10
Surveyed detailed strip.

Apr 11
Surveyed detailed strip.

Apr 12
Gonads etc made and changed all formalin pots and jars.

Apr 13
Surveyed detailed strip, cured coral. Made up lists etc.

Apr 14 Sunday neap
Morning diving in the anchorage. No difficulty about keeping
upright, but great difficulty to walk, one's effective weight is
so small that it is very hard get a push off for a step– finally
half swam over coral and fish. The light wasn't bad. Sun in
patches in 10 feet of water and the small fish in shoals around
the coral, all colours and patterns were just marvellous, and
they take no notice of one either. The coral itself was fine.
Read and washed wig and had a bath in the afternoon.

Apr 15
Cured corals - photographed *Actinoloba* [sea anemone] etc.
Went out after *Pocillopora* [stony or cauliflower coral], drew
Pocillopora etc.

Apr 16
Donkey jobs and drawing *Pocillopora* and gonads. Post day -
Luana is in sight rolling terribly in a high wind - everybody
amasses on the shore at sunset, including lighthouse families
and aborigines - it's the event of the week, and everybody
carries packing cases etc up the beach in the fading light and
tea gets cold as we sort the mail in the lab, and everybody is
silent as they read their letters at table.

Apr 17
Sunny but high wind. Donkey jobs before breakfast, out with
Stephen to the mangrove pond for *Pocillopora* and more
Diadema [sea urchin with long black spines]. Drew
Pocillopora.

Apr 18
Drew *Pocillopora* - cured corals etc.

Apr 19
Detailed survey.

Apr 20
Break in trade winds (SE). Hot clear sun and calm water, detailed survey and photography. Temperature 85°.

Apr 21 Sunday
Glorious calm day - photographed pen etc and slogged at detailed survey. Temp ideal at 85° once one's hide is sunproof.

Apr 22
Fine weather - calm. Detailed survey - mapped the pen.

Apr 23
Survey of anchorage started, immersed in mangrove swamps and *Alcyonaria* [corals with eight branches] - E.F. as useless as usual or more so.

Apr 24
Surveyed anchorage - literally up to our necks in water – photography.

Apr 25
Surveyed last few possible yards of anchorage and finished mapping pen.

Apr 26
Caught up with notes and graphs – fine calm, but neaps beginning. Debearding coral party at work.

Apr 27
Winds again and cooler weather - cold at 77°. *Symphyllia* [brain coral] gonads - hateful job and maps of survey.

Apr 28 Sunday
Neap Sunday - thank heaven - out diving after pots in the morning, afternoon duck diving after lost pot which was eventually found, I had to sit on the post marking it and its

water logged buoy and busted rope while Shiena went back for the helmet, dropped it on me and I sat on the sand at the bottom of the sea, tied the pot on the stake and refixed a new rope - ridiculous situation! Wrote 16 letters !!

Apr 29
Very busy day - rowed in "flattie" in a brute of a wind to the "clock tower" pen to fetch *Symphyllia* and manipulated the beastly craft back again with 6 pails of coral. Rest of day spent over *Symphyllia* gonads - foul job - while Anne, Allan, John and Michael prepared feverishly for Three Isles. So traverse graphs - cocoa and bed.

Apr 30
Still good neaps - cured corals and set to on Coral Pen Map - getting ink drawing done. Luana arrived early with post - two wks letters from home - loud cheers, tea late, and Luana reloaded with food and gear for 6 people on a desert island for a week. So to cocoa and bed v. late.

May 1
Less wind, arose by starlight at 5:45 to see the Three Isles party off. Boarded Luana at 6:15 and they sailed at 6:30 with motor and sail up. Magnificent sunrise and cloud effects over mangrove etc across the Anchorage, sun actually visible at 6:30 am. So to the days work now in charge of tide gauge - house keeping, aboriginal cook etc - not a little envious of the exploring party even if they are very seasick. Camp reduced to doctor, Shiena, Fraser, Self and Boys. Painted pen maps etc and photography printing orgy in the evening. Temp 85° midday and we played very energetic French cricket.

May 2
Scaled the tide gauge safely for making time mark. Getting on okay with Minnie and the stores. Finished pen map and and more printing - my coral photos in the Reef are a real

success and a credit to the exped. What ho and all due to Bibs' camera.

May 3
Redrew *Pocillopora*, which in 4 weeks had grown out of recognition, and in two weeks had grown new polyps from not even a bare space. Coral curing. Gonad Crabs.

May 4
Redrew *Pocillopora* - unexpected Daintree arrived + potatoes and eggs - latter very welcome. Had two birthday cakes, one made on the sly by Minnie, Shiena and Mrs Wills and another by Minnie after arrival of eggs - a great surprise the one without eggs was rather like fruit and toffee, but very good.

May 5 Sunday
Redrew *Pocillopora* – Washed wig wrote letters and photography in the evening.

May 6
At last spring tide materialised and work on deep anchorage traverse was begun and progressed well. Fine *Madrepores* [stone coral] and superior things like *Echinopore* appeared, and working conditions over v. irregular rocks with waist deep holes and scratchy brittle coral were difficult.

May 7
Continued traverse in anchorage - rocks regular and barer and scratchier. Rather strenuous going but very interesting.

May 8
Continued Traverse I outside rampart, wonderful corals *Favias* as well as *Madrepores*, especially well grown brackets and cushions round rocks of the [Boulder Zone], and manageable conditions up to one's neck in water. Fish numerous and not disturbed much and brilliant in colour.

Tide the best of the year so far. Echo and stores arrived, unpacked them and checked lists.

May 9
Continued Traverse I ending on [submerged coral boulder] dipping to neck deep water, high old time chipping corals off it underwater. Mapped near a [second coral boulder]. New moon, tripe hounds spawning in tank, fountains of eggs and clouds of sperm - marvellous site - also spawned on board.

May 10
Continued anchorage traverse to near its depth. The sediment pot sand deep. Finished map of other [Boulder Zone]. Weather hopeless for photography - strong SE trade blowing all the week and temperature cool. Tripe hounds spawning.

May 11
Mapped anchorage pen - strenuous day over odd jobs, tide gauge, curing corals, notes, labelling and housekeeping – did a little photography. Tripe hounds still spawning.

May 12 Sunday
Did the necessary coral curing and crab gonads and slept most of the day - dull, windy, some rain - letters and photography.

May 13
Neaps - thank heaven - Still no Luana - certainly must come today as stores should be fetched tomorrow. Busy with Survey mapping etc. No Luana by tea time so we flashed to P. Douglas asking a wire to be sent to Cooktown inquiring as to Luana's whereabouts. Luana was expected Friday and now it is Monday.

May 14
SE Trade persists and no Luana - rain and showers - more mapping - an endless job. Night so bad that flashing

impossible and no news of Luana. Otto continues to make a nuisance of himself and Orr and SMM bear up nobly.

May 15
Bad weather continues - no Luana - no sun therefore no heliographing. Getting really agitated about her as if in Three Isles still, the food must be getting short. Finally Orr and two aboriginals set out after lunch in the minute lighthouse dingy and sail and outboard motor to try and reach Port Douglas. We got the motor to go in the boat store, but it took one hour to start it in the sea while rain poured intermittently. I gave my oilskin to a boy. Finally they started precariously at 2:20, the water being very near the edge of the boat behind, one boy bailing continually, and the boat once out of the protection of reefs being tossed tremendously in a sea covered with white horses. All the afternoon we watched them with telescopes and glasses, as they were blown further out of their course. At sunset they disappeared from view and we anxiously awaited darkness – which comes rapidly in these parts. After tea the rain ceased and Curly Evans popped in to tell us that P. Douglas was signalling - off we trotted to the aborigines' verandah out of the wet - slowly the letters came and words were pieced together as we flashed back recognition of each word – the messages were as follows:-

Luana Luana wind bound off Cape Bedford three of party returning by Merinda tomorrow and reaching Low Island in Daintree that is all.
        "Has our dingy reached P.Douglas.
"Just arrived all wet
        "tell them to get wet inside
"Mr Orr has had three
        "Labour forty three etc (election results)
    Cheerio

So that was alright and proves Orr need not have gone at all.

May 16
Calmer weather, sunny, Merinda arrived with Anne, Allan, Michael and Iredale the morning, + gear - great excitement to see them back again and hear how they walked 25 miles to Cooktown with a black guide and then came via Merinda. Daintree, port and stores arrived in the afternoon with AP and aborigines - I helped unpack, wash - and did the stores - altogether busy with making lemonade and fruit salads.

May 17
Committee meeting on Lizard Island. I offered £50 in order not to be left behind.
Fine and calm, coral gonads, crab gonads, photography.
Good to have the others back again.

May 18
Good tides starting again and I did mapping in the anchorage (alone and unaided, cheers) and coral gonads and much photography. Glorious warm calm weather and no wind. Finished up as usual with cocoa squash in the Stevenson's cabin.

May 19 Sunday
Stevensons and co diving round outer side of ramparts took the telescope - hence I couldn't map so loafed the whole day - just great - little photography and collected gonad corals in anchorage - lunched at 2 pm - walked about reef to Northern moat and sand spit in bathing dress getting properly boiled to my great pleasure - huge massive *Porites* and *Favias* [stony corals] in North moat just fine 4 feet across. Returned - washed hair - and had a two hour spree with Mr Orr in Gannett and outboard motor. All round island seeing fine deep water coral - huge sprays - baskets and bowls and m. [massive] *Porites* 4 yards across - two blue sharks (5 foot) no giant rays - sun over mainland and fine clear air. Tide being up we then crossed the "flat" and went in and out the mangroves in the evening light - watching big fish and small

fish and little ones popping in out of their holes in the sand -
a great day.

May 20
Lunched at 11:30 and went out to map part of traverse in the
anchorage. Cold and rough, and telescope essential. I then
did 7 yards more of the traverse on the rocks single-handed.
F. out collecting or something. I saw lots of fish about me–
lovely things.

May 21
Out early after 11 am lunch with Dr Stevenson surveying
outside the NW rampart and boulders. Very scratchy going,
but a great day. I found a fine *Poripora,* cut 2 *Turbinarias* - a
brown coiled one and a coarse fine white one – A new
yellow tipped *Madrepora*, and a new coarse *Flavia* and a
huge *Polyphyllia* - quite a nice haul. Came in at about 4:30
and having been wet all day we warmed up with Cocoa
promptly.

May 22
Out mapping a rock in the anchorage in the morning while Dr
Stephenson started painting coral from the flattie - then I
proceeded with the traverse, another 7 yards and then the
downward slope made progress impossible. I fixed a 4 ft iron
stake and a line and swam off the coral edge, anchor and line
in hand. I forgot that hooked, gartered and anchored
swimming would not be so easy and I only just kept my nose
out! We returned about 3 pm.

May 23
Out, after daily jobs of coral washing, early to finish traverse
in helmet. F and Stephen came to cope and we got the boat in
position and anchored both ends when I found the lead
weight of the helmet absent - up we rooted the anchors and
had to go back for them. Finally we got fixed and down I
went with bucket, hammer, chisel, frame, pencils slates and

191

opal glass. To my joy it proved a workable scheme. First I lost the pencil tied to my middle - couldn't find it anywhere - finally I caught sight of it floating inside the helmet on the water surface! Opal glass proved very successful as the pencil marks don't rub off as on a slate with slate pencil. I finished the traverse in fine style (12 yards) – only once being hauled up when I didn't want to be – however these things will happen. Back we rushed I ate a huge lunch and so off with Dr S to the other side of the mangroves to continue outside rampart survey. We sat on the shingle beach and boiled in the sun as the tide went down – then set out in earnest – when up to our knees in water we were both promptly knocked down by the waves - notebooks lost and wetted - chisels spilled etc - then having caught one crab - we beat a retreat, went back to the flattie and rowed a zigzag course to [Wishatri] rocks where I remained with the boat and Dr S swam ashore. I surveyed [Vat] finding a few nice things, and then went over to the rocks outside our anchorage traverse with the flattie. There I made a fine haul of *Lobophyllias, Favias, Coelorias* and a huge sea urchin with striped fat spines and thin short ones and green ambulacial grooves. Later I got a spine in my finger - a most painful affair as the poison hurts like blazes. However it was dug out successfully. Evening spent mapping and pickling.

May 24
Coped with the vaste array of cleaning corals - 15 Kerosene tins and 2 baths - other odd jobs innumerable and inked mapped [sic] of anchorage rock. Afternoon spent collecting 12 *Symphyllia*, and laying line with anchors out seaward along traverse 1. More talk over the Lizard Island stunt - yesterday and today and tomorrow people have had to go in to P. Douglas and phone and wire etc - all too complicated for words. Developed films.

192

May 25
Finished up *Favia* gonads with the last 8 of the 24 - having
previously collected and parked them in the anchorage moat.
Afternoon spent in odd jobs in identifying *Madreporas* and
Favias on the blocks. Fetching in drainpipes and clam shells
for six months growth upon some and so on. Printed
photographs.

May 26 Sunday
Fine calm day and lazily spent - coral cleaning to start with -
a gigantic job now - washing prints and then under a bush in
the north west shore with a book - disturbed by goats, sand
flies and Stephen rehearsing for a corroboree [ceremonial
meeting of Aboriginal Australians].Helped Dr S with photos
and identifying corals etc. Cocoa party and to bed.

May 27
Cleaned vast array of corals, analysed Survey account etc -
fetched up *Symphyllia* for gonads *Diadema* gonads, Tripe
hounds spawning.

May 28
Gonads of *Symphyllia* - hateful job nearly reduced me to
tears, as the gonads were maturing and needed cutting out
and drawing with a camera lucida - finished at 3 pm - cleaned
corals, painted map etc. Merinda o.k. cheers. Did 74 prints!

May 29
Cleaned corals - went diving with Stephenson to get clam
shells, pipes and rock after 6 months in the sea, some fine
little corals appeared and small *[slimy]* *Polyzoa*. Continued
Survey analysis and attended to bleaching corals - 56 prints
and so to cocoa and bed. John condemned my cocoa
methods, as one has to watch the pan and stir it - we nearly
came to blows over it the whole room taking sides!

May 30
Symphyllia Gonads - finished in the morning - helped Anne
and Michael collect the goods for Lizard island, and a vaste
[*she often puts e on the end of vast*] pile it was too.
Continued Survey analysis and got it up to date so to cocoa
and bed.

May 31
Tivoli departed at 6:30 am. Morning spent over
Lobophytums [soft corals] etc making key and putting
collection to rights, crab gonads - out to erect flags on survey
posts. Out getting Yonge's corals in Helmet with Otter and
Stephen, as Maurice and Nicholls both have sores on their
legs, so fär my cuts and scratches have not got septic luckily.
Returned to my *Pocillipora* which have grown out of
recognition nearly.

June 1
Busy day - coral cleaning - diving for traverse outside the
rampart - and here struck the beginning of the mud and
thinning out of corals - most interesting. Afternoon spent in
analysing and writing up traverse and preparing for Lizard
island. Cocoa with J.

June 2 Sunday
Fine day and all off to Snapper Island. Just great. John and I
sailed in Garnett starting at 9 am and taking 2 hours arriving
10 minutes before Luana and the crowd. I learned a bit of
sailing and sailed the boat alone for some time - just fine.
John a very pleasant companion - even if he does harp on his
fiancée. Landed on a shingle beach of quartz sand, what a
change, and all the coral fragments were polished and not
rough as here. Bathed promptly diving in off Luana with
deep water 18 ft 4 yards from shore. A scouring tide sweeps
through the mile wide Penguin channel between Snapper and
the mainland keeping the shingle steep. Stephen went off and
cut wild paw-paws for dessert and we lunched on the boat at

12 am, looking at the proper *Liana* [a woody vine] infested tropical forest with large knoll 350 ft high at the W end. J and I set out in boots and climbed the barer E knobs - 4 of them, getting glorious views of sea, mainland, Snapper, Low Island etc. Also great area of muddy Daintree river water being banked up by rising tide. Climbed down to a rise above the E precipice and encamped, watching a celt [baby shark] basking in the sun and on the other side a big turtle 4-5 ft - seen clearly with its head out and flippers showing. Late afternoon lazily spent, then clambered down directly from E knob to beach rocks and had a mile v. rough rock scramble back to the W end between the rising tide and the cliffs. *Pandanus palloro* [trees with pyramidal root formation] above the beach showing mangrove root stump! So home at 4:30 on Luana - tea embellished by paw paw, and later cocoa with J and F. Previously John's *(words on Caty's gramophone)*.

June 3
Boiled unlimited numbers of corals, dived and got traverse on to barren mud debris areas. Did more boiling, washing, and preparing for departing to Lizard Island. Wrote up traverse, letters etc.

June 4
Set out in Luana at 9 am for P. Douglas - fine and sunny, rolling sea, not in the least cold with no coat and no vest. Saw Dr Buchanan as we trans shipped to Merinda amid the staring populace of P. Douglas. Encamped upon the ropes, diving helmet etc on the top deck and fairly boiled myself in the sun amid numerous offers of shade from the crew. The common herd travelled below under awnings etc. Again passed Lizard Isl. through penguin channel - coast from then on just fine, never more than 1 mile away, often quite close - hills <4,000 ft all the way with steep spurs going into the sea and all covered with dense rain forest choked with climbers. Passed a few mangrove grown river mouths, few islands and light

houses - Anchor point the only long arm of land offering sea shelter. Finally reached Cooktown at 5:30 with a setting sun across the sea inlet. The most being behind table mountain etc. On the sea were Japanese owned, aboriginal manned luggers looking most picturesque. Left Merinda for Sea View Hotel, a shack opposite, and I put on boots for the occasion lest I should be thought a tramp. Hoofed up the street after eggs and a cold chisel - good tropical veg. smell in the evening light. The whole town dead, but a shadow of its former self, grass everywhere, most houses and pubs closed - charming vegetation and avenue of tropical trees - monument to Capt. Cook who landed 1770. I can well imagine his thrill at seeing such a coast and such light effects. A little tin mining still seems functioning in the interior behind Cooktown. 'Tea' at 6:15 and jolly good too, best steak I've had in Australia, and very welcome. So to bed after a walk for one and a half hours in the starlight - the Great Bear upside down appearing just on the horizon.

June 5
Arose at 5 am and on board again at 5:25 - not without having to go back and look for F - the ass - late as usual. Left at 5:45 instead of 5:30 am, quite dark, a big king fish 3 ft long jumping out of the water along side and taking 2 leaps together = to the length of Merinda (60 ft?). The last star in the E faded at 6:20 and the sun was up and the light bright at 6:45. By 7:30 the sun was as high as it ever gets in Sweden in Jan. Coastline here very different, huge sand dunes looking like snow flecked mountains with grey peaks behind them. A fine pair of eagles over Cape Bedford. Breakfast on board at 7:30. So to Lizard island arriving 11 am - I fixed up flattie rollocks on board first and [rowed/moved] off the flattie full of gear. F and Hales to the shore. Tent and 'Kitchen' all nicely fixed up - and no note for Hales so I took him back to the Merinda and returned. A truly heavenly spot - bright white coral sand beach and high peak and shoulders. Scrambled eggs for lunch and started to climb to the top at

196

12:15. F. had to be waited for perpetually going a snail's pace - finally I gave it up and waited 3/4 hour for her at the top. Truly a heavenly view. Seawards the Great B. Reef with the open water passes between, showing up at the low spring tides. Shorewards two rocky peaks separated from Lizard by reef filled and sandy sea, all marvellous colours - other reefs in sight in all directions, either as dark patches in the water or sandy banks with or without Cays on them. Coast visible in distance and white sand of dunes clearly visible between the green covered part. So to sleep and down again by another route - a good steep rock scramble both ways - first a bathe and await return of party from outer barrier. Tivoli chugged in just after sunset - so to sort out the catch and cook the tea, write up, and so to bed at 10:30.

June 6

Anne and Michael arose at 6:15 - the alarm arousing me to see the sky, sea and shore in the pre-sunrise light out of the end of the tent - heavenly - Breakfast at 7 am, having washed in instalments. Washed corals, cleared breakfast, tidied away bedding of 5 in the tent and got off in Tivoli by 9 am for June Reef. Huge swell, and boat soaked with waves - arrived at marvellous waters behind reef 12 miles away, Michael miraculously steering to same place. Blue and green water took place of ocean colour and 18 ft water with sandy bottom looked like 10 ft - vast [weathered coral boulders] etc got in close as poss. and so to the flattie + goods I to map reef cut and outer moat - all too marvellous, fish a dream, likewise pacific breakers with refracted image of coral in the waves. Worked hard and in tide turning walked + gear 1/2 - 3/4 mile back to boat, lunch on Tivoli at 4 pm- and chugged home after sunset, to sort stuff - label it - tea at 7:30, and busy evening over writing up and and inking maps till 10:45, cocoa and to bed 11:30 very weary. The greatest day of my life - I love such a spectacle as the outer barrier unknown to science. Jim caught 3 different Parrot fish <5 lbs for tea - also made fine boots of canvas, planks and nails - uppers however came to bits.

June 7

Arose 6:15 - cleaned corals, tidied camp - breakfast at 7:15 - cleared - odd jobs - sailed at 9 am for June Reef 12 miles off. Michael miraculously steered to same spot exactly, near reef being [made of weathered coral boulders] like houses - I climbed mast for the view of the reef getting fine idea of shape of reef and mauled edges and seeing the reefs beyond N & S. Out in flattie to S. Horn and dumped Michael and Anne after much expostulation, as Butler wanted to maroon them on a rock, to wait for the tide going down. Self and F got off further N, me to do a map of inner moat and of "anchorage". Also some photography, probably spoiled by dropping camera and pack into the sea on way back from the dingy. Corals very fine at a v low tide, great range of fall, and corals greatly damaged by being uncovered as the tips die and are white. Fish in anchorage great. Flocks of 5 lbs Parrot fish, angel fish of large size, king streamers 1 ft long - small blue and green fish, box fish, brown ones with snouts. Spotty dog fish and 17 ft shark. Huge size of corals clearly seen for first time - *Madrepora, Juniporus, Favia* boulders etc, Lunch sandwiches on Tivoli at 4:30 pm - sunny day, little sunburnt, wore wool slip and bathing dress - fine and airy and warm. Tivoli chugged home in fine style with a load of 4 ft thigh thick *Madrepores* collected by Butler. No fish for tea. Beer instead! Sun set as we got in lea of Lizard island as the night before. Time saved by not having a proper lunch being neutralised by later tide. So to collections, retrieving coral tins from stream washed away by current and tea - welcome at 8:30 - mapping till 10 pm and bed 11:30 - most welcome. Bread needed colour plate for mould!

June 8

Arose 6:15 - same glorious pre-sunrise sea view out of tent - cleaned corals etc before breakfast at 7. Finished off labelling etc and loaded up Tivoli starting at 10 am. More wind and much rougher and difficult to steer the course, which however Michael managed with his usual navigators skill. Just great to stand any motion of the boat without feeling the shade of illness - had to hang on to seats on top of water tank and got soaked with sea. Went off to see N. end of June Reef for comparison w south end. All packed into flattie after lunch on board - with a very tricky entry among the house high [weathered coral boulders] in a foul breeze. Difficult row to reef runs Devil-Devil anchorage coral zone in foul wind all 5 on boat + gear. Took a few photographs with Stephenson of outer ridges etc and crest, and returned in flattie to huge [weathered coral boulder] near Tivoli when I mapped and Dr S surveyed and photographed. Almost the most amazing sight seen. Huge brackets of /wz/ 2 yards across. /W nubly middle, h2<2 ∏ r/ Stags Horn fields, holes infinity and all v solid, colours marvellous going against violent blue sea 2-3 fathoms, sedis precipitous! Took few photos - returned to Tivoli, climbed mast, took few snaps - so home - rather late, v rough, getting in well after dark. Cooked tea at once, fed hastily + /beer/ at 8:30 - cleared up - wrote up - to bed 10:45. Too weary to do maps or anything. Great day. Mouldy bread exhausted.

June 9 Sunday
Arose as per usual - late start at 12 for little near reef, intended doing maps and jobs first - much palaver over Anne's bloodshot eyes and sprained toe - Michael converting kitchen into outpatient's dept. Weather got worse and worse, wind and rain and cold. Mapping etc up till 10:45 and then we stretched out lazily in our beds and felt thoroughly happy - Anne in Michael's arms as usual. Dr S up the mountain painting. Gave up Little Reef in favour of fringing reef in anchorage bay and diving - lunch in tent on biscuits, jam, oranges and tea. Gave up diving re weather, and at 3:30 miserably emerged in bathing dress to crawl about fringing reef. V. cold, but awfully wonderful place and fields of

Alcyonaria – 4 ft clams common, nearly put my foot in one - horrid moment. Marvellous anchorage coral type - very little *Madrepora, Tubinarias, Tridacophyllias,* fringed starfish 15' across 20 arms, 3" spikes, wonderful photography spot - but no light and water rough.

So home - warmed up, cooked tea, fine stew and huge appetites fit to eat a house - braced up tent re wind - had to take table inside tent as plates and cups etc blew off table even in lea of kitchen screen. Dr S came home wet and so borrows my only pair of dry shorts! Wrote up notes all in blankets after tea - view across anchorage bay with colours faded on a dull day is v like Devon coast. Very pleasant to have had a more or less lazy day. Very thankful we had 3 good days on Barrier as we could not have got there today. Jim and Butler carry Doctor F's fish.

June 10

Wind still high limiting our activities although it was not like the preceding stormy night with the tent straining and flapping. Dr S finished picture from top of Eagle Island. We dived at face of fringing reef in anchorage bay, and cold and breezy it was too - reef face tiers of iv Pointes and v Pointes and cooked a fine lunch of egg sauce and boiled fish - fish being caught by Jim. V pleasant altogether - F having gone off on her own. Smoked after lunch and wrote up surveys and so off across island to the lagoon encirled by reefs at the S end with Michael and Anne. Bush and mountainous country varied and very attractive - passed through *Pandcross* grove with its famous water hole and bath rooms and wriggled through 6' grasses and light bush, the dense bush being quite impenetrable - descended to *Casuarina* bordered beach by lagoon - fine view all round. Broad beach was like a path in an elaborate garden with specimen trees drooping over it, *Casuarina pandermass*, the L.I. Rhododendron like thing etc - found a nautilus shell, and surveyed a small fringing reef very like L.I. coral flat . So home via the points and bays - cooked a vast tea, of fried fish and stew, and tinned fruit.

Wrote up survey and wearily to bed at 10 pm - quite nice and early for once.

June 11

High tide at 6 pm and wind strong so work effectively stopped. Started coral packing and walked to *Casuarina* beach with Dr S. Lunch on new good fish - common short with our 3 biscuit ration per meal and no bread etc. Lay on our beds and watched terns diving in the sea for fish outside, with an emerald green sea and reflections on their white feathers - glorious sea colours, vivid greens under a blue sky. Went out diving, not wet myself, having done my share of chilly wetting yesterday. Dr S tried to get a giant clam 3-4 ft going down putting boulders in its mouth and preparing to murder it with a long knife - mantle proved nearly as hard as shell and mouth wouldn't be wedged and whole show was impossible. Fine sunset, green sea, pink sky, pink sand (vivid) and golden flecked sky, just great. Very hungry and Michael made a famous stew of onions, vegetables (dried) and peas (tinned) decanned ham etc - very good indeed - tinned fruit and biscuit ration - fine meal. Inside tent as usual owing to high wind. Packed 6 more cases of corals. Lazily spent evening over pressing plants and pouring over charts for Tivoli's return passage in and out through the reefs - Michael and Anne going on Tivoli - lucky dogs.

First 3 days of exped were fine, and from work the last 3 petered out being wind bound - very interesting but very strenuous, not sorry in a way to leave after a week as the life is tiring doing all the camp running as well. However the whole show has been the most marvellous trip of my life.

June 12

Very rough windy night and most fortunate that we had roped down the tent with the dredging rope. Much rain. We awoke in "Timothy" shrunk to a soaking drizzle. Gloom fell on us as we thought of striking the camp in the wet. Lazily

201

we lay abed and then all 5 got up and dressed at once in the 12x14 ft tent! Dismantled beds, brought in stove etc and cooked within. Packed up gradually in the wet leaving the tent to the end. View with colours dimmed looked like Devon although the sea was a washed out emerald even so. Got gear into Tivoli, and on word that Merinda was in sight at 11:50 we pulled down the tent and left Lizard Island all piled up in the flattie. Merinda's crew fished unsuccessfully in the wet for a bit and we started in a howling gale and high sea and rain - we quite believed Holis reputation for washing his passengers from for' and aft! Tivoli was alongside for a bit, shipping far less water than Merinda, even the high ledge by the funnels was occasionally a river! Foul passage all day reaching Cooktown at 6:20. Felt illish for 2 hours at midday but recovered and was OK!!! Wonders will never cease. Walked into Sea View Hotel barefoot in oil skins and a south west hat. Ate a huge tea and to bed early. Miserably cold (about 70°)

June 13
Arose at 5:30 and sailed in Merinda at 6 am. - weather just awful - and motion incredibly bad - one of the few v bad passages she makes a year. Again I survived and was quite fit and hungry for lunch although I refused breakfast. All passengers violently ill. "Flat calm week off Lizard Island in lee of Low Island", at least it was so in comparison, quoting Olley the helmsman. Dropped us two hours late at 2 pm in flattie and we found L. Island surrounded by the wildest roughest sea I've seen there - that was our comparative calm! Dull weather like England showing faded colours made me fully realise the ordinary tropic brilliance of the place which one gets so used to as to not notice fully. Had good lunch - washed clothes - which stood up on their own accord with salt and dirt, and hair - there are great advantages in a more permanent camp than that of Lizard island. John had shaved!!

Developed two packs and four dry plates John doing the washing for me. So to bed very late after cocoa in the dark room to help in the last lot. Cold temp not above 70° for two days!

June 14
So to chores - getting stuff ready for packing, gonads of *Diadema* - maps etc. Weather cold and grey, but not wet - wonderful light effects as air v clear when clouds not on horizon cutting out view.

June 15
Bad weather, rough and cold - chores cleaning corals, gonad animals, maps etc. Tivoli arrived at 8 pm John and I surveyed the shore by moonlight looking for them.

June 16 Sunday
Perfect day, still calm and sunny. Unpacked Tivoli and corals from Lizard Island etc in the morning. Afternoon S, Anne and Michael went diving and John and I abandoned work for sailing. Scarcely any wind and we got becalmed, so merely lay in the sun and basked. Printed Outer Barrier negatives.

June 17
Cleaning corals, perfect day, finished muddy end of traverse 1 in helmet - cheers. Chores, - very busy. Had the fright of my life when a big teleost came and looked at me, all I could see from the helmet was the vast fish head making straight for me!..

June 18
Mapped face of [boulder zone] in calm weather in morning. Continued coral gonads and finished the horrid things. Post day, much nice letters.

June 19
Out with Anne and Michael and Stephen doing level section
of anchorage traverse - cold very wet and spiky job - took
ages - perfectly foul. Chores - coral labelling, cataloguing.

June 20
Finished traverse 1 level section - fouler still - beastly wind -
and alone by soundings - having marooned me on [a huge
coral boulder] temporarily, not to lose the place! End of my
work was 18.5 feet at low tide i.e. usual working distance
about 24 feet below surface - I had no idea it was so deep.
Chores and coral packing.

June 21
One day off the moon and tides not too good, foul wind, so
that outside rampart work impossible. Lab day in transverse
and section notes coral packing and cataloguing etc.

June 22
Day spent map making etc.

June 23 Sunday
Hopeless rough day, mapped in morning and walked right
round island for the first time with John and so to mapping
again.

June 24
Bad weather continues - mapping and indoor jobs.

June 25
Mapping - post day - Michael acquires huge case of tinned
fruit! - very merry cocoa party.

June 26
Awful day mapping all day, orgy of packing etc on verandah
all my 450 corals labelled and catalogued I got let off

packing - 1lb coffee arrived, fine change, and we coffeed after lunch - cocoaed in my room, J and I finishing up!

June 27
Less windy, cloudy and warmer - Daintree trip probably off but J and I have wild dreams of sailing there on Sunday if Luana can fetch us back.
Interviewed my growing *Pocillopore*, who continues to grow amazingly - so to packing - loathsome job.

June 28
Weather breaking, and sun shone and temp rose to 80°. Loud cheers. However my jobs became more and more domestic with Wishart kaput with a fever or a bilious attack on Luana, Mattie in bed with a temp and a throat and Shiena in bed with a budding abscess or something in her leg which I poulticed with antiphlogistine. All went well until Mattie got up and tried to operate on Shiena - it took me 1½ hours to divert her intention and get another poultice on - so to cocoa, having odd jobbed and packed and considered meals and invalids all day. Went out with John diving in the morning and took flashlight photos of [*Lobophyllia*] with Dr S at night.

June 29
Mattie better and Shiena worse - Wishart was tended at night by AP and was improved. Fine weather - decided to go to the Daintree on Sunday and Shiena and Mattie went off to Port Douglas Hospital. AP. wouldn't take John unfortunately as he had previously refused to take Mattie - all too silly as there is pots of space. Morning spent with Michael, Anne and Stephen making a level section and lists of corals on windward side of island in an oily flat calm - first with theodolite then soundings - clarity of water made diving unnecessary mercifully - fairly strenuous business hauling up 15 feet of line etc and coping with steel tape, until Michael read distances with the sextant. Mapped after a late lunch pudded with Michael's tinned fruit and my coffee. Typed

coral catalogues with John and took more flashlight photos
and wearily to bed.

June 30 Sunday
Chores and off to Daintree at 10:45 w Mr and Mrs Wishart,
A.P. [Orr], Moorhouse, Nicholls and self. Perfect day,
negotiated a creek near the mouth for Moorhouse to do
oxygens, pHs all right - lunched on board again - and so 8-10
miles up river nearly to the settlement. Glorious river - rich
mangroves gave way to tropical rain forest of great
luxuriance in palms, climbers etc but few flowers and all
same green - beyond banks of forest peered forest clad ridges
and beyond again rose Mt Thornton 5000 feet and less high
mountains to the south. Winding wide river, but shallow.
Abandoned AP and Nicholls in Garnett outboard motor and
gear to go on and do their 24 hrs observations. So down the
river to the creek by the mouth - had the Kingfish we caught
en route for tea - marvellous sunset - gold purple and red,
blue mountains and black mangrove forests and great
reflections - seascape being cut off by Port Douglas coast.
Feeling a little lost without Anne or John and only having the
very Australian unattractive minds for company.

July 1
Left Luana after breakfast on a glorious proper tropical day,
and boots, J's puttees, lunch and camera. Walked along
glorious beach of quartz sand and sparkling mica round
mouth of Daintree and northwards opposite Snapper. Met 6
ugly evil snappy hounds and a wild aboriginal who called
them off, quite a chatty aboriginal whose grubby but
attractive wife soon followed for conversation.
So up inland over the promontory opposite Snapper -
grappled for 2 hours with true rainforest, up by grassy glade
to near the top of the ridge and down t'other side, hitting a
dryish water course which made the going possible. Great
thrills to be really among such vegetation. Extraordinary
climbing palm like thing putting out "crawlers" 14 feet long.

206

Stuff with reflexed barbs (layer vine), so climbing forever upward through the vegetation - festoons of climbing ferns. Stag and other epiphytic ferns, five palms of various sorts, big leaved things, gums and leguminous affairs with giant seeds. Suddenly without warning I burst upon the beach opposite Rocky Island! I could never see more than a very few yards ahead. To start with I thought I was following a path and kept on losing it - possibly someone had been that way before. Very dense going, tommahawk really needed as it useless to argue with even the thin string-like climbers which tie themselves round one at every turn. Buttress roots extend like ribbons over the ground. Spent the middle part of the day on a glorious rock and sand beach like a primitive savage in the sun, having hung up what the forest left of my raiment to dry. All round the dense forest came down to the beach on the steep cliffs, which appeared quite impenetrable. Saw a shark, 6 foot perhaps, close in shore, after I had finished my second swim - reluctantly dressed and departed back the way I had come about 3 pm. Returned fairly quickly, not stopping to photograph the jungle. Over the ridge and down t'other side, and along a path among more open forest with grass glades (6 ft high) and giant cycads. I climbed one to get some sporophylls and fruits for Bibs. Path took me too far inland so retraced steps and broke off path and scrambled through forest and mangrove forest belt, eventually reaching beach, covered with mangrove wood stains. Beach deserted and tide high so bathed again and returned to Luana, passing aborigines on the way. Left at 5:30 and sailed up river in the dusk until we met Garnett, Orr and Nicholls. Anchored for the night one mile below settlement. On seeing tropical rain forest again one noticed many things missed on the previous day, the river too bore many floating Hibiscus blooms of large size. To bed at 8 pm, and at 10:15 could stick Vidgen's [part of the the boat party with Mr Wishart] snoring no more so went on the top deck and curled up on the ropes. Later mist became thick and fairly cold.

207

July 2
Left on the tide at 6:30 am breakfasted near mouth and AP made 10 ft boring in mangrove mud, pumping out contents of the bore tube, mud for 9' then shingle. Left at 11:30 for Port Douglas - sea roughening all the way. Reached port at 1 pm, and lunched, Stephenson coming to see the animals feed. Visited hospital to see Shiena and Mattie, Shiena's abscess had been opened and was very deep- Mattie's throat worse. Hospital awful - goats, cats and fowls everywhere. Saw Dr F, Anne and Allen off on Daintree - weather then very rough. We left later with the two hospital patients and Mrs Curtis. Rough and I wasn't happy a bit - old Wishart refusing to put up a sail. So cocoa with John and Michael - having put the invalids to bed. Mattie now really bad taking no food and with a temperature.

July 3
Not liking the responsibility of Mattie's illness a bit but fortunately a doctor came across on Echo and removed her. Shiena in bed can be coped with. Day spent on outside rampart with John and Michael. Writing up, communal printing etc with John.

July 4
AP now joined ranks of sick list having caught a chill up Daintree, and Nicholls I tried to send to bed also, but he soon recovered. Outside edge work continued with usual assistance. Writing up and cocoa and printing with Michael - poor boy rather worried about things in general. No Daintree appeared for trip north.

July 5
North trip hopelessly planned. Maurice as weak as water and all undecided. "Daintree" turned up about 11:30 while Luana had gone out to do a station - hastily we decided to lunch at once and go as soon as possible - Luana arrived and Vidgen proceeded to collect stores at that 11th hour - finally we got

208

off at 1:30 - AP, Maurice, Moorhouse, Nicholls, Wishart, John, Michael and self. Bad weather - dull and windy – Daintree, a 20 ton cargo boat, deck and hold only - no shelter of any kind. John, Michael and I sat up forward out of engine smell in the spray, until we made out the Bloomfield river about 5:45 pm where we anchored for the night. Cooked a meal and so to bed, rolled in blankets about the deck, Michael and I sharing a ground sheet. Night v cold, with heavy dew.

July 6
Arose at day break and sailed at 6:30 as light crept over the river mouth, a picturesque spot with a pair of "heads" at the entrance. "Elam" had crept in during the night and was sharing the anchorage. J, M and I made breakfast under way, and we soon felt the warmth of the open sea upon the land. Passed close to sand bay in Pickergill Reef and into Ruby Reef, arriving about 11:30. Caught a King Fish en route which I fried for lunch. Went off in two boats to reef, a long stretch. Garnett being towed by Daintree's motor boat. Reef in structure like June Reef, but largely devoid of coral. Got back to Daintree, and anchored for the night among the giant [weathered coral boulders]. M, J and I made communal beds on the hatch and lashed the groundsheet over us to keep us from falling off as the boat rolled. Horrid wind and high seas.

July 7
Arose at daybreak and shifted south to Escape Reef. Similar anchorage and programme. Reef richer in coral, but not a patch on June Reef and no anchorage coral zone. Mr Moinian, the 65 years pilot a great character - old beche de mer fisher and reef navigator, a fine old man. Night very rough - everybody in the hold except John and Moinian - had to be lashed in firmly as there was danger of slipping off the hatch - missing the scuppers and falling into the sea as the boat rolled in a moderate gale of 45 miles per hour and heavy

sea coming over barriers at super-high tide. Kept each other warm and slept partially.

July 8
Shifted off south to Undine Reef, arriving 12 am. Lunched and worked a small patch while other folks went to main dull sandy reef. Patch is like June Reef [boulder zone]. Left about 5 pm and pointed home against wind and weather arriving back after 10 pm v cold and wet. Had a row with Vidgeon - so J and I took out the black flattie - getting soaked standing up to my waist launching boat in sea - eventually to cocoa v late - then almighty row and free fight between Vidgeon and J - so finally to bed about 1 am.

July 9
Packed before breakfast - and goods off by Luana. Painful morning apologising to A.P, and Maurice - all blew over by lunch. Pleasant coffee party w Michael and John, chores all day, and developed film packs in evening - so to cocoa. Michael discussed 'points tables' till 1 am - poor fellow.

July 10
Chores, notes, packing etc and exposed 4 colour plates with Michael. John did his vertical distribution station and arrived back at 12:20 am instead of 10 pm - Michael and S had kept his cocoa in vain, as I upset it all over the floor. Orgy of printing and Michael developing.

July 11
Neaps well in - developed colour plates before breakfast, most of day used in photographing Shiena and A.P.'s sediment experiments at intervals - developing at intervals. Evening spent on notes - Michael printing and John developing. Getting nice and sunny and warm again and winter over.

July 12

Developed colour plates before breakfast - finished A.P's photographs of the experiment - the *Favia* having completely cleaned himself of sand and the *Fungia* starting to climb out, his surface being clean. So to notes - diplomatic letter to Anne, by Friday boat - having given up intention of leaving today, going via "Bump" to Cairns and seeing Yungabarophyte, instead leaving next Tuesday - more for poor Michael's sake than anybody's. Afternoon spent in packing corals - etc after prolonged coffee party - all of us being rather weary. So to chat with Michael.

July 13

Developed colour plates at 7 am - so to notes of Reef work, packing corals with M. etc. Coffee party as usual. Wind suddenly violent after few days calm. Afternoon over mapping. Very glad indeed to be here and not away on the mainland alone, as I seem to be Michael's only pillar of moral support. Printing evening.

July 14 Sunday

Morning spent with Michael photographing map - Prolonged coffee party, as all three of us are rather fagged. M and I put light house panorama of his together, and we spent 2 hours before tea sitting in the sun in the lee side, Michael and I - self patching his shorts. Printing and so to Carter's for gramophone and tea - thus to bed.

July 15

Last day at Low Isles - I could weep - helped Michael pack in morning - afternoon coffee as usual - J one side and M on the other. So to chores - Vid and George clearing up etc. Printing in the evening, cocoa with John and Michael. J to his letters and later Michael to his thermometers. Both such dears in their different ways.

July 16

Arose at 4:45 - cleared out room of sheets, and conveyed foods to Michael's and John's hut - boarded Luana by starlight with rucksack etc - and Harry's kerosene tin butterfly! Started finally at 5:40 all on board and Claud and Minnie and the kids. Everybody except J, M and self in 'respectable' clothes to go to sugar mill and polite lunch at Mossman. As I had sent all my clothes to Cairns, so had to back out - and J, M and I spent a very happy day together on shore away from the madding crowd. Arrived at P Douglas at day break just before 7 am - saw off the folk on the ridiculous 2 ft gauge train and wood fueled engine - breakfasted at the hotel, little shopping at Jack and Newells tin made store and, provided with chocolate biscuits, we walked along the beach south - glorious beach and trees, *Casuarinas* etc - fine day, cool air, dead mud around fringing reef exposed at low tide - found 2 rivers, fish trap of large size and queer 'barrier' of mangroves. Michael and I extremely happy, and John also - so glad we missed the Mossman show - back to P.D. and by 'Daintree' to Cairns – 4 pm – 10 pm. Roughish at first - seasick folk on all sides, and rather cold. Had a spherical meal at Michael's café - so to bed rather weary and terribly sad at leaving Low Island and the friends with whom I have been so happy.
Photographed moving regiments and battalions of blue round crabs!! Wondrous sight, especially seeing them dig themselves in.

July 17

Arose at 6 am - hiked off to the Daintree in shorts to get a package - by then my trunk was at the "Strand" so I clothed myself in civilised "decency", breakfasted just after sunrise, and so to the Townsville Mail. Did not catch the peculiar "Australia in the early morning" smell as at P.D. - a smell peculiar and not to be forgotten. Journey to Townsville very tiring - these trains are first class uncomfortable and no doubt about it, and I was tired too having had 5 hours in bed after

arising at 4:45 the previous day. Reached Townsville at 6
pm - strolled out and saw no Jim or Butler - so fed at the
station and walked about the town afterwards feeling blue
and lonely. Suddenly I met Jim and car - marvellous
recognition on his part of me in the dark in a hat and civilised
clothes. I was whisked off to the Butler's house - Mrs B
being away - all most charming - Mrs and Miss B and a
friend went to the pictures and Jim drove me around - finally
gave me coffee and cakes at the poshest Townsville
restaurant, so seeing me off!! All most touching - meanwhile
he explained the family affairs - Jim being Butler's brother in
law and the three having just inherited £12,000!!! The actual
rail journey was v interesting after previous Queensland
experience, the sugar cane was being cut, pineapple orchards
showed autumnal colours - tropical rain forest appeared an
old friend as I recognised its constituents - far more fan palm
than I had seen near Daintree river, then bush with ground
covered by "grass palms" 4 feet high was very astonishing.

July 18
Slept like a log through vibrations and violent coughs of my
compartment companions. Far more comfortable coaches on
Brisbane mail and scenery more monotonous - distant
mountains fine at times, but an abundance of open bush
country prevails, grass covered below the trees by constant
firing. Some inferior canes ripening - saw wallaby or
kangaroo - many big grey cranes with red heads, huge black
and white curlew like birds - few eagles and many jackasses.
Wonderful view and lights at Cardwell across Hinchinbrook
Channel. High imposing mountains on the island itself. Fine
sunset through the bush - a glorious red - so to feed at
Rockhampton, and to bed, with the whole compartment to
myself. Guard hailed me as 'Low Island' recognising my
rucksack!

213

July 19

Whole compartment to myself and slept exceedingly well.
These two nights in the train have been my best for a long
time. Very cold however, and the bush was white with frost!
most unusual occurrence. Scenery less interesting,
monotonous open bush with ground covered in places by
'grass palm' bearing huge bullrush like heads up to 14 ft
high. Arrived in Brisbane at 12:30 - collected my baggage
and was met by Miss Bage who whisked me off to the
college. Afternoon spent in vaste shoppings and fixing up of
tickets, boats and baggage. Dr F arrived in the evening from
the south and was also staying at the college.

July 20

Dr F. not at all well. Retired to bed with a temp of 102° and a
pain. Shopped in the morning and addressed a female coffee
party gathering of graduates at the Lyceum club - awful
nuisance in the middle of a Saturday morning, but otherwise I
did not turn a hair. Afternoon spent out in car with two
students Mr Longman and Miss Bage to fetch Mrs Longman
from a show - then a picnic tea on a beach of Moreton Bay.
Glorious sun, but air cold, and very cold in mornings,
evenings and at night. Returned about 7 pm - and found
verdict of acute appendix for Dr F. We motored her off to
Hospital at once.

July 21 Sunday

Dr F. operated on successfully. Thank heaven she did not die
on us on Lizard Island or in Java. She was apparently in a
bad chronic state and another attack would have burst it. Day
spent letter writing and packing.

July 22

Off to Nieuw Holland after breakfast, and sailed at 11 am.
Miss Bage motoring me down and thrusting custard apples
and strawberries and cream upon me. After 5 hours we
cleared Moreton Bay and shed the pilot. Fine near view of

Glasstop Mountains and fine Low Island type of sunset with a huge moon of similar appearance half over the eastern horizon. Made a perfect glutton of myself over the glorious confections of the Chinese cooks and the custard apples! Boat crew all Chinese. Super marvellous vaste single berth cabin, best on board after cabin de luxe. What a difference to my last night at sea on Daintree in a moderate gale! Folk on boat most revolting, empty headed highly civilised oily creatures of emaciated hues. A jaundiced outlook doubtless due to my missing J and M etc. Met the Captain dancing in the evening, gave him a photo of his ship from Low Island when she passed close with Prof Goddard on board. Promised to pass near Low Island again. Awful wireless dance music.

July 23
Fine and sunny, air still cool, but warmer. Sent a wireless to J and M saying we were deviating to pass near L. Island. Saw porpoises playing with a baby one close up. At 12:30 we passed North Reef, the beginning of the Barrier, with lighthouse, lee sand cay and wreck at S.E. end, 9,000 ton boat been there 4 weeks - could have been salved, next day, but crew refused to work overtime even at double wage! Washed, ironed, developed a pack in ship's darkroom.

July 24
Warmer but less sun, calm. Inspected charts etc on the bridge - learnt that we pass L. Island at 4 am, a miscalculation previously of the chief officer's. Very sad, as I had been looking forward to seeing the place - and more particularly my little friends. I seem to be the honoured passenger and authority as to reefs and ship's position for all and sundry - rather a bore. Had a very pleasant tea with Capt. Bauer on the bridge in his sumptuous cabin, a most cheery soul - spent most of his life in these parts starting as a cabin boy in a sailing vessel. Told of adventures of his first captaincy 80 miles up a river in Borneo getting stuck for 40 days, being

the only white - and when the natives got dangerous he gave them dutch rum which quite incapacitated them.

<u>July 25</u>
A truly wonderful day. Arose at 4 am to see the L. Island light [house] and the ghost of Snapper Island pass in the darkness. A rather morbid proceeding, so back to bed till 6:30. Dressed and saw anchor point abreast of boat, Mount Cook loom up and Cooktown Bay, although only the beacons leading to it could be seen. So watched Cape Bedford pass from the bridge - the scene changing so rapidly at 15 knots compared with my usual speed in these parts. So to Breakfast as we passed between Three Isles and Low Woody. Fine bird's eye view of Three Isles, high tide with the lagoon full of water and Michael's map just shouting itself aloud. So past Woody, Two Isles and Rocky Isle, N. and S. Direction Islands in the misty distance, the mainland standing up finely with the snow cap-like sand dunes. So to Cape Flattery a welcome old friend. The tide being high and just past full moon we took the shallower inside course within the Turtles, rather than the 10 mile longer route between Lizard Island and Eagle Island. Eagle Island could only just be seen with glasses on the horizon. N. Island was on the horizon and clear, while the Turtles were close on our starboard bow. Later passed the Q Islands to port. All these islands low and wooded. Day gloriously sunny. At 2 pm I went on the bridge by invitation and remained for the afternoon. By 2.15 we were close to Cape Melville, wondrous pile of innumerable boulders. On the seaward side was Pipon Island. Very like Low Island on a larger scale. Rampart mangroves, flat, sand cay, gorges in rampart and S.W. projections and angle in rampart all the same, anchorage appeared small. Unattended light fixed up in rampart. So across Princess Charlotte Bay and close along side the Flinders Islands for my especial pleasure. Two fine rocky piles of land with queer weatherings and a fine wave cut trench at the foot. So past the Flinders at 4 pm and up the track again passing numerous

islands of the L. Island type, with or without trees (palms etc) and mangroves and showing sand cays in corresponding stages of development all most fascinating and so darkness descended once again. A wonderful calm sea all the way - how unlike my earlier impressions of this part. What elementary geography lessons in weathered shore and embayed drowned coasts etc. Flat topped inland mountains plateaux etc.

July 26
Another great day. Passed Cape York about 8:30-9 am an inhospitable stretch of coast - less high and rugged, smoothly weathered knobs of land - very bare. Passed similar appearing Mount Adolphus Isles to starboard, and turned westwards round Cape York towards Wednesday Island, a large bare rocky patch. So on towards Hammond Island with Thursday Island lying behind it. Navigation precise, with reefs, shallow patches and [boyed] rocks on all sides. Previous night Captain Bauer spent on the bridge, but clear atmosphere and moon made all well. Occasionally if visibility is very bad - if it rains or an unattended light is out they drop anchor. Bays and channels between the islands fine. Two humps on Thursday Island with houses visible in gully.
Pearl luggers anchored nearby. Actual Torres Strait very narrow between Hammond Island and North Reef to the south - a huge wide and very long reef appearing nearly dry, no breakers on it and another reef beyond and parallel to it. So on past the Hammond Island - two very old wrecks on rocks on next island. Fringing reefs clearly seen around the islands, fine wave cut benches, familiar green shallow water etc. Past Booby Island and its lighthouse and so farewell to the Pacific and to Australia and out westward towards Timor. Spent the morning on the bridge until we entered the open sea. Getting warmer, but still pleasant. Passed "Cape Lewin" the lighthouse boat in the Torres Straits.

217

July 27
Started to be hot, but clouded over with misty rain at times
and pleasantly cool later. No land in sight, quite uneventful.
291 miles. S.E. Trade persists.

July 28 Sunday
Uneventful warm day, in morning flocks of 50 - 100 flying
fish about 8" long continually rose from the water like a
cloud of swallows looking like silver streaks in the sun. Sea
flat calm - slight swell of yesterday being absent - water here
deep. Played very good and strenuous semi-finals in deck
tennis - just winning 6-5 6-5 with Mrs Reid.

July 29
Another wonderful day. Awoke to find us alongside the Letti
Islands - 3 large mountainous piles to starboard. By 10:30 we
were close along the coast of Timor, at times being within
150 yards of the shore over very deep water (more than 100
fathoms). We spent the morning following the embankments
of the northern coast, and from the bridge the view was
fascinating - mountainous country 1100 meters, steep
wooded slopes showing fine weathering dissection. Coast
dips at once to deep water leaving a clear wave cut bench in
most places, with occasional narrow sandy bays with
coconuts behind and a small fringing reef in front. Few
habitations, native kampongs with picturesque huge thatches
were visible among cultivated patches of coconuts on the
slopes, a few white pleasing habitations of Portuguese
governing officials lie near the shore along a coastal road. Up
the slopes of the mountains were seen old wave cut benches
at higher levels, several being visible one above another.
What a geography lesson! Passed close to the settlement of
Lautain with its fort and white walled thatched buildings of
the Portuguese and the native huts. So we fired a salute to the
gazing populace and fishers on the shore and turned
northwest away from Timor. All day fine mountainous
islands were visible on both sides and at sunset we were

218

passing away from the last of these, glorious sunset and heavy clouds after misty gloriousness of mountains in the bright sun. So to a fabulous fancy dress show and horse races - only commendation being my wearing my reef clothes. Won finals of deck tennis!

July 30
Warm and sticky, light clouds about. No land in sight till late afternoon. Developed films, washed, ironed, packed etc. Marvellous sunset as we approached Salayer Straits between Salayer Island and Celebes. Heavy black clouds, black islands ahead with overlapping narrow neck between them, sky vivid crimson with a black frame and next door vivid orange in a similar frame of clouds. Over Celebes it was impossible to tell where mountains ended and where clouds began. Colours changed, and rock became vivid red between black land and gradually the first lighthouse of the Straits appeared.

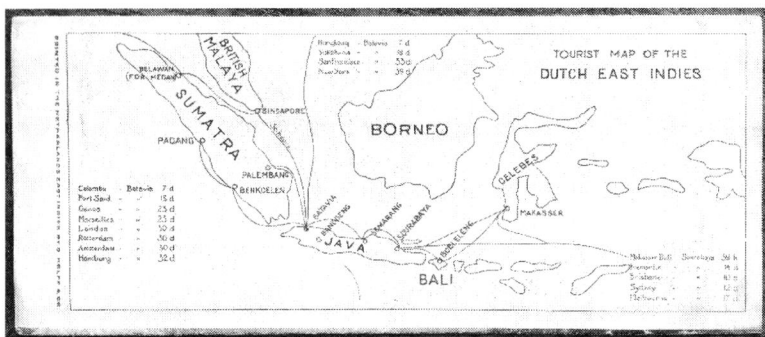

July 31

Amazing never to be forgotten sunrise as we entered
Makassar harbour. Half the eastern sky was brilliantly
coloured and half was pitch black cloud over the mountains
of the island. Native dwellings appeared on the shore and
numerous queer sailing boats and palm covered islands out to
sea. Just lovely. Breakfast at 7:30 and about 8:45 was
introduced to the harbourmaster's wife on the bridge. She
took me off the boat and motored me to the Orange Hotel and
then round and about the place and out to native villages in
the suburbs. I was too thrilled for words at seeing the native
houses of bamboo with palm thatches all raised on piles and
the swarms of Malays and Chinese, dusky with purple
sarongs. Coconuts and bananas and bamboo groves abound
along the roads and round the native kampongs. So to the
hotel for lunch at 12:30. My room spacious stone floor with
balcony plus w.c. and bathroom (no bath) but basin, trough
and shower. Afternoon spent fussing over luggage - ok in the
end and N. Holland sailed at 4 pm. Tea on verandah -
overlooking a palm filled court - very warm. Walked from 5
till 6:30 among the Malay outskirts of the town, perfectly
fascinating with the natives coming home carrying fish, food
in banana leaves etc and all with sarongs of mauve, purple
and magenta - few of other colours. Developed a pack and so
to dinner at 8:30 - hideous hour after 12:30 lunch. Met the
three Yanks and arranged a motor stunt for tomorrow.

August 1

Breakfast at 6:30 after a delightfully cool night, could have done with a sheet, but no covering provided. At 7 am we motored to tombs at Dongaÿa, where we photographed the natives and a choice small infant. Then on to Soeggoominassee to see the biweekly bazaar, arriving about 8 am. Place just fascinating. Walked about photographing for two hours, and were great centres of attraction as we inspected Chinamen selling cocks, fruit, queer vegetables, fried bananas and cotton goods. Several tiled rooves protected some goods from sun, and the rest of the show occurred below a bamboo grove on a high bank of the river. Malays both dark and light thronged in hundreds, buying and selling. Very well behaved and friendly and vastly inquisitive. The Yanks in vast plus fours and hats a yard wide and 'Moovie' cameras were very conspicuous, while self in shorts (my pandering to civilisation in the way of clothes lasted 1 day!) passed little noticed. My burnt skin and decayed topee go a long way towards inconspicuousness - my legs are the same colour as the paler Malays! So on to the Bantimoereng waterfall - 30 miles. Fall itself not exciting but country very much so. Flat inland from the coast with rice fields, bamboo and coconuts and house thatch palms near water - then suddenly gold limestone cliffs with 100 foot or more vertical sides and trees on top, all deeply dissected and segmented into blocks - truly surprising with stalactites galore from undercut edges etc. We followed up the stream ½ mile having climbed up alongside the falls by steps. The valley or cleft between these limestone tables was fine, dense tropical vegetation and shoals of huge yellow, yellow tipped and speckly blue and black butterflies drinking on the wet mud edges. So passed through fine caves in the limestone tables full of glorious stalactites and spanned by vertical roots 30 feet long, like pillars, from trees above, and passing across the mouths of the caves. So reached two small lakes where the stream rises bubbling out of caves and holes in the limestone at water level. So back to Makassar to lunch at

221

3:30 and to tea with Mrs Harbourmaster *[Boeveie]*. Then enquired about boats for tomorrow. 2000 local sailing trading vessels deposited their cargoes here last year, copra etc from Celebes and other islands - the boats are native made of hand hewn planks on the plans of the Dutch and English vessels of the 17th Century (!) with high stern and low bows. Average temperature here is 80° - and cool nights make the climate pleasanter than Surabaya or Batavia which are hotter. 10,000 Chinese in Makassar, 1000 Europeans and many Malays - chiefly outside the town. Developed 2 packs.

August 2
Breakfast at 6:30 am - left at 7 am and went for a row in the harbour and outside the sea wall with 2 Chinese-Malays. Tide low and 1mile about from shore, bottom was shallow and sandy and spattered with coral rocks and living favias and *Heliopora* and *Porites* with occasional foliose *Montipora* and *Seriatopora*, in deeper parts inside sea wall. No other branched forms. Early morning haze fairly thick. Chased various native fishing and trading craft to get photographs, all most interesting, passed chinese fishing in sailing canoes with a boom of bamboo for stabilising on the opposite side to the sail - canoes same both ends. Trading vessels with square sails and larger boats built on the plans of 17th century English and Dutch trading vessels with high sterns and big lee boards behind. So back at 11 am, changed to civilised clothes, drinks and lunch at 12:30. Then out by car to explore native kampongs around Makassar. Penetrated a village entirely under palms near a creek with waterways and sandy lanes through it, all perfectly fascinating. Mr Ostenheusen talks mixed Arabic and Malay to the natives of Arabic extraction with great success getting a volume of replies and much merriment. He is a character and no mistake, looks like a tramp - no teeth and not even false and earns his living by travelling and lecturing on his travels in the States. Developed a pack. Dinner at 8:30 and listened to Mr O's talks of formal feasts etc of old Constantinople.

Temperature less than previous days - must have been 68-65°
at night. In harbour was a sunken schooner - sunk when
Chinese boatman was 'me small boy boat down' 30 - 40
years ago I suppose. It had a thick growth of massive corals
on it - *Favias* 6 inches, *Madrepora* (of similar size), coarse
hefty varieties and other blunt branching forms possibly
Psaninserias etc.

August 3
Arose early, breakfast at 7 am - so to some horse races with
the Koenigs. A most entertaining morning. The Celebes
horses are minute and ridden bareback by diminutive boys
each in vivid coloured shirts to distinguish them and decked
with ordinary sarongs and head rags etc. One urchin must
have been about 10 and weighed 40 lb so had to wear a huge
belt of lead to bring him to minimum weight. His horse was
wild, and threw him off before the start - however he won the
race finally. The boys keep beating the horses with a switch
in their right hands and hang on to the reins and mane with
their right [?] - or don't hold on at all! Horse owners started
the beasts all in bright colours, a fine opportunity of seeing
the natives. Sailed at 5 pm on S.S. 'Melchior Treub' 3,000
tons. Glorious sunset giving a beaten gold appearance to a
broad bank of cloud stopping short of the horizon leaving a
band of marvellously coloured sky as a red sun streaked with
grey cloud rapidly plunged itself into the sea. After 7 pm hit
a strong W wind as we steamed south - and I went to bed
immediately with no dinner and stayed fit - the motion was
nothing compared with Daintree or Merinda, but v. different.

August 4 Sunday

Fine day, no land in sight. Old Mr Koenig a fearful bore, being decidedly senile, but other two Yanks improve on knowing, especially *[Ostrander]* who talks wonderfully of his travels. Sighted Bali at 9:30 am as a high mountainous mass appearing below and above clouds. Landed at 4 pm. Horrid Yank endless haggle over price of cars - eventually started with a 7 seater car and an admirable English speaking Chinese guide - drove through Sinparadia behind Bochleng *[Buleleng]* saw girls with grave offerings in huge covered stemmed vase on their heads - drove on upwards through irrigated rice fields and then coffee plantations - rice field temples most charming, wonderful sunset through palms as we looked back over Bochleng far below us and the open sea. Past very deeply cut water worn valleys with precipitous sides and deep side valleys. Then up to 4,000 ft in the pass across the E. W. mountainous ridge and in the dark arrived at the government rest house at Kintamani. Native women half naked and men dressed. 75% population women.

August 5

Awoke at 5:45 to find a thick mist, so that it was useless to get up and see the sun rise over the volcanoes etc. Breakfasted at 6:30 - and mist cleared enough to see where things were, but it never got brilliantly clear. The crater is miles round with a huge rim upon which we stood. A lake occupies the eastern side of the crater and the cone or cones of the Bantoer Volcano stood up from the crater with a steam of cloud arising from it. East of the volcano arose the steep slopes of the highest mountain, and between the two stood out the distant peak in Lombok. Started about 7:30 to 8 am the road going a few miles along the crater edge where the new village now stands. From a view point we saw the black flow of the 1926 (August) eruption which destroyed the village, inhabitants being saved and building a new village up top. View magnificent, but badly lit. So on down the slopes to the south, passing alongside a 6 mile crack due to an earthquake in 1917, crack now 150-200 ft deep with precipitous or slightly weathered sides separating similar flat fields on either side. Investigated village of Bangklet where we entered a house inside its walls - all village houses having a wall along the road with fairly elaborate gateways. Household consists of closed hut for married folk and girls and open shanties for men and open kitchen - row of private Hindu shrines behind, one for each major member of the family. Houses of native brick and here shingled with bamboo instead of palm leaves, as it stands wet mountain climate better. Two men let their roosters fight for our benefit - roosters being in Bali more vital than wives - we photographed the half naked girls and folk - girls having palm leaves etc rolled in huge holes in their ears. Looks of many natives spoiled by betel chewing - So on downhill past mountain rice fields all water supplied, and increasing cross paths to Bangli. Here we entered a high caste Balinese house with beautiful carved brick and sandstone porch and screen behind it. Within were several huts and roofed verandahs and we photographed a beautiful high caste girl weaving etc. Whole household pleased and hospitable. So onto Kloengkoeng [now Klungkung] where the Javanese first made themselves at home for a while. En route we passed marvellous terraces of rice fields all sizes and shapes, beautifully levelled with raised edges to hold the water and water falls from one terrace to the next. Pleasing deep river gullies and natives washing etc. Kloengkoeng a fairly large place, we looked especially at a beautiful square roofed dais or local assizes with wonderful brick and stone carving all round. Chairs of painted wood, and fine ceiling decorations of painted stories depicting heaven and hell. Nearby were lovely gardens and ponds beside the "Holy Gate" of the "Old Palace" where the Rhaja formerly lived - this is a fine carved gateway - but the place teems with wonderful gateways - temples - shrines etc. So retraced the road and hurried on to Den Passar for a late lunch, passing entrancing scenery of padi fields and dense palm groves, coconuts, sugar palm and bamboo, water courses and views of the sea and everywhere beautiful native women with goods on their heads and large and small shrines to the rice fields on all sides. Spent some time at the temple of Soekawati over the wonderful carvings of the gate, walls, and outer pillars, natives, and inside many shrines to sun god etc - all Hindu. Started off at 2 pm and saw some fine shrines to the rice fields and to the earth god. (Rice goddess is Dewi Sita) so through rice fields - palms shady and open roads - past the small market of Abian Sismal with its rice barn and into the Sacred Wood of Sangeh. Here as usual we found a beautiful half bare girl who took us to see the sacred monkeys who run wild and feed from corn out of our hands - the trees in the wood had a fruit spirally falling and growing immensely high - highest in the island. Shrines and small pagodas lay in the heart of the wood. Had to hurry on, as it was past 4 pm, and went to the Giant Banyan Tree of Bonghasa which covers an acre - bigger than Ostander had seen in India or anywhere in the world - fine glimpses of native life. Turned homeward and stopped by a gamelan playing outside a house, a long stripped bamboo or tree palm stood outside bearing a white paper bird lantern and flag. It was a funeral, the gamelan of bells outside and about 30 operators was strange if not too tuneful - we went inside and on a bier wrapped in white was the corpse surrounded by about 200 Malays another smaller gamelan played next the corpse (died yesterday) and the smiling and laughing relatives crawled under the bier - women covering themselves, as a mark of respect - more singing and jingling, but the crowd sat quietly on the ground. Then the corpse was seized and much squabbling to help carry it into an inner court where it was put in a house (no walls) on a bamboo frame inside a bamboo basket covering and more cloths applied. We were welcomed right inside this house, and the folk seemed more pleased than otherwise that we should watch the proceedings. In the house the body is mummified by salt, lime and vinegar and kept for a year or two years, continuously tightening the wrappings. So we went out, and a procession formed lined by men carrying poles with women carrying things on their heads and the visitors following. Determined to return the next afternoon as it was too dark for photography. Truly a wonderfully impressive dream like spectacle. Previously on the way we had stopped at a village house and inspected its constituent parts within its outer walls - we also through the guide got invited inside the house of the Chief of the village, a fine figure in red and white jumper and gorgeous sarong and nails on left hand 2" long to show his nobility in not working. Many buildings to his house, and in his sleeping house, open on three sides - were some palm leaf books, with Malay writing - these said to last 200 years. In the rear two new shrines were being built, sandstone blocks and bricks all mud cemented, and when dry carved. We bade him a cordial farewell and met him later at the funeral. So to dinner at 7:30, and out afterwards to the market opposite. Here another gamelan was playing. The corpse having been kept two years was about to be cremated along with bones of dead younger members of the family. A huge wooden cow by way of a coffin was ready. Alongside a performance of "Shadow Dancing" started at 9 and proceeded till 12. Another fascinating show. A man sits behind an oil hanging lamp with a white muslin screen in front - a pile of figures with moveable arms etc made of hide and wonderfully cut and stencilled and painted, sticks working the arms - aided by mystic forms etc he sat working a local mythical story, telling it first in Sanskrit which nobody understands, and reenacting it and telling it in Malay with the aid of two clowns impersonating the real characters. He keeps up a perpetual banging of a wooden clapper held in his foot in a box with big crashes for battles etc. Very strenuous performer - aided in the rear by four operators of bells. On the ground and on bamboo poles sat the natives quietly watching and laughing at intervals greatly absorbed. After standing 1 hr the local agent and one time king sent us a stool. Another crowd of watchers pressed round the near side of the screen equally enthroned, while folk sat all over the "cow" at the side. The

227

shadow dance was in honour of the funeral the Balinese
having learned the art from the Javanese, a wonderful show.
A wonderful day from 6 am to 12 pm.

August 6
Breakfast at 7 am and out to market opposite photographing
"Cow" and natives - tower of 11 storeys and wings being
made for funeral procession, also straw elephant heads and
fine wood carved dragon head to be carried in procession. On
through the village to another more elaborate market under
permanent roofs and concrete floored and so by car to
Kedaton village to see Balinese dancing. The dance costs f15
paid to the temple, the dancers serve three years to the temple
(everybody serves a period of 5 [years] temple service) and
dance gratis, clothes being provided by the temple. Arrived
at 8:30 and saw elaborate dressing and painting up of girls in
house yard, really beautiful damsels shown off well by hair
dressing, trace of powder and blackened eyebrows and
forehead streak. Before the dance extensive and prolonged
prayers were said to the shrine. The dance took place on an
open space by the roadside under the shade of a huge banyan,
with a fine carved archway on one side and native village
stalls on the other. Dancers sat on mats in a square, 14 girls
plus 8 boys. Orchestra of gongs in the rear. "Dancing" was
largely posing and chanting for most, two girls at a time
dancing in the central space. The dance depicted the
"temptation of Aijuna" a 2,000 year old story put in dance
form 30 years ago and now very popular and has therefore
been annexed to the temples. This story we saw the night
before in the shadow dance only more of it. After about 20
minutes dancing and singing a beautiful high caste girl
dressed elaborately as Aijuna appeared and performed in the
central space in slow beautiful poses and finally sat on seat,
[very sorrowful at loss /death of his betrothed princess].
Then he is tempted - firstly by two dancing girls who comfort
him and make love to him in restrained poses. He remains
unmoved. Finally the devil appears, easily recognisable in

228

detail of costume and mask from shaddow show and carvings etc. He and Aijuna fight and Aijuna shows fine acting and different expressions and shoots the devil with an arrow. A wonderfully artistic and beautifully stately show. Damsel acting Aijuna was called Goesti Poeto Bai. So we left and went towards [Kampakosining] northward, passing a tower used for sounding the tom-tom in a village. Fine rice terraces and palms everywhere. Country hilly and magnificent round the elephant cave, a Buddhist cave with heavy carved entrance on the face of a cliff built 1,200 years ago. Inside the cave, a tunnel in the rock enlarging into a chamber was a five foot statue of an elephant headed god - Goa Gajah and before it various offerings of food etc on palm leaves. On thence up to [Kampakosining] rest house high above a fine rivered valley terraced with rice, sweet potatoes etc and below lay the Holy spring and washing baths and temples etc. Lunched hurriedly to the foul squawk of dance tunes on a bad gramophone and down to the springs. Some natives from the north were there with solid gold goblets of fine workmanship, embossed and lid bearing stones, for fetching back the Holy water. Baths were fine - stone made with carved water spouts - natives were there, bathing, washing and combing their hair etc. Next stop was at the Palace at Oebod, a fine set of courts, gateways, walls and houses, with and without walls, elaborate stone and brick carving, and deep wood carving around doors, windows and pillars supporting the roofs etc. The prince - Tjokordo Agoeng was away - he is the Balinese member of the Java parliament. His brothers and sisters and wives were there. We were welcomed and no objection was made to the intrusion. Then on to Abian Semal to catch the funeral ceremony, but nothing much was happening; however a procession left the house for the sea three miles away led by banner poles, women with burning incense and offerings in bowls on their heads - women with paper ? wood and bamboo images on their heads and men with long legged sunshades, followed by the crowd - about 80 - 100 folk. The dead man was the head priest - we

229

saw another head priest officiating from a neighbouring village - no man can be a priest until his wife ceases to bear children. Death is regarded as a joyous release and great expense is incurred willingly over a funeral. Balinese men and women are all carvers and weavers respectively, and a truly civilised people in their own way, and quite a good way too, as far as clothes and morals. Balinese girls chose their husbands, court a man who proposes or otherwise, if she accepts and subsequently changes her mind he kills her - 90% of the murders are due to this - the girls know the consequence and accept death willingly. A man has to make a separate house for each wife. Before lunch we went to see the tombs at Goenoeng Kawi, descended a steep valley luxuriantly terraced with a tumbling rocky stream at the bottom. Fine views up and down the valley, and elaborate irrigation streams for the terraces. On either side of the stream at the bottom were 1,200 years old Buddist tombs, upright huge carved monuments in alcoves cut in the rock face - kings on one side with inscriptions in a dead unknown language, and warriors on the other side, walls and shrines abound. A deep tunnel in the cliff face leads to the tomb of a king, only discovered 30 years ago under rice fields and now it is full of offerings from the natives! Nearby is a court open above composed of meditation chambers cut in the rock all round with a central block of stone left. In the evening a native dance took place outside the hotel at Don Pasar - very different from the morning's dance. A beautiful set of gamelan gongs made of silver etc. lay in 3 sides of a square, led by two drums in the central space and large gongs lay behind. Really beautiful music, tuneful and wonderfully performed. Periodically a dancing boy in wonderful sarong and narrow cloth wrapped round and round his middle danced with a fan - mainly sitting down. Very effective pose dancing with rapid arm movements and face expression.

<u>August 7</u>

Mr Ostrander and I went on to Boeleleng leaving the Koenigs. Started at 7:30 and stopped among the rice fields and palms and fascinating low land villages and markets to photograph. It was essentially a day of revelations in temples by way of new sights although the scenery as we climbed up and up to the mountains and upland villages and down again to the sea was marvellously beautiful. At Mengwitani two temples lay on either side of a side street, both with fine carved stone doors and wood inset carving. The second showed an elaborately painted and carved inner shrine with gilded door kept covered by a bamboo screen. At Dakdakan, where we met girls with huge piles of earthenware pots on their heads, was a fascinating temple on a hill with fine doorway, and carved screen behind it (to keep out the devil who only walks in a straight line). On this screen and covered by a bamboo fence was a painted carved God of astonishing design. Shrines within were elaborate. At Bandjor anjor, a sizeable place, was a vaste truly unspoiled native market. Ducklings and pigs and seaweed were on sale besides the usual other goods fruit, fish and dry foods - also stores of white men's goods, pocket knives, chain and picture hooks. Farfi bought silver inlaid iron betel cutter. Ostrander buying candy attracted half the village! Still 92 km from our destination so hurried on leaving the lowlands behind us. The mountain villages soon appeared and the long house walls of thatched mud became fewer and shorter, roofs of bamboo shingles instead of palm thatch appeared. A wonderful temple of reddish stone we found at Desa Goebock, with a main archway and two side ones with no lintels, truly beautiful steep flight of steps led to the middle gate - the walls bore high relief medallions of dragon like beasts painted. The inside was just as beautiful. So on down deeply cut valleys with marvellously engineered rice terraces - like machine made frills, all in different stages of rice growth. Beautiful views across valleys and down them - the ever present "giraffe of vegetables" of which one never tires for

231

its beauty was always in sight. At Desa Ringdikit we found a wonderful temple with two high pagoda shrines overlooking flooded rice fields, and another gorgeous archway (only Hindu Pagodas in existence). So on to the sea, passing seedling rice plots from which the bright yellow green plants are pricked out into the fields. Passed kite flyers - kites being a national hobby - size huge taking 6 men to carry them, string being of bamboo. Reached Boeleleng at 2:30 and went into Meh Patimah's house at Singaraja. She is the Princess of the island, owner of the silver mines and ours and other cars. Her house was like a large high caste establishment with a wonderful <u>wooden!</u> rice barn with painted carvings on it. In buildings and on verandahs we found men and boys making hammered silver bowls and silver stoppers and her daughter doing gold and silver silk and cotton weaving. A breadfruit tree stood in the court. We then came back to Boeleleng to another house to see her wares and just fine they were too. Never have I seen such beautiful weavings, I longed to buy it all - fine hues, swords of water marked steel with gold hammered handles. 8 inches long set with stones, silver bowls and bottle stoppers. Patimah herself is charming and knows how to show her goods and please her customers. She gave us coffee on the verandah and very good coffee too - most coffee here is absolute poison - (due to bad roasting as coffee beans are excellent quality). Later she dressed me up completely in wonderful woven pieces, a fine strip wrapped round and kept there by a 5 inch batik band wrapped tightly round and round my middle and thus another fine broad strip wrapped round my upper wrists. Those weavings of glorious colours and gold and silver thread tastefully applied were a revelation. We reluctantly left and arrived at Boeleleng about 4 pm. We walked about till 5 and then boarded the Van der Lijn, 2,000 tons the "Pig Express" - 4 passengers, 1,500 pigs in baskets for Singapore plus 300 bullocks and a smell!!!
So goodbye to Bali - truly named the Enchanted Isle and Heaven on Earth - people charming in disposition, boys smiling and attractive and women marvellously beautiful.

Only regret is Betel chewing and barking dogs. Exposed 13 days negatives in Bali - could go home now without a murmur so full am I of wonderful memories and marvels. Forgot to mention our admirable guide Tan Hock Ban, Chinaman speaking English, Balinese Chinese and Malay and learning Dutch and of great intelligence, likewise wild monkeys darting across the road and beautiful Frangipani trees in blossom on the shore at Boeleleng - flowers and no leaves on the tree and the flowers are sacred and worn in the hair of the dancing girls. Developed 6 packs and 2 doz plates! To bed at 2:30 am.

August 8
Arrived in Sourabaya at 11 am and motored to Gnemplak [real name Ngemplak] Hotel. Rest of morning in shopping collecting letters etc. Afternoon to Zoo to see giant lizards *Varanus komodoensis* [Komodo dragon] 10 ft long and fairly active. New well built aquarium in London type but after the Barrier Reef it was tame. Fine tubeworms and *Bispina* and one living *Favia. Dinkias* were very pale. Mr Potter called at 5 pm and gave me tips about travel. Motored me round Sourabaya and arranged to fetch me at 8 am and put me on the train to Solo (Sourakata). On getting back I found Ostrander had scooped a free 7 seater Buick for two days to go to Tosari offered by the Orient touring company on agitations unknown to me by Capt Bauer of the Nieuw Holland. Too good to miss so arranged to cut off a day at Batavia and cut out Sourakata and go. If ever anyone fell on their feet it is me! Washed hair, developed 4 packs.

August 9
Arose at 6 am and left at 7 with Ostrander for Tosari. Drove about Sourabaya for 1 hr and then inwards across the sugarcane covered plain behind S - much being cut and factories busy. Few Tapioca plants and cotton trees, the pods forming stuffing known as kapok, trees have very few leaves and these all at the top. As we climbed and left the plain the

233

country became more wooded, many bananas, cotton trees and finally casuarina woods with lovely views on either side as we climbed up the spurs of the mountainous region which starts abruptly from the plains. Arrived at Tosari through the casuarinas at 10:45 am and found a charming Dutch hotel with glorious flower gardens, canas, 4 ft begonias etc and rooms at f6 instead of f10 at S. and 12 in Bali. A new posh Hotel lies higher up. Arranged to walk to Bromo instead of on ponies. Left at 11:45 with guide, me in shorts and *[Yokohamas]*. Glorious 3 hr walk to edge of Bromo. First past cultivated flat slopes at incredible angles, soil fine volcanic dust, hence peculiar weathering, then through Casuarina forests, vast tree ferns about and glorious views across v deep valleys to other spurs, but soon clouds marred views. Path drops for some distance and then rises steeply until the Moengal Pass was reached and we suddenly from the crater edge looked over the vast sand sea far below us - 5 miles x 3 and 10 miles in circumference, the largest in the world. Crater rim precipitous high and vast - in the crater opposite was the huge dead cone - Battok (4 cones all of them) fluted regularly all round by rain on the fine volcanic dust. Other similar weathered slopes abounded, and the Bromocone partly hidden behind Battok was sending up volumes of smoke. Some of this settled down in queer towers and masses on the sand sea, and the volcanic sand itself was blown into clouds in places. Vegetation of sorts on the Battok and grass in places on the sand sea. The soil all the way up was simply volcanic dust, hardened in places, but then scratchable easily with a finger, going very dirt and occasional whiffs of SO_2 filled the air when miles from the crater. Left Ostrander on the crater edge and descended 1,000 feet to sand sea with the boy. Long dusty walk across the sand, round the front of the Battok to the Bromo. Weird weathered spurs of the Bromo on a huge scale, climbed up these and finally the last lap by 240 concrete steps to the edge of the cone. Edge narrow, black soft dust underfoot, and one looked down thousands of feet into a steep sided funnel from

234

which came incredible volumes of smoke, soft and curling and solid looking. Gurgles and crashes were heard and many minor land slips of inner cone face clattered down. Visibility across the crater poor owing to Bromo smoke, but sun penetrated in places and the spurs of volcanic dust, black, grey and whitish and the fine cone of the Battok and mountainous crater edge beyond are never to be forgotten. A torrential downpour of black smuts drove us hastily down the cone to the sand sea and back. Very stiff climb up to the Moengal Pass, where I drank tea and ate bananas and sat down for a few minutes. So we started back and half way left the main track for a steep path among the cultivated slopes, cabbages grew in that too! Past hedges of fuchsia and wild castor oil trees - and so into the clouds again reaching Tosari at 5:30 in time to see a gorgeous sunset behind lumpy clouds below and level with us lying over the plains, and flanked by wonderful mountain silhouettes, pinky grey cloud effects unlike anything I have ever seen. So to washing filthy and slightly weary self.

Bromo is connected with the Semeru to the south, highest Java volcano 12,000' high.

<u>August 10</u>
Arose at 6 am - but no fine sunrise owing to cloud. During the night a thick layer of black dust had settled over everything, dust contains iron and kills flowers etc as it lies on the petals. Left Hotel [Kario] at 7:30 - a very nice hotel with dining room decorated by really fine painted panorama looking over plains to the sea and round over the Bromo. So down through the misty casuarina forest - the most beautifully graceful tree in the slight haze and the huge red flowered Dadap trees - great bushes of trumpet shaped white flowers 7" lost and epiphytic ferns - all growing on loosely binding volcanic dust. Went S.W. to Malang at foot of mountains - fine road through sugar country, bamboo and palms everywhere. Back to Sourabaya - to bank, shop and to lunch with Mr Dubois - owner of car - there to learn that that

ass Ostrandes had *[wrecked]* the trip more or less, we ought to have gone up another mountain, remained till darkness and looked down into fiery crater <u>or</u> gone up to Bromo before sunrise and further going to Malasy on main roads was fatuous stunt, we ought to have gone through side roads and villages. He is extraordinarily helpless although a 30 yr world traveller. Mr Dubois very helpful over detailed itinerary of Java and Sumatra. Ostrander off to Borneo. Had a mango for lunch! Not very thrilled thereby.

<u>August 11 Sunday</u>
Woken at 4:30 am and caught train for Djarkarta arriving at 11:30 am. Country at first flat with endless finely cultivated canes and rice fields with bamboo and coconuts between. Over a short stretch was a forest of big trees with gigantic leaves, deciduous and largely bare, and lots of that glorious red flowering Dadap, all the upper branches being solid with flowers. A few wild monkeys scampered about the branches. Sugar mills dotted the plains. Hazy mountains appeared from time to time, not far away and arising abruptly from the plain and girdled with white cloud strips. Between Sourakarta (Solo) and Djokja line passes close to long mountainous ridges richly cultivated in terraces reminding me of the Aosta Valley. Reached Hotel Toegoe opposite station, lunched, and it being Sunday Batik and Brasswork not open. I spent the afternoon in driving about in a Sado at 75 cents pr hr. Visited the 'Water Castle' or home of Sultan 300 years ago. He was the first sultan and now the 18th reigns. Place rambling with courtyards and banana lined lanes and native dwellings between - mostly badly ruined but very attractive in spots. Women at work over Batik and I made 2 purchases - several week's work for f6. I think. So on through the mature old town - huge spaces enclosed in white walls with white gateways and lined all round with old banyans, chipped with middles cut out and leaves forming tubular screen. A fair of mixed European and native sorts was in preparation. Native streets charming - houses with plaited bamboo walls and tile

or thatched roofs but not on legs as in Celebes or open all round as in Bali. Batik sarongs of natives glorious and all subdued in colours, so back to Hotel and out walking for 1 hr to the old town. Usual blasted developing of films. To bed early for 1st time for weeks, rather weary.

August 12
Arose at 5:30 and caught 6:19 train for Moentilar, being the only white passenger. Slow train through glorious country, far more interesting than previous rail journey. Agriculture magnificent, usual cane and rice and sugar mills, molasses containers lying about the rails. Sugar being reaped and also young. Halts frequent in minute villages, train passing the doors of bamboo plaited houses with tiled or sugar leaved thatches - Javanese people here different in looks and language from the Madurese of Eastern Java - short, not good looking, wearing dull brown sarongs and black jackets and black shorts. Some heavenly valleys with streams and rice terraces and nearby mountains. Reached Moentilar at 7:45 where train goes down a mile or two of village street. Was met by car from the Borobades Hotel and drove out the remaining 14 km, arriving at 8:15 am - Walked about the temple till 12:30 - first with a guide and then alone taking photographs. Wonderful view - mountains on 2 sides and overlooking plains on 2 sides - misty distance and Merangi volcano not visible. Cool in early morning but temple very hot in the middle of the day. 4 wonderful galleries of frescoes depicting lives of the Budda pictorially. Lowest gallery without a balustrade was added later for strength and so covered up carvings depicting the lives of sinful man. 2 miles of frescoes showing fine workmanship and durability from 750 – 850 AD. Kalasan gargoyles and door decorations - glorious gateways - over 500 Buddahs, in different attitudes, according to the points of the compass. (E right hand down on knee, palm downwards, 'meditation' symbol of thought above. W hands crossed - symbolised charity. N right hand raised, calling east to witness. S right hand on knee - palm

upwards - dispelling fear). The whole is not impressive as to size from a distance, one must walk its galleries and climb its steep stairs etc to realise its vast proportions. Slept from 1-3:20 pm - really slack and weary for first time since Makassar, due partly to attenuated nights. Spent another hour at the temple - saw the misty sunset and perused literature on temples and Javanese culture at hotel. To bed early.

August 13
Arose at 5:30 to see the sun rise. Night quite cool and blanket needed 1/2 the time, went to sleep with the moonlight on the temple from one window, and through the open door I saw fireflies, two white cats, and heard a distant gamelan orchestra. Climbed to the top of the temple, and there to the east where I thought was endless plain, loomed up the huge symmetrical cone of the Merapi volcano, black against a faintly coloured sky. To the left of the Merapi lay the more cumbersome mountain Merabo /Merbabu?/, likewise invisible in daytime. The Merapi was smoking magnificently. The sunrise colours were nothing much, but the spectacle of the Merapi and other mountains was magnificent. The sun rose finally right over the sharp peak of the Merapi as a red ball. At first the plain was filled with low clouds, pimples of hills and heads of coconut palms sticking up through it. As the sun rose so the mist dispersed, and as the sun became visible above the Merapi, so the Merapi and Merabo silently vanished in the haze - a marvellous revelation, or rather the opposite, Merapi only about 15-20 miles away. Left at 8:30 for Moentilar and arrived in Djokjakarta by 10:35. Rest of morning spent buying and seeing native handicrafts. Lunch at 12:30 and out by car to temples. First to Kalasaan, a perfect gem of a Brahmanic temple near the road side in process of restoration, piles of carved constituent stones lying about - carving exceptionally fine, detailed and deeply cut. Makaras [mythological Hindu sea creatures] at foot of steps on four sides. So on to the Prambanan Temples. These lie in a vast low walled enclosure, one huge temple in the middle and a

238

ring of temples round it - then a wall and a triple row of 12 smaller temples on each side of the square. In the middle of each temple within the wall is a high room reached by stairs and galleries, open or closed to the sky with an opening or doorway into it on one side. Within is a statue of Brahma or a sacred cow etc. In the central temple are three other small rooms on the sides which do not open into the central room. These contain one elephant headed god and two Brahmas respectively. Galleries round all fine with glorious deep carving of the story of Korma and Sita, beautiful stairways - door lintels and makaras of various kinds. The whole group of temples are being reconstituted - heaps of Malays being busy sorting out the piles of loose carved stones and wall carvings. Temporary bamboo scaffolds being erected. Had to tear myself away, one could spend days there, and go to the Sewoe temples. These are a huge group of private shrines, a large central one, a square space and low wall and rows and rows of surrounding shrines, all richly carved, but in very bad repair and many in ruins. All Brahmic temples in the Prembanan plain and all built of loose uncemented blocks as the Borubudur. Wonderful preservation of carvings.

Forgot to mention temple at Mendoet visited between Borubudur and Moentilar - fine temple completely restored as to shape with blocks of identical rock, new rock left plain in place of lost flat relief carvings, although some makaras etc have been recarved. A fine piece of restoration. Inside a huge Buddha on throne, back and sides formed by makaras, figures and below surrounding elephant. On either side a Boddhisattvas [a buddhist divinity] of unknown significance. Went to the Kraton in the evening after dinner - having developed 3 packs. Tried to find native dancing, but only discovered a semi European fair of huge dimensions - having gone to the wrong event.

August 14
For once did not get up early - breakfasted at 8 am - went out to the workshops of the native art place and saw the women

doing fine Batik waxing both sides, scraping some wax off with knife after first dip getting rid of wax with boiling water on cotton or petrol on silk. Buffalo hide work in progress and brass work. Wax moulds made, and covered with a muddy granular looking clay - dried for three weeks spouts cut and wax melted out and brass cast. Most primitive turning lathes of bamboo foot pedal - string and bamboo spring pole outside - carving on brass then done by squatting Malays.

Left by 11:35 train - the train I had taken from Sourabaia. Fascinating journey reaching Garoet at 7:20 pm. During the greater part of the day the country was flat and intensely cultivated for cane, rice, tobacco and a little tapioca; lovely wooded bits of the usual coconuts, bamboo, "thatch palms" in wet places - also red dadap trees etc. A little monotonous if beautiful as the rice had mainly been reaped and the fields were dry and brown. One hour from Tjibatoe great changes occurred, country became gradually alpine in topography, fine hills, valleys, gorges, streams and mountains the line winding in and out. Vegetation glorious - elaborate rice terraces everywhere, newly planted and flooded and older and brilliant green, a green never seen in Europe either in paint or nature. Description cannot convey the the gloriousness of alpine rice terracing on a vast and elaborate scale. Terraces smaller with less high steps to the next than in Bali. Sunset behind grey mountains in all directions. Found that Gramplang Hotel 4½ miles from Garoet at 4,000 ft was full, so had to stay at Villa Dolce 2,400 ft in Garoet itself. Arranged to climb Papandayan tomorrow by aid of 15 florins' worth of car to start with. Developed 3 packs.

August 15
Arose before sunrise and left before 6 am by car for the village of Tjisoeroepan at the foot of the Papandayan volcano and the Thkorai mountain. Glorious road up the Garoet valley for 30 km or so, winding in and out along the stream passing heavenly rice terraces all green and much bamboo, but few coconuts. Mountains in the perpetual haze loomed up

all round, and the opening to the crater of the Papandayan was visible afar off as a huge gash in the side of the mountain - yellow brown in colour of bare rock. In 1772 it erupted badly, blew its top off and one side, leaving a lateral crater with three gigantic walls - more or less perpendicular towering up hundreds of feet. A really charming hotel at Tjisoeroepan (4,200 ft) provided a native guide, and I left the car there at 6:30 or so. I had to refuse stoutly offers of horses and sedan chairs and set out in Yokohamas and shorts. Walk up took only 2½ hours, fairly steep and switchbacky and gloriously beautiful. First through bamboo tunnelled lanes and native dwellings, then bamboo, banana and tea plantations appeared, a lake and chincona trees etc. As we reached the cloud zone dense high forest and cool dampness were found - dadap and vast trees, 30 ft tree ferns, epiphytes, huge leafed ferns as in Queensland forests, glorious selaginellas and lycopodium, white trumpet flowers but no lower vines and vine like climbers as in Queensland. All this with the morning sun filtering through it and dispelling some of the haze - the stream rippling and butterflies like plates and violently coloured flapping round. Higher up the trees became bushes and much fern abounded. Two hot springs trickled over areas of rock which were quite bare of life and much eaten out by the sulphurous water - only a vivid green alga seemed to grow there. The vegetation thinned to bushes (rhododendron?) and tongue ferns of small size as we approached the white brown rock of the crater. Here was desert, watered by warm streams. The path led ever upward through the missing side of the crater - and here emerged much noise and clouds of steam. If the crater had been an Earls Court Exhibition show it couldn't have been arranged better. Here a pond of boiling grey mud with a fountain playing up through it - next two ugly deep holes full of boiling surging mud and gushing steam and splashes, further on a mound of sulphur, yellowings of crystals 1-2 yards across, middles being steaming tracts of burnt sulphur dark in colour. Further on up a hillock an extraordinary miniature

241

mountain of sulphurous mud the size of a house with stalactite like process and a yawning hole spouting steam and jets of H_2S. Behind this lay a hill of pure sulphur, the face being filled by caves and holes, beautiful with yellow crystals and spouting the bulk of the steam from the crater. The insides of the sulphur crystal caves in the sun were marvellous. Then came a hole in the ground spitting out pats of grey larva, like the subsidiary crater I saw in Vesuvius, the grey larva here covered a small area forming mounds. More stifling jets of H_2S greeted us, more boiling mud, and cascades of hot water passing down as the main stream, and finally a small but perfect sulphur cave and mound emitting an awful steamy stink. Finished drink and a banana the boy had been carrying and started down again. Fine view of Mount Thkorai girdled with cloud, perfectly shaped cone with richly terraced lower slopes. However the haze almost entirely wiped out the view of the Garoet valley itself. Downward walk quite as delightful as the upward and I was cool all the way, thanks mainly to sensible clothes. Passed the horse - sedan chairs etc. on my way down - still struggling upward. I had overtaken them before on my way up. Reached Tjisoeroepan at 12 am and had to wait till 1 for my car - delightful drive back, seen to greater effect in full sunlight. Idle afternoon spread in a capacious chair on the verandah with a fine view of palms, poiniema and bamboos and distant mountains. Near sunset had a stroll for 1½ round Garoet - exquisitely beautiful country, as good as Bali terraces, bamboos, people and houses and gorgeous mountains all around and a fine sunset - and what would man desire more? Indonesian here better looking than Javanese of mid Java, and dress in brighter colours, mainly reds.

August 16
Started just before 7 am to walk to Lake Bagendit - heavenly morning, just 3 km along road from which I saw the sunset - now brilliant with crowds of natives walking towards Garoet all brilliantly dressed in sarongs and jackets. Next 12 km

242

along a lane through rice country - richly watered with field like reservoirs, possibly just deeply flooded fields, covered by *Azolla* like floating ferns and other things, and fine palms and bamboo all round. Pleasant villages some houses being really well built, slightly raised (1½ ft) walls of bamboo weaving, tile roof and good wood doors, windows and verandah etc. Then endless and beautiful rice terraces and streams, hundreds of ducks about being driven for miles in batches of 50-200 - no wonder hotel duck is a muscular product! Kept mainly for eggs I believe as the natives won't eat hen's eggs. Finally reached the lake - not very impressive, although interesting for fleet of canoes of hollowed trees, two tied to a platform carrying chairs constituting a ferry - many fishers out casting nets from the canoes. Nearby women were threshing rice. Mount Throrae dominated the scene at all time, and Papandajan crater showed up clearly in the early morning. Turned back and plodded out the 13 km - although the last 3 were an effort - reaching Garoet at 11:45 - lunched and left by 1:35 train down the valley again to Tjibatoe. Heavenly scenery of terraces, deep stream valleys etc. On to Bandoeng by 5:23. Beautiful country all the way. The line climbs, winding in and out for some time, and one looks down and over the main valley surrounded by hills and mountains over a pass in the hills and down a valley to Bandoeng - wondrous journey. Very cool in Bandoeng - 25° for developer of 2 packs!!

August 17
Arose late - having slept extraordinarily well - breakfast at 7:45 and at 9 am out by car to Lembang Village at 4,000' up the side of the valley overlooking Bandoeng. Glorious view of the valley and the mountains to the south of it. Valley quite flat with hills rising straight up - must have been a fjord once I should think. Lembang Village very attractive - full of colour with a lovely market. The sarongs here and at Garoet are redder and usually printed flowery patterns compared with the excellent batik of brown and blue at Djokja. Views

243

to the near and far on the road between Lembang and
Bandoeng fine. Returned to Bandoeng - nothing to do in the
town - washed hair, wrote home and caught 2:21 for
Buitenzorg arriving 7:15. Marvellously beautiful journey all
the way, climbing up and up along the sides of valleys
getting fine views down them - carried on high bridges across
deep ravines with streams and rice fields and luxuriant upper
slopes - or across deep precipitous gorges - through passes
between hills and slowly down through stream watered rice
and bamboo country, plants of tapioca on the higher slopes.
Extraordinary steep cultivation of cabbages etc on high
mountain slopes rivalling that of Switzerland. Hotel Dibbits
full - so to the expensive and bad Bellevue.

August 18 Sunday
Breakfast at 8 and out to Zoological Museum - found no trace
of Dr Dammerman to whom I had sent Prof Goddard's letter
of introduction with time of my arrival - very poor welcome
so I did not even go into the public part of his beastly
institute and merely left a card to rub it in. So off to the
famous Botanic gardens - a great disappointment after one
has seen 1) real tropical forest, 2) private gardens a riot of
colour, 3) Kew Gardens, - here are nothing but trees and
flowerless climbers - water lilies, *Victoria regias* - hundreds
of orchids grown on frangipani trunks - practically none in
flower. The trees are very fine - but when one realises what
might be done with flowering shrubs, trees and smaller plants
in such a climate and abundant cheap labour - the present
exhibit is not creditable. Frankly bored all day in Buitenzorg.
Sat about the gardens - had a beastly lunch, sat about that
loathsome expensive hotel - until my train left at 5:38 for
/Wetteouder/ arriving at 6:45. Lovely journey again - chiefly
due to magnificent sunset - subdued purple and red over
distant hills one behind another and pleasing agricultural
foreground of the usual type. Villa Park a cheap nice hotel -
found that Dr Delsman had called before I arrived.
Telephoned Delsman and arranged trips etc. and to stay with

244

the Delsmans - a royal welcome after the entire absence of any welcome at Buitenzorg, even after posting letter of introduction and time of arrival to Dr Dammerman.

August 19
Was fetched at 6:30 am by Dr Vervey, a red headed young and cheery Dutchman - a very good zoologist I should think and very pleasant. Took lunch and heard about plans for 2 days on the reefs and islands in the bay. Left surplus gear at lab in Batavia and started off in a small motor boat with a foul smelling engine and two boys. Passed out through the old harbour of Batavia, now only used by fishing boats, the new harbour being some miles away at Tandjong Priok. Very amusing fishing boats etc all with a face painted on the prow or at least two eyes. We passed out between two long sea walls enclosing a dredged channel. Islands were in sight everywhere and the shores of the Bay lined by a deep belt of mangroves. In 1½ hours we reached Haarlin Island - just as I felt I could stick the motion and smell no longer. Charming small island, sandy and densely vegetated, a rampart of sorts on the windward side and a lagoon behind it (moat) freely open to the sea on the lee side. The rampart gradually fizzles out as a submerged flat of debris covered by luxuriant life. On the lee and last side part of debris flat was a carpet of *Helianthopsis* an anemone grey or green 2" across - really a solitary coral with a minute internal basal skeleton - usually rare and here abundant. Much brown *Xinia* and black urchin with white long spines *Actinothryx*. Fine big anemones and commensal damsel fishes, branched corals but few massives and practically no *Favias. Madreporas* of unfamiliar varieties, and many staghorn forms with windward side outside the ramparts. *Junipora* was here flourishing, but no fine varieties of *Madrepora* -α was recognisable, or rather some of the smaller varieties of α. No π^2 but other very lofty varieties, small massive *Pocillopora, Montipora foliosa* in abundance outside rampart on windward side, but no loftier varieties of *Montipora. Goniopora* brown in colour is

common. In the lagoon were few *Hiata, Synopta* and *Montipora* (*G. poites*), but very poor growth of coral owing to excessive heating of water in a small lagoon. Spent much time lying in a 'hot bath' and watching commensal pair of *Alphids* [prawn] and a *Gobie* [mud skipper] living in holes in the sand everywhere. The fish comes out, or sits in the entrance and the prawns forever dig out the burrow as the movement of the water fills it up with sand and stones etc. They rapidly come to the opening with chelae-fulls of sand clasped as an armful, and chuck it out in front, or put a pebble ½ as big as themselves on the pebble heaps on either side of the burrow. On the side opposite the sand heap is usually an elevated stone covered with algae on which the alphids feed from time to time. The fish waits till food comes within close reach and darts after it, and always returns backwards down the burrow. We walked round the island, ate our lunch under a bush out of the full glare of the sun which was burning my hardened hide. Then off to a river in the coastal mangroves. At first lies a deep belt of *Avicennia*, the *Rhizophora* not occurring until far from the shore. *Thalassinia anomala* makes huge mounds - 2 foot high by 1-2 yards in the mud of the mangroves, and on higher ground and therefore also in mounds of *Thalassinia* lives *Sesarma taeniolata* [a crab] burrowing in ground. Saw a monkey (macaccas) in the trees, huge herons or stork like birds, a vast *Periophthalmus* 1 foot long swam across the stream with its eyes and upper head out like a rat. We landed and got devoured by mosquitoes - don't worry - says Vervey - it's only *Culex* - no *Anopheles* here!! [malaria carriers]. So we left the mangroves and went on to Onrust Island a quarantine station where we were the guests of Mr and Mrs Steinfortd - charming folk. We saw a most choice aquarium there of 6 tanks with corals, anemones and fish doing magnificently. Damsel fish living in commensalism with anemones had bred there, the eggs being fixed to the walls and giving a pelagic stage, so that the small fish living with large ones in an anemone are newcomers, not the progeny. *Amphiprion sebae* [clownfish] black with white vertical stripes, was fed with small fry, it dashed out, seized the dead fish and gave it to the anemone, plunging it into the tentacles near the mouth, and went off for another and another !! a wonderful performance. *Premnas biaculeatus* [maroon clownfish] large female and small male with red stripes had laid a batch of eggs under lee of its anemone and was guarding them, getting very excited if anemones turned so as to uncover eggs. The three other commensal damsel fish occurring in the bay of Batavia are *Amphiprion percula* - yellow, *Prochilus ephippium* - red and dark ruddy purple - vicious beast which bites your boots, and if met in numbers bites unpleasant bits out of your legs. *Amphipiron akallopisos* has a horizontal white stripe. *Acanthaster* (15 armed starfish found on Lizard Island coral reef) lives well and normally is a great enemy of coral as it eats off the soft parts. In the tanks one anemone reproduced vastly and tends to cover everything. Fine *Fungias* and *Herpetolithas* [solitary disk coral] feeding also on sprats. So to tea on a paved tree shaded court effect with house on two sides and overlooking the sea - just perfect. Then to a bath and civilised clothes - saw the sun set over a near island and the thousands of *Diadema* [long spined black sea urchins] and luxuriant corals growing by the vertical built face of the island. To bed early.

August 20
Was on the Onrust reef at 6 am - swimming about with Vervey with our noses in the excellent inverted bucket telescopes. Low tide at 6 am - and fortunately a full moon and spring tide and calm weather - phenomenal luck as usual. Reef here very fine, luxuriant corals, branched and massive - all living with a sand foundation visible in spots - not a skin of living stuff over debris as on Haarlem reef. Huge *Tidacophyllia* patches. Vast boulders of living *Porites, Symphyllia, Favia, Platygyra, Coeloria, Meandrina, Lobophyllia* 4 ft across (free, long corallite variety) *Bispina* and a huge tube worm on the massives - anemones and

damsel fish - huge *Turbinarias* of new and very solid varieties with coralites like half pennies, large areas of branching *Hydrophora*, green and brown, and branching *[mendis]* (as one of the aborigines got at L.I.) *Goniopora*, branched poritis β and γ and on the outer face of the reef going to deep water tiers of *M. porites* and some *Mandroporas*, stag horns etc. *Mandropora* brackets scattered about, mainly of unknown forms (to me). Altogether a revelation in massive and superior branched corals - much *Montipora foliose* and *Millipora* of various [fancies] little *liliopora*. Returned ravenous for breakfast at 8. Took few photos and off to Hoorn Island. Spent about 1 hour there swimming over the reef outside the rampart on the weather side. Huge massives and much branched coral - outer barrier like plates in shape etc exactly as W^2 but branches looked like α. Staghorn types - *Junipora* etc, but no fine varieties such as W.T.0.9. large honeycomb growth of *Millepora*, flanges 8-10" long and all 6" across - nasty stinging variety. *Aglaophenia* 1-2' long also strongly stinging. Various branched *Millipores, Heliopora etc* - anemones and fish in abundance - a glorious reef. Lagoon typical - see congress pamphlet. So back to Batavia, saw the aquarium and the lab - wonderful spitting fish, who spits a jet of water at a fly 4" above the water and never misses! Lunch with the Delsmans. Slept shortly in afternoon - tea and after out in car with Dr Delsman around town. Dinner at 8 pm and out with a friend to Tandjong Priok Yacht Club and sat on the beach in the moonlight and drank coffee etc and saw the fishing boats of the Makassar type sail out on the light land breeze starting about 10 pm. Truly delightful and cool. So back and to bed very tired at 11:30.

August 21
Breakfast at 7 am - and out to KPM and bank, lunch and so motored to Tangjong Priok by Delman, Vervey joining us. Sailed on Melchior Treub at 4 pm - and passed the familiar islands of the bay. Passed Krakatoa at night. On reaching

Sunda Straits foul roll developed which kept me awake nearly all night.

August 22
Awoke to a dull cloudy day, the first since Australia - sea calm, slight swell and much roll making walking very difficult. I don't mind it this time a bit. Coast of Sumatra barely visible - no flying fish. Developed two packs.

August 23
Arose to see the sunrise over the mountainous island fringed coast of Sumatra - great sight. Many coconut covered islands near the shore - presumably coral islands. Emmahaven very fine with imposing coastline on two long sides. Coast forest covered - embayed and non cliffed (fringing reefs?). Landed at 7:30 am and in virtue of Sumatra time being quarter hour behind ship's time I caught the 7:33 train for Fort de Kock. Only European passengers - all other folk being road hogs. Six hours run for 70 miles and very pleasant too. Line at first traverses Padang valley - rice and coconuts and bamboo - mountains on both sides with wisps of white cloud hanging about the hollows - all perfectly beautiful, grey buffaloes bathing in streams with their noses out - natives at the village stations selling goods - neat packets of heaven knows what done up in banana leaves, banana fritters (cold), meat stews and orange gravy, heads of corn, bits of roast bird, fruit peeled and like a hundred flushed orangey lurid pink drinks, catherine wheels of stuff like pineapple chunks, pastries, bread fruit etc. All carried on trays or in basins on their heads or hanging from a bamboo shoulder pole. Dense foresty bits and the most beautiful and abundant Stag horn ferns on the branches. The whole very wet after nights of thunderstorms and smelling simply delicious. Sumatra has rain all the year round while Bali and Java have had already 4 months drought. The rail and road lie close together and a steep climb leads to Padang Panjang at 780 metres. Train crawled uphill 4-6 mph on a gradient of 7/1000, topography and water

like the gorges of Gondo and heavenly tropic vegetation superimposed, forest climbers, tree and other ferns, *Selaginelles* etc. - blue water in the rocky streams etc just heavenly. Reached Padang Panjang at 12 am and was scooped out of the train into a bus on the same ticket reaching Fort de Kock half an hour earlier. Followed the line across gently rising plain, rice and maize crops and Merapi and other volcanoes rising all round and hiding their heads in the clouds. Menangkabau houses visible - Many with fine external carving. Others however making their beautifully shaped roofs out of corrugated iron - what a crime. The walls are either wood or woven bamboo, decent window frames often pleasant and elaborate porches, steps and verandahs. Quite the best native houses I've seen. So to Park Hotel and lunch. Then out for a walk along the edge of the Kerbouenjat - wonderful canyon - cultivated in the bottom where a stream meanders, and showing sinuous vertical walls - a perfect revelation. Path along the top delightful, shady with bamboos etc. 5 ft veronicas and many native houses, plantations and rice barns about. Rice barns particularly beautiful with carving etc and houses much plainer as to walls and decoration than those lower down the valley. F.de K. at 3,000 ft and climate fine - feels like winter after sea level, yet thin clothes sufficient. So back around the town - very charming and the end of a perfect day.

Malay Vocabulary

AT LUNCH.

Where is the menu?	Mana soerat makan?
Bring me some soup first	Bawa sop doeloe
I don't want any rice	Tida makan nassi
Let me have some rice but none of the hot dishes	Minta nassi, tapi tida maoe sambal
I want only chicken, eggs, and fish	Minta ajam, telor dan ikan sadja
Let me have some beef-steak and salad	Minta biefstuk sama salad

IN A CARRIAGE.

To the left	Kiri
To the right	Kanan
To the British Consul	Pigi di kantor konsul Inggris
To the German Consul	Pigi di kantor konsul Djarman
To the French Consul	„ „ „ „ Pransman
To the American Consul	„ „ „ „ Amerika
You know where it is?	Kwe tao di mana?
Go back	Balik
Go home	Poelang
Go on	Madjoe
Stop	Brenti
Bring me to the Concordia Club	Pigi di kamar bola Concordia
Bring me to the Harmonie Club	„ „ „ „ Harmonie
Wait till I come back	Toengoe sampe saja datang
Open the carriage	Boeka karetta
Open the hood	Boeka kap
Clean the seat first	Bekin brissi bankoe doeloe
Go to Kemajoran station	Pigi station Kemajoran
„ „ Weltevreden station ...	„ „ Weltevreden
„ „ Batavia S.S.	„ „ Batavia S.S.
„ „ „ N.I.S.	„ „ „ N.I.S.

GENERAL.

TIME.

Good morning	Slamat pagi	Last week	Mingo doeloe
Good day	Tabeh .	Last month ..	Boelan doeloe
Good evening .	Slamat malam	Last night ...	Kemaren doeloe
Good bye	Slamat tingal		
Periodical time	Temponja	Midday	Tengari
All night	Sotoe malam troes	Month	Boelan
		To-day	Ini hari
Day after to-morrow	Harie loesa	To-morrow ...	Bissok
Day before yes-terday	Kemaren doeloe	To-morrow morning ...	Bissok pagi
Evening	Sore	To-morrow evening ...	Bissok sore
		Yesterday ...	Kemaren

DAYS OF THE WEEK.

Day	Hari	Thursday.....	Hari kemis
One day	Satoe hari	Friday........	„ djoemahat
Sunday	Hari mingo	Saturday......	„ saptoe
Monday	„ senen	Every day....	„ hari
Tuesday	„ selassa	One week.....	Satoe mingo
Wednesday ..	„ rebo		

1929 Phrase Book Extract

251

Malay Vocabulary

AT THE HOTEL—continued.

Have you got them.........	Soedah ada?
I want some tea or coffee....	Saja minta te (koppie)
Is there no barber?.........	Tida ada toekang tjoekoer
Yes, sir, he will be here after a while	Ada toean, nanti detang
Call the washerman for me. ..	Pangil menatoe
Here, washerman, are 20 pieces, I want them back in 3 days; that means on the 29th, at 5 o'clock in the afternoon..	Sini, menatoe doewapoeloe potong, minta kombali dalem tigi hari, djadi hari doewapoeloe sembilan, poekoel lima sore
All right, sir................	Baai Toean
Boy, I want some writing-paper, some ink, and a pen.	Jonges, minta kertas toelis dan penna tinta
I want some icewater.......	Minta ajer ice
I want a bottle of apollinaris.	Minta ajer blanda
Where is the W.C.?	Mana kamar ketjil?
Where is the bathroom?......	Mana kamar mandi?
Open this bottle............	Boeka ini bottel
Open this trunk............	Boeka ini kopper

IN THE EVENING.

At what time is dinner, boy?..	Poekoel brapa makan, jonges?
Don't forget before dinner to clean my bedcurtain properly from mosquitoes	Djangan leopa bekin brisih klamboe baaibaai deri njamok
Remember, if you don't look after the mosquitoes, you don't get your tip	Ingat, kaloe kwe tida djaga njamok kwe tida depat present
Yes, sir, I will take care......	Saja Toean, saja djaga
Wake me up to-morrow at six o'clock sharp. I want to leave by the first train to Buitenzorg	Kassi bangoen bissok pagi poekoel annem betoel. Saja maoe pigi di Buitenzorg (Bogor)
Allright, sir	Baai Toean
Can I have some breakfast before I leave?	Bisa depat makan doeloean?
Yes, sir; breakfast is always ready at 6 o'clock	Saja Toean. Makanan deri poekoel annem soedah klaar
Shall I order a carriage for you to bring you to the station, and a luggage-car for your luggage?	Apa saja misti pesen karetta boewat pigi di spoor dan karetta bagazie djoega
Yes, I want a carriage and a luggage-car	Ja, saja, minta karetta dan karetta bagazie

AT DINNER.

Boy, I want some bread......	Jonges minta rotti
Let me have the wine-list....	Bawa soerat anggoer
Bring me a bottle of claret, No. 10	Kassi satoe bottel anggoer merra no sapoeloe
Give me some ice, boy	Minta ice, jonges
Give me some fruit	Minta boea
Have you a match for me?...	Kwe ada korrek api?

<u>August 24</u>
Arose late and to the biweekly market - the biggest in
Sumatra. The town is just charming and the Menangkabora
people quite different from anything hitherto seen except that
they wear the same Sarongs as in Garoet - Batavia – i.e. the
printed flowery variety, although good batik head wraps and
saris are common. Much more intelligent folk I gather, and
rich ones dressed beautifully with silk jackets over fine
sarongs, sandals, sari over their heads instead of the hefty
head wrap of the common folk, much gold ornaments,
bracelets, hairpins etc. Market in a space bordered by quaint
houses, on ground floor having [inset] covered way opening
by arches, and within, open fronted shops housing numerous
Singer-machin-ists, cotton drapers, shoemakers etc. Several
streets of these buildings surround the market within which
are many huge covered areas divided into numerous stores
for food, groceries and cotton goods. Roundabout under trees
and huge yellow umbrellas sit the vendors of goods and
crowd the buyers, both coming from long distances. Striking
absence of nakedness, everybody clothed up to their eyes.
Walked through bamboo basket and halters, fruit like coarse
jack fruit tubers, piles of coconuts, cooked foods of every
kind and eating places for natives, nuts, pastries and queer
solid cold foods - rice cooked in banana leaves inside a
hollow bamboo - contents 4" diameter being slipped out of
charred mould and cut up. Piles of pineapples, longitudinal
cut peeled pieces 1 cent each - <u>v. good</u>! Then on a terrace at a
slightly lower level was a fascinating and unexpected fish
market. Piles of split dried fish of every size and piles of
dried shrimps whitish in colour - these spread on banana
leaves and in baskets lined with banana leaves, rows and
rows of live and semi live fish - the display being renewed
from kerosene tins of fish in water. Catfish up to 1 ft long
very active, big gold fish - red and brown carp over 15" long
- fat beautiful creatures, brown muddy looking fish, big
flattened forms and eel like things. The smaller gold fish are
slung on bamboo strips in bunches. These tropical fish seem

253

to keep alive merely damp on banana leaves in a merciless sun! The fish are all fresh water forms and come from the lakes up to 34 km off. Low parapets limit the market and its terraces and from there one has a fine view of the flat plateau around the hill on which the market stands, and the surrounding mountains and clouds - great! Three flights of steps by way of streets lead up to the market in the cliffed sides of it. Another terrace lodged vendors of red chillies - beautiful colouring of chillies - yellow umbrellas and native dress, and then came the meat and poultry terrace - piles of wretched ducks and hens lying about with their feet tied together and panting in the sun, being carried about by the feet all unprotesting - probably past it by then. At the foot of the south Steps is a 'buffalo-wagon-park' the two wheeled wooden carved wagons and buffaloes being let loose all together. By another flight and in the town square opposite the market were hundreds of Sados - which had brought the elite natives from far and wide. In side streets and along the main street were rough native buses, packed as only natives can squeeze themselves and goods, bound for distant villages. Finally in a field at the foot of the hill was a buffalo and humped cattle market - also housing a few goats. The market was at its height at 11 am and so not an early morning affair as other markets in Makassar etc. Afternoon spent in sleep and in walking to James and Storm Parks - reserved beautiful hill tops overlooking everything about F. de Kock. Had been fine and mainly sunny all day rain only started at sunset, Dr Stomberg - a friend of Delmans from M Treub turned up at hotel for the night. Arms and legs getting a foul irritating rash - heat? or excess of anti mosquito oil? can't be heat. So to bed very full of beans and pleased with life. Developed two packs.

August 25 Sunday
Morning cloudy and slightly misty - although Menapi and Sinjgalang had their heads clear of cloud - the one irregularly flat topped and the other a peak. Morning spent hoping

254

weather would improve for excursion to Lake Manirdjcu-walked round the Westenerksche Paadjes and the Karbouingat again after reviewing the landscape from James Park - round by the road and through the town, taking a few photos of natives and back to lunch. Then spent a glorious afternoon by car - ostensibly to see the lake, but the route left one perpetually gasping with wonder, and finally came across a perfect Minangkabau village of carved painted houses - just great. The road to Matoer passes up giving a broad view of the F. de K. plateau, a former lake bottom probably, with the Karbouergat to the right and slopes of M. Singgalang to the left. So up a wonderful watered rice terraced valley with mountains on either side - then a narrow canyon with nearly perpendicular walls - then through a pass - having wound in and round mountains hillocks and down a wonderful valley - road carved out of the mountain side - below stream fed rice terraces and on the other side deeply dissected weathered spurs at right angles to main ridge, breaks up whole surface - making it very beautiful - with villages of typical roofing both thatch and iron dotted about. So passed vertical rock faces and road cut deeply through a hill and descend to Matoer village - spoiled by the replacement of thatch by corrugated iron on half the houses - however the next village Lawang is a gem - or rather its outlying parts are. A newer large village green and market lies below a smaller green space lodging the village "Balei" or assembly hall and the tom tom. The former is a fine carved and thatched affair open on four sides, and the latter a long tom tom 12 foot or so with bladder over one end supported horizontally under a thatched roof. Roundabouts were some delightful carved and painted houses and rice barns. Further in a shanty lodged a man and woman making treacly cakes such as I saw in the F.de K. market. The road degenerates to a track between cane fields and finally lands you suddenly at Poentjak Boekit overlooking lake Manindjan - marvel of marvels! A precipice at your feet descends 1,600 feet to a vast lake, a little flat ground between the water and the precipice was glittering

255

with wet rice fields, like an aerial photo, and villages etc. Mountains wall in the lake on all sides the water lying at 1,900 feet, tropical mountain vegetation all round, and the Antokan canyon to the west breaks through the mountainous wall and the distant Indian Ocean glimmers through the gap! The most stupendous sight in lakes I've seen without snow (blue and green Norwegian lakes). A haze destroyed the proverbial brilliant blue of the water etc. So we retraced our steps - at Lawang I went inside a house devoted to weaving - four looms in a room rich in painted and carved pillars, screens, roofing etc - the floor was of woven bamboo - like many walls. In the "hall" at the top of the entrance steps was a huge bunker of rice grain. Passed many buffalo wagons on the road, evidently returning from yesterday's market. It must take them two days to do the 30 km or so between Lawang and F. de K., usually amid typical wares on the wagons was a sheet or two of that precious corrugated iron - hateful anachronism. The road has only been made since 1926 - how unspoiled is Lawang - first comes the lack of carving then the use of iron for thatch - then the abandoning of traditional shape and formation of rectangular iron roofs and woven bamboo walls - such as European clothes follows European development, even if we do give them roads, railways, bicycles and sewing machines. Round F. de K. saw some charming mosques, charming inspite of corrugated iron on most of them, and all standing in or by a pond. In Java the mosques are hidden and never meet the eye, but here the mosques (Missigit) are seen everywhere. Developed 2 packs - plagued to death by skin rash and mosquitoes.

August 26
Left Fort de Kock at 7 am by the road post bus - whole front seat to myself - no trouble about weight of case and rucksac - natives bring cartloads of goods with them behind. Arrived at Kota-Nopan at 4:15 having had a marvellous journey. First few hours climbing up and up and winding in and out of the Padang Highlands. Gorgeous mountain scenery of the

wildest, scarcely a trace of cultivation, and a wonderfully engineered - if dangerous road. Alternate views of Mt.Merapi, Singgalang and Ophir 8,000 , 8,000 and 10,000 feet behind wonderful rough foreground and marvellous vegetation and water. What a large portion of each 24 hours I spend gaping with wonder. Then we went down hill a bit - crossed the Allahan Pandjang River near Bondjol where the road for miles is cut through dense jungle - quite impenetrable near the ground - few wild monkeys scuttled away as we passed. Birds of all colours and sizes of the kingfisher-jackass build. Minangkabau houses - some well carved and painted, along the way, but everywhere the regrettable sight of corrugated iron rooves. A flat plain hemmed in by mountains lodges the village of Loebock Sikaping where I lunched at the rest house - not without difficulty as I did not realise I should have gone to the store and selected the tin of food I wanted warmed up!! However a Dutch dame assisted me, and I managed to get pea soup and sausages and some bananas eaten before starting again at 12 am. Shortly after 12 we crossed the equator on the east slopes Ophir Volcano - and the coolest day I've spent in the D.E.I. I had a coat on half the morning. On then through forest region and more monkeys - (terrible tendency to sleep between 1:30 and 3 pm). Then down a long luxuriant valley at first the weathered dissected ridges being grass covered, the forest having been cleared a long time ago, except in steep places and in hollows. These ridges were remarkable in being knife edged - some a few inches or 1 foot across, and the flat faces sloping steeply for great heights. Natural grass downs never like this - ridges always rounded. Valley opens a bit, and rice fields lie on either side of a meandering stream. The Poengkoet and mountains rise up on both sides. Villages losing their Minangkabau appearance, square wood and bamboo houses being thatched by square roofs. Rest house at Kota-Nopan pleasant, surrounded by palm trees and native dwellings - an open plot in front and the mountains all round. Driver nearly distracted by this - rash on my legs and arms -

257

and got bitten on the arm by a <u>most</u> venomous insect, brightly coloured, hornet size and sting hurt like anything but seems recovering fairly rapidly. Sad to think I am back in the N. hemisphere. Rain in the evening. Very welcome dinner at 8 pm after soup at 11 am and bread at 6:00 - I ate a whole jungle fowl - a little tough across the grain but very good!

August 27
Arose as usual at 6 - breakfast at 6:30 - put my foot in it by asking the only other guest (a Malay) for my bill! Left at 7 by the same bus. Cloudy and cool - clouds are only 50 -100 ft above us. Road continued along the valley, and great views with the sunlight bursting below the clouds here and there in the distance. Gradually we rose to the top of forest cleared ridges, getting above the clouds which lay below us in various valleys - a broad view being opened up with mountains in and above the clouds all round - really magnificent. Forest and mountain scenery continue, lovely but not as grand as the Pedang highlands. Wild monkeys of various kinds - and tame monkeys and gibbons tied up to houses and being used to pick coconuts in the true lazy fashion. More nakedness about and the people better looking than most Minangkabau which are not handsome as a race. Lunch at Padang Sidempuan, not very attractive coconut shaded town full of flies innumerable. This time I knew the choosing of the tin technique for getting a meal! So on again at 1:15 and continuing along a lengthwise valley of the Boekit Barisan mountain range, fine wooded country, beautiful tumbling rivers of now fair size. Jungle cleared in places and for miles the road passes under the shade of rubber trees, mainly well kept plantations - few native rubber forests quite unkempt. Giant 2 ft lizard scuttled off the road. Villages very attractive, the road being merely a track between the palm trees and thatched square logged houses. The 'flowery printed' type of sarong becoming more artistic in colour and patterns. So west to the coast which we reached suddenly - a wonderful view of the blue Indian ocean

between shore palms, showing the great Tapanoeli Bay and many islands to sea, and fine mountains inland. Progressed round the bay for half hour to Sibolga getting heavenly views seawards. Arrived in time to see the sun set over the bay - one of the grandest sunsets I've ever seen. Fine shore lined by fishing boats, light boats without booms, canoes etc, - houses and palms bending over the waters edge much as at Makassar, a fjord like arm of the sea running inland with a mountain beside it - behind fine tropical vegetation in rising hills and to sea was pure glory - island beyond island - blue - purple and mountainous, few bits of sea open to the horizon and green coconut island edges on the near ones - behind the lot a marvellous sky as a red sun dropped behind the furthest blue island. A tiring day from 7 am – 6 pm and oh these Dutch habits - no dinner till 8:30 - and I was ravenous at 5:30. Watched geckoes chasing each other and biting one anothers' tails on the walls and ceiling - likewise scores of fat yellow and brown frogs (or toads) emerged from below the plant pots on the hotel verandah and spread all over same and dining room catching flies and winged ants - phenomenal sight. That cursed rash still plagues. No blanket needed or provided as on previous 2 nights on either side of the equator up in the mountains.

August 28
Arose at 6 - took some unsatisfactory photos of the bay. Left by bus at 7 - already it was sticky hot at that hour - Sibolga must be a warm spot hemmed in closely by mountains and shut in a bay by islands. Road climbs marvellously to Bonern Dolate, 1,400 ft up a precipitous valley, road tunnelling the rock in places, and engineering rivalling anything I've seen in the Alps - perfectly gorgeous scenery all the way up with glorious views over the Bay of Tapanochi and its islands and the forest clad mountains. Road now traverses tops of things - through dense jungle clad slopes and countless twists and turns of the road. Beautiful valleys succeed one another and in the depths the streams roar and waterfalls tumble. Descend

to Taroentoeng, lying in a perfectly flat bottomed valley between 11 ranges of mountains (old lake or sea floor?). Taroentoeng is the centre of the Toba Plateau, full of people with a fair on - gay flowery sarongs or sarong trousers - women mostly with tidy hair in buns, and carry a sun shade or wear a thin sari or scarf over their heads instead of the usual hefty head wrap. Batak people here. Left at 11:20, passed up the valley and over the heights with fine views behind over Taroetoeng. Here the road passes over entirely new type of scenery to Lake Toba - waste mountain region of Barisan rather like high rolling moorland with distant ranges of mountains on all sides and clouds above and below us afar off. Land fern and vulgar grass covered, a few "funny" palms, but not banana or coconuts - little bamboo. (Has virgin forest been burnt off???) probably. Then we zigzag on mountainsides and a fine view of Lake Toba and mountains round it bursts upon us. Down and down goes the winding road for another 10 km or so and finally the bus deposited me at the Toba hotel just outside Balige (3,000 ft) on a high spur overlooking the lake and commanding an incomparably magnificent view of the lake, island and its reflection - mountains - terraced rice lower slopes and a "heroic" sky. Truly a spot belonging unto heaven - and to think that I am here alone and in 1835 the first explorers, 3 French and Americans, were cooked and eaten long before they reached the lake, a sacred object not to be looked at by foreigners, and in 1863 a Dutchman (Dr A. Neubronner van der Tuuk) reached the lake, but had to beat a hasty retreat owing to hostile cannibals! So to a welcome lunch - only one other guest, and my room in a house by itself surrounded by open land. Afternoon spent by a glorious never to be forgotten walk seeing Batak villages or compounds - a mud bank and trees (bamboo) hedge effect on bank planted with aloes or the like encloses a squarish space a few acres in size, usually surrounded by shady trees inside the bank. Inside is a double row of buildings facing one another, the centre ones on each side usually being the most magnificently carved and painted.

260

May or may not have windows with shutters. Those with no windows have a "loft" opening - sort of balcony, door is usually a hole in the floor accessible by a ladder. The rice barns are like the houses only the loft is the only enclosed part. All perfectly fascinating - likewise a graveyard on the hillside. These house compounds visible as groups of trees dotted about the rice terraced lower mountain slopes at the side of the lake. Sarongs here grubby looking - some weaving being done in a few of the compounds. Developed two packs. Usual mild evening thunderstorm it has had one every night since I left Batavia.

<u>August 29</u>
A most enjoyable day spent at Balige. Misty morning and wonderful to watch the cloud and mist roll off the lake and mountains - all being brilliantly clear by the afternoon - far more so than yesterday. Spent the morning walking through the village and over a rice cultivated promontory investigating the native housing schemes and photographing the carved painted houses - only decorated the side to London - the other end facing the surrounding bamboo is plain. Much weaving being done, but natives unattractive - preponderance of grubby European clothes, only made popular, be it noticed, by the introduction of the sewing machine. Many Singer machines being found in every village in Sumatra and Java. Fishing activities along the coarse white sandy beach - very light canoes carved out of a trunk used, and at either end is cut a projecting keel and fluted tip, canoes small and easily carried, the sides being very thin - not much over half inch. So back to lunch at 1:30. A car full of folk were lunching at the hotel - and the conversation in French centered about Richmond! Afternoon gloriously sunny and clear, and light on the lake and mountains and reflections of the islands and promontories and the cloud wisps about the hollows were pure undiluted heaven. Put on a bathing dress and walked down through the rice terraces to the shore - about quarter hour - rice now harvested, it must indeed be

glorious hue at the prime colouring of the rice fields. Swam in the glorious warm lake - attracted attention of a few natives from the near compounds who appeared amazed at my swimming - they themselves bathe occasionally, but mainly to wash round the shores. The natives do plenty of washing or rinsing of themselves, their babies and buffaloes in the streams. I've never seen so many babies - every woman carries one, and there are enough to go round for the aged wrinkled women to carry them too! Developed two packs - washed hair and clothes. Wonderful evening fork and sheet lightning behind first clouds over the lake.

<u>August 30</u>
Arose at 6 and left at 6:20 armed with camera, 3 bananas and a welcome hanger on in the form of a very nice dog. We climbed a mountain (Dolok Tolong) about 5,000 ft on the east side of the road reaching Balige through the mountains surrounding Lake Toba. It was a heaven sent morning, slightly overcast and misty, the lake and distant mountains being shrouded in subdued light and mist, with low clouds scattered about. The path up a spur of the mountain was clearly visible so we barged off through the rice fields as the crow flies, between bamboo hidden house compounds, over streams until we reached the foot of the mountain. Light was streaming over the lake, and the clouds and mist gradually fading. My companion chased and chivied some foals and young buffaloes in an alarming manner, however all was well. The climb up was steep, we did it in just over 1 hour – 2,000 ft up - my shirt was sopping wet at the top, but I must be in perfect training as I was not out of breath or in the least thirsty! Halfway up we got the heavenly view NW up the major stretch of Lake Toba with the mountainous island Samosir 28 x13 miles lying in its middle. Mist hung in the NE arm, the only part visible from Balige, for a considerable time. From 7:50 to 9:40 I contemplated this roof of Sumatra. Gradually the sun rose and the clouds and mist departed eastwards and all was bathed in an undiluted tropical sun.

First the far western ranges were caught by the rays, and gradually all was lit up as the clouds passed eastwards. Round the lake shores and flatter slopes lay dotted Battak house compounds surrounded by their rice terraces. South lay the winding road by which I had come and vast expanse of rolling mountain tops of the lower mountainous lake wall to the South East. The mountain itself was covered by a dense growth (more than 5-6 ft) of fern and tea tree with lovely lycopodium like miniature fir trees. At this end of the lake the mountains are devoid of forest - due to the hand of man I'm sure, as elsewhere the mountains are forest clad, and effects of current and past fires could be seen on the journey to Prapat. So down again – lunch at 12 and off by bus to Prapat. A charming ride - saw the market at Babgi in full swing - nothing was doing while I was there the two previous days. Real Battak costume visible unspoiled by contact with whites. Typical weaving worn as a flat head gear with the ends hanging behind, colours decidedly somber and faces not beautiful – loads of babies being carried on backs and streams of natives walking home along the roads with palm leaf sacks on their heads. (Car park of native buses near the markets also). On leaving the lake shores the road cuts off the long promontory opposite Balige and climbs a mountainous region on all sides. Batak compounds become fewer and finally we descended suddenly on to the lake again at Prapat - situated on a small promontory bagged by the hotel. Thankfully there was no room there - it is a beautiful spot - like the Norwegian fiords, mountains rising steeply out of the lake leaving no broad rice land between - simply the idle rich weekend spot– nothing but civilised pastimes, no native villages etc– and I had already seen a view from the mountain which could not be bettered of the lake. So on to Penatang Sinantar arriving at 5:15. Route pleasant - cut into mountain halfway up above Lake Toba, tunnelling through rock, and superb views over the lake and Samosir. Rose to 4,800 feet and turned north east, through wooded mountain scenery - then much rubber and tea country is traversed and palm plantations. P. Siantar a mouldy hole and hotel bad and drear - what could have been more perfect than Balige, my room a separate little house - whole hotel situated in the middle of the rice fields and surrounded by fine Battak villages and glorious scenery. Battak architecture entirely deteriorates between Toba and Siantar to the square shack with a characterless thatch or tin roof. At Prapat I watched an ugly betel chewing woman wait for ages with four children, she carried number three, and number four was tied onto number - one a nice little girl of about nine. Finally the village tap became free and she washed the family hair and all - just a rinse and a rub - no soap! Number four (six months) scarcely whimpered at being held under a very cold stream of water! A little rain in the evening and thunder. No grub till 8 – I lunched at 12 too!

<u>August 31</u>
Mum's birthday, what ho - spent a miserable night - people singing and playing the fool loudly till 3 am keeping me awake, also mosquitoes inside the wire gauze and the electric light ceased to function so I couldn't swat them - misery and fuming intense. Got up at 5:45, breakfast and caught the 6:30 train for Medan. Changed at Tebing Tingii on to the main coastal line. Arrived at 10:10, passing through endless rubber, tobacco and palm oil estates, and uncultivated dense scrub. In Medan - a hot European town with endless chinese shops, I K.P.M.ed [visited shipping office]- and shopped, but all offices were closed as it was Queen Wilhelmina's birthday - and flags flew from nearly every window. Strange to see all the chinese about, and rich chinese houses and consulate. In Java the most prosperous store in every village is owned by a chinaman, but hitherto in Sumatra the natives keep their own shops and the chinese have not penetrated throughout. No point in getting drenched with perspiration seeing the so called sights of Medan - so I got thoroughly bored at the Grand Hotel from 11:30 – 1:15 over a lemon squash and a lunch - be it noted - only my second extra drink

in the D.E.I. [Dutch East Indies]. Left by car - a veritable "fur lined" 13 seater instead of a broken down old bus, for Brastagi and Kabanjahe at 1:30. Four other passengers and stuffy hot across the Medan plains covered by tobacco estates with huge tobacco barns - walls and roof of palm thatch, by the score. Dense edgings to the road and deeper plantations of Jetti trees with leaves like tea trays. They are grown for poles for the tobacco barns. Then we climbed a bit and passed a Battak village with a fine market roofage in the village assembly hall (Balei). Further between 2-3,000 feet we crossed an immense tea estate with hideous "state" houses for the tea labourers. Then came the fine portion of the route - dozens of hairpin bends as we rapidly climbed up to 4,818 ft going up an apparent mountain wall and getting an immense distant view of the Medan plains fading away in the mist. The sun was fully out at 10:30 - the early morning being overcast. Brastagi, on the edge of the plain reached after the climb, and surrounded by mountains has a marvellous situation - inspected hotels as we passed. Sulphur and steam visible on mountains near the Grand Hotel. So on to M. Kaben Jahe to Hotel Frisia, got an upstairs room with low ceiling instead of the usual hot weather bungalow- a fine balcony overlooking nice country and beauteous mountain with its table cloth on straight opposite. Arrived at 5 pm for tea. A little tired after many early starts and wretched night at that loathsome Siestar- and they charged me for a lunch I never had too - a slug like custom.

September 1 Sunday
Slept like 10 logs far into the day and did not finish breakfast till 8:30! Had a sheet and a blanket - unique in the D.E.I. - oh no - except for Tosani and Kintamani. Glorious sunny morning. Went out to see the native Kampong of Kabandjahe. The volcano opposite (Delery Sinaboen 2,451 m = 8,039 ft) was very clear, a peak with two great gullies emitting steam and showing yellow sulphur - fine sight. Further north could be seen the volcano and steaming sulphur

265

cleft above Brastagi. Kampong a revelation. Utterly unlike Balige Batak villages. Whole Kampong of about 50 houses enclosed by a bamboo fence to keep in the pigs etc, you open a gate or rather climb over the fence at stated spots and you arrive by a lane through houses into a dry dusty open space. In this are fenced banana plots - the dove cot and balei and the houses scattered about around without order, several balei present and 2 rice pounding wall-less buildings - squared trunks with pot holes for pounding being built into the platform below the roof. Houses of various types - often very large, square 40 ft or 70 ft by 50 ft sort of thing, altogether bigger than the Balige ones. Doors at one end in the sloping wall and outside a bamboo verandah reached by steps or a ladder. Few or no windows - no loft opening, and no floor opening. No elaborate painted carving on walls etc, and gable decorated by woven bamboo painted often gorgeously. Roof however is the great attraction - may have a straight or slightly curved ridge with a horned buffalo head at either end. The richer man's house has marvellous gadgets on the crest often with carved wooden figures. Roof may have a gable built on either side at angles to the primary end gables. Rice barns stand about - proper ones, and round bamboo tub like affairs with a protecting roof of thatch or bamboo-a-la-corrugated-iron. Natives grubby and ugly and quite spoiled by visitors - hoards of cheeky children clamouring for tips and being a perfect nuisance. Left the Kampong and was followed by insulting little boys for half an hour. I wandered along a side road over agricultural country uphill a bit getting a huge open view of this high plain and the volcanos and mountain ranges around. Much corn grown in the wetter season and natives busy tiling <u>dry</u> ground, going along with a sledge hammer breaking the clods and smoothing it with their feet. Clouds of dust blown up from the soil - very different from the rice country soil which dries like a stone and is never dusty. Passed a wavy sided roofed building (tomb?). My tame Hoojinx led my blind footsteps straight to another larger Kampong about 3 miles away - a wonderful surprise

266

and a fine Kampong with unspoiled inhabitants who merely looked at me like an escapee from a zoo and that was all. Lingga by name and comprised perhaps 80 houses, several beautifully carved and painted on the horizontal wall beams. The walls in both Kampongs were decorated by plaited black palm hair in a universal pattern - end resembling an animals foot perhaps. In both Kampongs two rich men's houses were joined by a roofed passage, and a wonderful gadget sat on the passage roof. Dying of cotton for weaving was in progress and hanks of dull blue thread were stretched between bamboo poles on the verandahs etc. Walking through the dusty but clean open spaces and passages between the houses, barns etc of this great village was too wonderful to be believed - it seemed like a super White City and unreal in its marvellousness. So back through the fields - past a pond full of wallowing happy buffalos with the tops of their heads out. On the roads humped draught cattle are more numerous than buffaloes and they don't wear sandals here as do the draught buffaloes in other parts. Marvellously cool - my topee forming a halo of shadow round my feet, and walking I was barely sticky - at least not streaming with stick. Lunch at 1:30 - lazy afternoon on verandah contemplating the view and volcano - now provided with a cloud cap, and a short walk round the modern village - just a collection of chinese shop shacks and a market place. Developed 3 packs.

Sept 2
Left at 8 am by car with hotel keeper to be shown over the leper settlement at Lao Simono a few miles away. Fine and sunny and very interesting indeed. The place contains 400 lepers, and is arranged in Kampongs - similar small typical Batak houses around a grassy space containing a pond in case of fire and often a balei and dove cot. All most spic and span - white walls and thatch roofs, mostly of palm leaves, but the chief of each Kampong has a black "brolly" roof as Batak roofs at Balige. Gable at either end decorated with coloured patterned woven bamboo, every house different, and a carved

painted beam below. In the rear are chicken huts etc. They have a shop, with grid for exchanging wares and wash pots for leper's money. They have their own allowance of rice, fish etc - I went into one house, up a short ladder to a small verandah - in at a wall door to the single room - bamboo mats on the floor, a mattress and mats on one side and a cooking place in a corner - no chimney, 2 windows wire netted to keep out fowls, and a few shelves and things hung about. A non-compulsory church officiated by the missionary in charge, a wash place, school and medical store and a grid and pasanggrahan [an indonesian guest house] for visitors of patients from distant parts completes it. The Kampongs are freely open to the road, but nobody attempts to go away - and I don't wonder with all a Batak needs provided and also wireless, cinema and electric light in every house! A few industries in progress, iron work and weaving. Place financed by State, Missions and Rubber and Tobacco growers etc. A missionary here is doing good work but he certainly isn't in Australia etc. I also learned that August-November inclusive are the wet months here and folk are agitated about the nonappearance of rain, as there has been none worth mentioning yet. What luck for me - imagine trying to see Batak Kampongs in tropical deluges. Potatoes and cabbages are exported largely - to Singapore. So back to Kabandjahe and to the weekly market. Again my tame Hoojinx came up to scratch and I promptly met Dr Stroomberg (friend of Dr Delsman, on M. Treub, and met again at Fort de Kock) He and his friends had unearthed some Batak mask dancing, how greatly warming, and the show was to begin shortly! A phenomenal performance - orchestra of gongs and miniature drums, a queer noise not unpleasant, but not music as is the Gamelang - Dancers were 3 rogues in red and blue gowns, wearing huge wooden masks and wooden hands with handles held inside the cuffs or huge fingers of wood in gloves. Two yellow faces and one black. They merely moved slowly about in grotesque attitudes gained by hand positions and knee bending. No order or programme - indeed the dance of a heathen savage on feast days compared with the perfect ceremonial, historical and religious dancing of Java and Bali. The masks etc were packed off to Holland - how glad I am to have seen them in use among the bamboo trees instead of as meaningless objects in a museum - and soon that will be the only place in which to see such things. So back to the market, bought some weaving and took photos - all ugly folk and clad in dull blue and black. What rot it is to say Europeans find the Balinese attractive merely because the women are half dressed - the Bataks here are interesting, but not attractive - rather repellant with or without clothes. Incidentally they speak a different language to the Baligi Bataks. The Balinese on the other hand are the most beautiful people I've ever seen. Afternoon spent on balcony over nothing in particular. Developed 2 packs.

Sept 3

Left Kabandjahi by bus at 8 am for Brastagi. Arrived at 8:30 at the Grand Hotel - said to be the finest hotel in the East - I dug myself in for F11 a day - not too bad - and had a fine view of the volcano Sibajak (6,868 ft) from my window. Hotel marvellously situated overlooking the high plain here fringed with mountains and fissured by young canyons. Sunny and clear, so started at 9 am with guide and lunch for the craters of Sibajak - a v solid 2 hours climb. The way led over a steep forest clad ridge separating the valley at the the base of the volcano from Brastagi - a choice path cut in the forest, fine trees and a wealth of huge epiphytic ferns and glimpses of a great view over the Brastagi plains and the mountains bordering them. Over the crest and steeply down and down to the valley at our feet getting lovely views of Sibayak with the foaming sulphur coated cleft outside the crater. The valley contained a small typical Batak village, much cultivation, a fresh stream and a very hot SO_2 smelling stream from the volcano - I could only just bear my hand in it, and it left a greenish coating on the rocks over which it flowed. Then we entered dense forest over slopes of Sibayak.

The ground ulidge was cleared leaving a tunnel below the 15 ft fronds of ferns - fine - became very steep - steps all the way held up at the edge by roots. Top slope rocky and steep to the edge of the crater - down one looked to a deep basin walled by ragged sulphur coated rock, yellow and green, and by high precipices to pinnacles at the edge. In the middle below was a grey muddy lake - boiling and surging, but too high up yet to see this. Opposite were two huge yellow caverns emitting clouds of steam, and similar jets of small size were present all round. The cliff above the main jets was yellow with sulphur glorious in the sunlight. Then we walked into the crater and along its lowest edge, running and choking across a belt of suffocating steamy H_2S and SO_2 -a gully leaves the crater rim here flanked by a huge crest raised in pinnacles. Glorious view across to Sinabung Volcano steaming gently, out over the Brataji plains, and on the other side of the crater edge a marvellous ventilation - endless expanse of Deli plains far below at sea level and the Malacca Straits losing itself in the misty distance - all the nearer ranges and peaks etc stood out strongly against the wonderful distance - one of the first 360° views I've seen. Got bushed in fearful scrub and prickly *Pandanus* in the guide's endeavour to reach another peak - lunched and returned the way I had come - back at 3 pm - and luxury of luxuries in the tropics- - unlimited hot water - I simply wallowed in it slopping buckets over myself for half an hour - only a Dutch bath of course. Tea and a walk to buy Batak weaving. On returning I met Mr Mouzilly St Mans - seen on Mt Treub - at Baligé and Siantar and talked about G.B.R. They were vastly keen to go there - would have built the G.B.R.E. a boat as bought one for £500 at Sidney!!! I broached the small hoped for revisit to these parts and they have guaranteed the boat and we will all meet 15 months hence in London!!!!! Marvellous - we only got into conversation as they took my fancy for nice folk and I said good evening at Siantar instead of my usual mannerless proceeding of avoiding fellow travellers. Dined with them and talked ad lib. Gosh - and I'm only here in virtue of

270

missing Prapat owing to the hotel being full - my tame Hoojinx again!

<u>Sept 4</u>
Arose betimes to say goodbye to the St Mans folk but missed them - was wondering how to spend the day when two girls greeted me - they were on the N. Holland and were going riding for 3 hours. I have been pining to ride and had not the courage alone so promptly tacked on and 5 of us went off - along lovely lanes and paths through the forest and fields - winding about. I clung to the saddle in front like grim death to start with - finally I managed better and only bumped every other time in the proper fashion and ceased to hang on with my hands - I felt unexpectedly stable especially when galloping - my beast shied once at some red frocked children, and when nearly back he chucked me off after shying at a red flag marking a landslip and my urging him on. However all was well and for £2.50! I enjoyed it no end, but did not let on it was my first appearance in a saddle - I said I hadn't ridden for 12 years - perfectly true! How wonderfully my Hoojinx arranges things! Overcast today, Sibajah in the clouds - perfect for riding, and yesterday marvellously clear for the view and crater! Also I neatly missed the hooha over the Queen's birthday at Kabandjahi, while this hotel was full last weekend and is now half empty!! Lunched very well with that choice Victoria.plum coloured passion fruit-like fruit. Slept off some of the effects of climbing and riding while it rained between lunch and tea - my first rain, fine for a walk round the village between tea and sunset - and then a pouring wet evening - doubtless all arranged for my benefit by my Hoojinx! Forgot to mention the absence of coconut palms trees on the Karo plains although bamboo present - too high and cool for them.

<u>Sept 5</u>
Arose early and caught the 8:30 bus for Medan. Abandoned my faithful Yokohamas, the component parts of which -

271

having taken me up my last mountain - began to dissociate. Raining early and overcast till the afternoon, cloud hiding all view - what luck - and it doesn't matter today. Reached Medan by 11:15 and this time wasn't a bit bored there till 3 pm - shopped sarongs in the native market in a charming Chinese shop effect, and had great difficulty in explaining that I wanted sarong trousers by signs! So to the Grand Hotel for lunch, off a very muscular bit of buffalo I believe - then I found a Punch of Aug 7th!! Quite recent and I laughed till I was nearly ill, chiefly over "On living Alone". I was in the mood to be easily amused. Left by the 3 pm train - only Europeans as usual, and some difficulty in discovering which of the numerous Belawan Oceanhaven halts to get out at - got on board at 4 pm. Harbour surrounded by many rooves and drowned thatch palms - "Duymaen van Twist" delayed till 7 pm unloading coconut oil and those palm oil seeds the - filthiest smelling things imaginable - the ship reeked of them - far worse than the harmless "Van den Lign" farmyard smell of pigs and oxen. Hold empty, except for cabbages, and we rolled a bit. Smallest K.P.M. I've been on - 7 passengers - minute deck space. Fine evening lightening over the sea and behind the clouds.

Sept 6
Got up at 6 am as we neared the rocky high tree covered islands around Penang and approached the Malay coastline, uneven high and rugged. Beautiful sunrise and island charming as we passed quite close in - with sandy bays, native villages, coconut and banana plantations etc. Anchored in the bay outside George Town. Penang at about 10 am - passing a big fishing fleet all drying their bamboo supported sails in the still sunlight, and the smoke of the steamers at anchor went directly upwards. Landed at about 10:30 in a launch - gosh and I felt quite at home - arriving here only 3 weeks from London, a purely chinese town it is true, but a 'beach street' greeted me - likewise a G.R. pillar box and a "Stick No Bills" - no more "Verboden Toegangs" and

272

unpronounceable Malay road names - I leaped into a rickshaw with a lovely lacquered peacock on the back and went to the cheapest of only two hotels, vaste palace, just as if it was the ordinary thing to do. I got the mouldiest doghole of a room, small permanently shuttered there being no windows, an earthenware water pot trough for a bath - and would anyone believe it - no drains!!! All for the trifling sum of 8 dollars (£1) a day! Help - and to think what I got in the land of recent cannibals for much less cash. The dog hole more over was in an annex across the road in an extremely decayed chinese house with the typical gloriously carved wooden door and gilt carved doorway. Interviewed shipping offices, found my luggage at the K.P.M., and walked on a precarious row of planks forming a long chinese jetty to get photos of the boats changing their sails etc. Some queer chinese houses on poles opened onto the shore end of the jetty. Chinese restaurants, boat building sheds - wood choppers abounded and I watched busy loading and unloading of cargo canoes and barges, and jostling wagons with two bullocks each, white or grey and humped and longer horns than D.E.I. beasts. Usual chinese streets, shop lined, covered by chinese gilt signs, the first floors projecting over the pavement which opens to the street by a series of arches and into which many shops spread themselves liberally. Many of those striking handsome dark skinned men about with curly hair - perhaps Tamils. Saw a few in Medan, after this hair is long and beards frequent. My bottom garment and half my frock were wet, but I scarcely felt hot - so to lunch. Again to the town after tea - my spending becomes more reckless daily - I bought a choice blue cashmere dressing gown with lovely patterns for Mum, still can't find a mortal thing for Pa. Saw the sunset from the hotel garden - a choice seafront, below palms and frangipani trees overlooking an apparent bay flanked by a promontory of irregular heights to the west and a long low palm coasted island to the east. In front a fleet of sailing boats were going out for a week's fishing, and the high irregular Malay coast and road out beyond. So to dinner - the electric light and fan in my doghole fused halfway through the evening - blast it - likewise that dammed P&O boat is a day late and won't sail till Sunday night instead of Saturday (tomorrow) morning and leaving me 3 days here at £1 a day and no drains. The warmest night since Low Island.

Sept 7
Hot and sunny. Took a rickshaw or more properly a Jinvikisha to the Ayer Itam temple at the foot of the hills behind the town - at least I meant to get the tram, but chinese thought otherwise and ran the 5 miles each way for choice for 1 dollar. A pleasant method of locomotion, but I can't resign myself to the poor devil in the shafts - fully dressed, soaked with perspiration, and dies at 35-40. Very interesting drive past wealthy chinese mansions, then black-native streets and endless coconuts covering the low land up to the hills. Among them a few palm leaf habitations of the tall dark folk - Tamils - men with hair in a bun and women with at least 3 gold ornaments through their noses. Temple recent - finished 1905, but now putting up a pagoda - really a Buddhist monastery. Built in terraces up the hill, sacred turtles 250 in a pond - showing real McB green weakness - with goggly eyes! - sacred Shanghai goldfish and endless Buddhas from India, Siam and China in various attitudes. Some huge gilt ones treading on small figures representing mankind's vices such as drunkenness etc. Squalid living quarters mixed up with the temple rooms and queer incense burners here and there. Prayers carved in Chinese cover bare rock surfaces of boulders and huge stone wall plates and pillars. Visited the zoo on the way back hoping to see perhaps some indigenous East Indian fauna but no - the European Stork, Australian black swan and Brazilian marmoset greeted me! However that marmoset and especially an "American golden lion Marmoset" were most healthy, free from tears and very charming - likewise a nice black faced sandy gibbon who put out arms and legs and back to be scratched and a white

274

prehensile tailed monkey. Lazy afternoon, washed hair and clothes - tea and out to my pet chinese shop in a back alley. I returned a belt as he had given me two by mistake - the chinese knocked half a dollar each off two cashmere kimonos I bought. I vastly enjoy my Eastern shoppings, it's such fun acquiring heaps of lovely things, even to give away.

Saw the sunset again over that delicious view from the hotel lawns - developed 1 pack, dinner, and talked to a nice scotch girl and her husband, in rubber and coconuts, also waiting for the Kashmir to meet a friend. Changed half a £5 note for dollars, and was a country cousin enough nearly to refuse the £2-10-0 in strange and unfamiliar English notes!

Sept 8 Sunday

Hot and sunny - 90° during the day and about 86° at night on the boat and previously 83° at the hotel the night before - very damp air getting misty at night. Wandered off to the Kashmir in the morning and found my baggage delivered ok but I was feeling that boarding this boat was indeed the end. In the afternoon I went by tram to the Air Itam, an hour's run for 9 cents and much entertaining native scenes through the poorer Chinese and Tamil quarters - then by the Penang Hills cable railway 2300ft up to the top of the hill - gradient 1 - 1.9 - a fine view of Penang - Georgetown, and the low coconut land and hilly promontories - Malaya opposite (the flat land is no island but the mainland) and the high ridges beyond - lovely sea views out to the Indian Ocean and across the Straits - had tea there, but my thoughts were far away, on a boat near South Africa. Back by 7 pm - dark and I was glad the tram brought me near the boat - queer Eastern places and strange folk black and all colours are all right in the day but they give me the creeps alone at night. Very hot on board and loading of tea and rubber etc proceeded till 1 am.

Sept 9

2nd class on this boat (8,000 tons) just odious, only helped by scarcity of passengers (30) - and having a 3 berth cabin to myself. Saloon a mere nursery full of babies, cots and kids, architecture everywhere that of a rabbit hutch - food bad and little deck space - I have no use for the folk and went to be alone with my treasure house of memories and hopes. Distant coast of Sumatra visible - in the evening I discovered that they thought I was a missionary - it had permeated to all the passengers!!! Warm day fairly sunless.

Sept 10
Out of shelter of Sumatra, roughish - gave up breakfast for a deck chair and day spent uncomfortably getting used to the motion, eating with difficulty and preferring the horizontal.

354 miles.

Sept 11
Same as yesterday - deck chair and bunk the only places - however after getting battered trying to have a bath over the screw, I quite enjoyed dinner and achieved a walk or rather a stagger about the deck afterwards. This weather likely to continue to Aden - too rough for a swimming bath.

335miles.

Sept 12
Thank goodness now no longer "this side up with care", and I again enjoying the sunlight on the ruffled ocean and the rainbows in spray and the flying fish. Made Columbo at 10 pm - and post arrived from Hilda to say she was in Kandy on 11th and would meet me if boat was late and two letters from home - the latter came like a thunderbolt upon my pleasant dreaming - news of the Cornwall move, death of Miss Allen and Mr Nicol etc. Went ashore in case Hilda was there - she was not - walked about Columbo in a dazed sort of manner couldn't pull myself together enough to make my intended purchases and returned to the ship at 11 pm and went to bed - lay awake most of the night, porthole shut owing to cooling and anyway sleep wouldn't come easily. Wonderful

phosphorescent "cricket balls" in the sea below the surface like translucent globes on approach to Columbo.

Sept 13
Sailed at 6 am. Usual sort of routine to pass these interminable days - morning knitting - afternoon reading and sleeping, after tea knitting, washing, ironing etc. Not so rough but much rolling of boat. Endeavored to dance on slippery rolling deck.

Sept 14
Passed Minicoy [between Maldives and Laccadives], palm covered cay on reef 7x3 miles in the morning - otherwise one more long day ticked off and one more oz of wool converted into sock.

351 miles.

Sept 15 Sunday
Another day ticked off and half a frock made for Bibs.

345miles.

Sept 16
Wind dropped and a dead flat calm, sea oily at times, and gentle puffs here and there marked its surface. Really pleasant, but for the smuts with no wind to blow the bulk away. Dancing not up to much owing to eternal vibrations which is very tiring - I have no energy for games after a little knitting and sewing done.

353 miles

Sept 17
Foul wind and roughish water and detestable motion - missed breakfast and languished on deck in the morning and almost came to blows with the ship's doctor who maintains this is a fine boat which doesn't roll, and runs down the Mooltan - that steady comfortable palace. Towards evening this infernal SW monsoon wind abated a bit.

325 miles.

Sept 18
Steadily calmer and warmer - very warm and calm by
evening, as we got away from the SW monsoon and neared
African coast for Aden.

295miles.

Sept 19
Calm and warm, reached Aden at 1:30 getting fine view of
the rock as we approached, perfectly bare and much degraded
- my appreciation of weathering is much increased by having
read so much of Davis on coral islands etc. A desolate place
indeed - very hot but a cooling sea breeze - dusty houses and
roads without one blade of grass anywhere around
habitations or on bleak sun baked rock. Went ashore and to
the tanks once more by car with the Jones family from the
boat. Interesting to see it by day after my previous moonlight
visit with Polly. The village proper of Aden is some distance
from the port and lies in the old volcanic crater - flat
bottomed rimmed by rock most of the way round, the tanks
lying in a gully of the crater wall. Through the gap in the
crater wall could be seen a vast expanse of beach with white
piles of prepared salt. Spent an amusing time bargaining with
the Arabs. Left at 6 pm - slept well - without a stitch of
clothing and all the fans going - temp at 5 pm - 8 am 90° and
fairly damp.

349 miles.

Sept 20
Passed volcanic promontory on African coast at 9 am,
showing fine valley filled with a black lava flow going down
to the sea - all bare burnt dissected rocks - what a coast!
Cabin nice and cool all day (91°) with draught (and dust)
catcher and all fans on. Stuffy hot on deck and a cheesy hot
wind - lovely I sat and stewed and sewed revelling in the last
warm weather I shall get for heaven knows how long.

333 miles.

Sept 21

Wonderfully cool - 90° all night and breeze on deck got it to 87° at breakfast time - warmer later - no shores of Red Sea visible, damp haze everywhere - feeling really frisky for first time since Penang, and played tennis - barefoot in shorts to most people's horror! Helped make the doctor lose his temper by rubbing in the rottenness of this boat - it isn't even trying now the mails are gone - 337 miles and calm - however vibration is far, far better now.

Sept 22 Sunday

Fairly hot still - I'm sorry for the boats going the other way with the breeze - their smoke goes straight upwards - decks must be warm! Glorious moonlight still in the evening - I couldn't bid the Southern Cross farewell in consequence of moonlight. Night temperature 90°.

Sept 23

Jumped into temperate non tropics - temperature down to 80° - I nearly put on a woolly coat, but just managed to exist without. Now in the Gulf of Suez, with its terrible eroded bare mountains and narrow alluvial belt and delta like accumulations at the foot of the deep weathered bare gullies - sandy waters and red rocks. Reached Suez at 6 pm - wonderful sunset of that desert and Arabian type seen nowhere else - red-purple-brown mountains, vague mist and festival theatre sky of red purple indescribable colour. Took our place in canal boat queue - 500 yards between each - moon on the wane but bright entered the Bitter Lake by 10:30 when to bed, a regretful and final farewell - perhaps for ever, to the miraculous enchanting FAR EAST - such is life.

Sept 24

Traversed the canal in less than 12 hours (14 expected) and tied up at P. Said by 8 am - went ashore - lovely and hot for the last time and fairly went on the bust this being the bitter end so to speak - in 2 hours I had acquired 2 carpets, numerous silver and copper inlaid brass trays, woven stuff etc and having spent £12-12-0. I hastened to the boat before I broke the bank. The trouble is I buy things for gifts and then can't bear to part with them and buy more to substitute on the next opportunity and then do the same thing again. Sent a letter home by airmail. It's a wrench to go from the heat and sunlight and dust of even the near east. Two letters from Pa arrived just on sailing and brought me to earth again. Home is really now "in sight" - likewise much work etc. The canal passage presented its grandeur - by night lit up with search light and the moon and at sunrise when a cheesy red sun rose behind a low grey cloud belt into a bright copper "festival" sky over the ruddy desert. The sun got up at 5 am - horrid shock after 6 am sunrises for so long.

Sept 25
Cooler by far and calm - had to put on a wooly garment - hateful. Finished the two frocks and 7 pairs of socks - for which relief and much thanks - wonderful Mediterranean blue - unlike any other sea I've seen. Getting suddenly excited about journey's end - 3 more days at sea - what ho she cried and waved her wooden leg. Did the 10 months accounts and spent £430 - Gosh help - but worth it and more.

Sept 26
Woke early to get a blanket and later again to shut the port hole owing to cold wind - arose to a horrid sea and gale - with us fortunately dressed in winter undies and skirt and leather coat but cabin temperature 70° what shall I do at home! - rain followed - and having covered an extra 17 miles by aid of the wind we went dead slow for 2 hours through sheets of rain and mist. Passed closely to a French mail boat, 6,000 tons battling against the wind - we saw daylight for 20 ft under the bows keel as she plunged and emerged from the sea - thank heaven the Kashmir was not so badly behaved. Lunch to dinner spent revelling in the Celebes and Java reading "Tide Marks" and gilding my own romantic

memories. I was excitedly spellbound reliving it all until my
bath time arrived at 7 pm. However I could write a far better
book that is if it could be put into words - at any rate I have a
finer supply of material and greater appreciation of
comparative cultures and architecture for the D.E.I. Fancy
saying Makassar is the most entertaining town or that a
season in a back street in Makassar would be greater fun than
exploring every tomb in Egypt! (p141). He got a very feeble
impression of Java, although he admired it tremendously as
one of the most wonderful countries. He never even saw the
Borobudur and Prambanam Temples. His impressions of the
Red Sea and Gulf of Suez exactly correspond with mine.

347 miles.

Sept 27

Awoke to see the Italian coast afar off, and we passed
Messina by 11 am. Cold cold day - miserable, odious and
hateful cold - my cabin thermometer said 71° - I should say it
was a lie if I did no know the brute to be true. Put on all my
winter clothes, including thick coat and shivered with
benumbed hands on deck as we passed Etna, stately, with
little snow and her head in the clouds. The Eastern sky was
yellow with cumulus clouds and the rest was dull with a spot
of blue over Sicily - you never see a sky like that in the
tropics - passed 2 masted sailing boats - but oh how
European! Coast lines fine - deeply and steeply dissected,
bare - vine terraced - olive and cyprus grove bespotted, and
very steep ribbon like wide water courses - must be cataracts
after rain, winding down to the sea. I've seen nothing like
them before. Passed Stromboli at lunch time - volcanic cone
steep, but showing "abrasion cliffs" on bluffs of lesser
inclination (been reading Davis!) Sea getting rougher. Packed
and washed. My mind is a gorgeous muddle of romance -
lucky I'm not in control of this ship or it would never get to
Marseilles. Oh to be in Singapore with 6 months to spare -
Malaya, the Moluccas - Burma and even China and Japan.
Not to mention Borneo and Celebes - but come to earth -
hateful is cold air to the skin and before you know where you

are you will be smuggling carpets through the English customs.

Sept 28
Warm sun helps to disguise the chillsome air - I couldn't get my cabin over 68° even with the porthole shut - and it was miserably cold in bed and getting up. Off Corsica by 10:30 and middle of the day spent in the Straits. Corsica and Sardinia looked fine in the sunlight - rugged - savage cliffs showing horizontal strata - white and brown and mountains beyond. Sea calm. Shall I or shall I not catch the 6:50 am train tomorrow?

Sept 29 Sunday

[the rest was blank, no words entered]

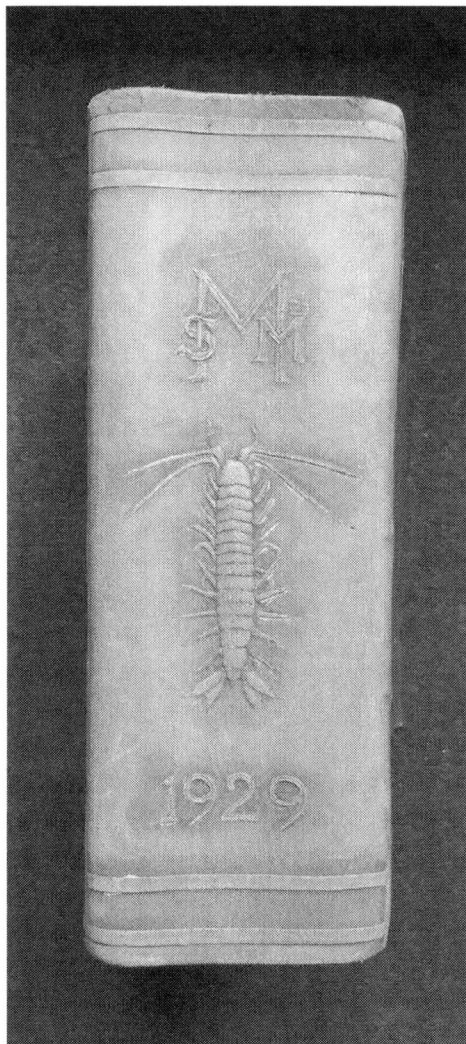

Spine

Front and Back Covers

She made an album with embossed calf skin covers for her
photographs from the expedition.
Here follows a selection.

Sidnie Holding Brain Coral
The wooden cases were originally for kerosene tins

286

287

Corals at Low Tide

Sampling tools

Corals on Concrete Blocks
to study Growth Rates

The Quadrat

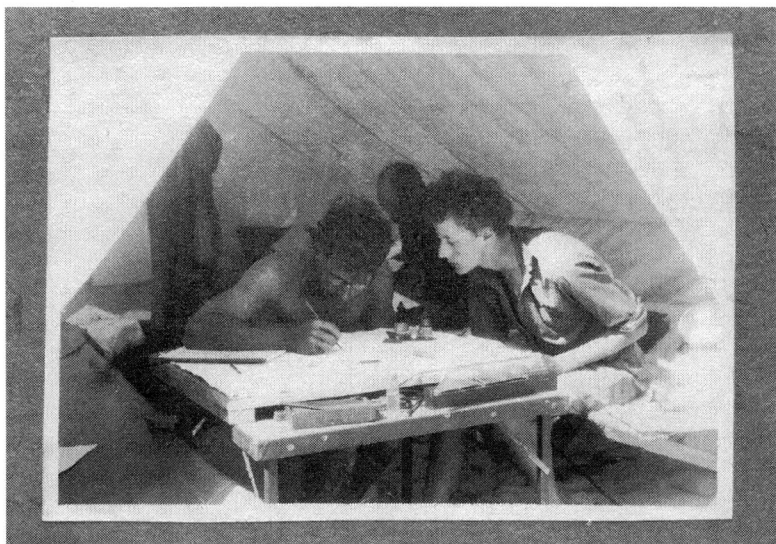

Michael Spender, the surveyor, drawing up a map watched
by Anne Stephenson with Dr Thomas Stephenson at the back
of the tent

Scientists at Sea (possibly aboard Tivoli or Merinda)

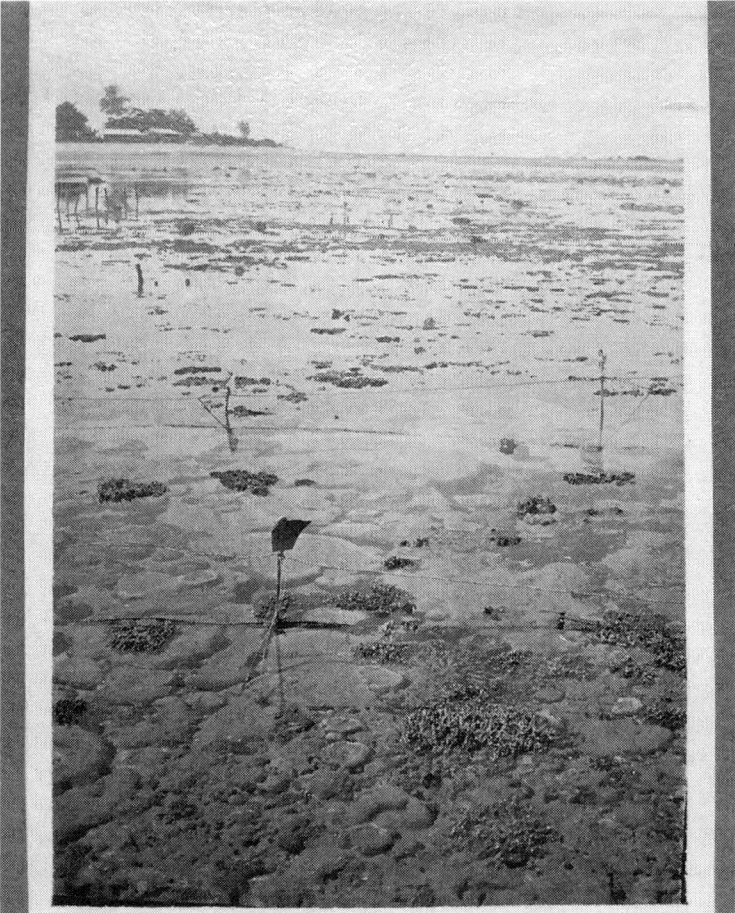

Surveying Lines
(Low Isle in the background)

Tripod at Sea for Measuring Tides

Sidnie surveying (on left)

Sidnie and a Packhorse
Hartz Mountains

Sidnie Rowing

French Cricket

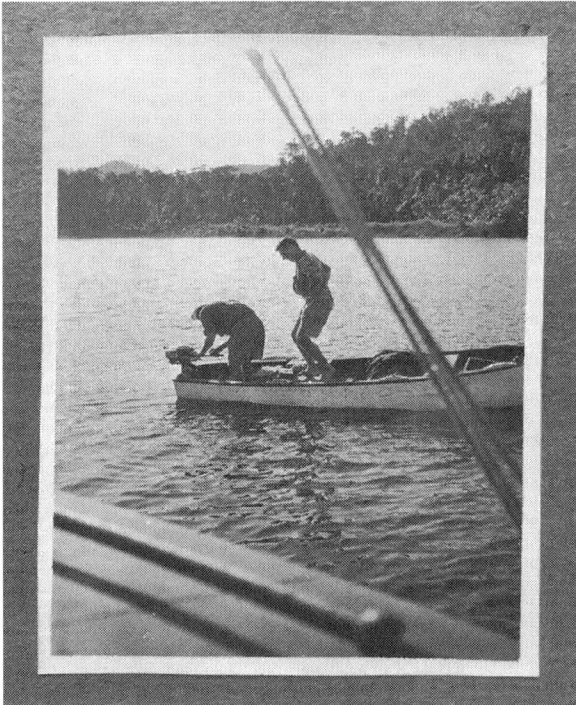

Trouble with the Outboard

BIOGRAPHY

Sidnie was interested in zoology from an early age and made hand bound albums for her detailed water colour paintings of flowers, butterflies, fungi and trees.

She painted this butterfly when she was 14.

She became a distinguished young zoologist who was recruited from the post of Demonstrator at the University of Cambridge to join C.M. Yonge's eminent group of scientists on the long awaited first comprehensive expedition to observe and record the ecology of the Great Barrier Reef, about which very little was known. Yonge noted "Sidnie did as much in those few months as the rest of us did in 4 times that period" adding that "this was no reflection on our activities, just an indication of the exceptional intensity of her own". He also commented "her exceptional capacities for observation, and for illustration were given the fullest range in this wonderful ecosystem", where the surveying part of her work was not confined to surfaces exposed at low tide "but continued down the seaward slopes by means of the simple diving helmet which was all that was available".

The whole of Australia was excited about the long awaited Expedition and her letters describe reporters greeting the scientists at every port. Many newspapers appeared in London and across Australia about the scientific studies and life on Low Isle.

Sidnie was a towering figure in the twentieth century history of arthropod biology, as the leading and most forceful proponent of the belief that arthropods have evolved several times independently from worm-like ancestors. She was an inspiring teacher at the University of Cambridge and later at Kings College London. She could draw very rapidly and could use both hands simultaneously on a black board. She went on to become a much admired, and most distinguished, if sometimes controversial, zoologist. She was elected Fellow of the Royal Society in 1948 being one of the first women to be admitted. The Linnean Society awarded her its gold medal in 1963. She received an honorary doctorate from the University of Lund, Sweden in 1968 and the Zoological Society awarded her the Frink medal in 1977.

Her energy was ceaseless, she never stopped working. Parts of her final book "The Arthropoda" were written from her hospital bed, she was still full of ideas. In 2018 The Journal of Animal Ecology created a prize in her name. There is a "Manton Crater" on Venus shared by her equally eminent sister Irène (Botanist and Fellow of the Royal Society).

BIBLIOGRAPHY

Barrett C (1943) *Australia's Coral Realm* Melbourne: Robertson & Mullens

Bowen J & Bowen M (2002) *The Great Barrier Reef History, Science, Heritage* Cambridge: Cambridge University Press

Fine M, Hoegh-Guldberg O, Meroz-Fine E, Dove S (2019) *Ecological Changes Over 90 Years at Low Isles on the Great Barrier Reef* Nature Communications (https://doi.org/10.1038/s41467-019-12431-y)

Manton S M (1930) *Notes on the Feeding Mechanisms of Anaspides and Paranaspides (Crustacea, Syncardida)* Proceedings of the Zoological Society of London Vol 100, Issue 3

Manton S M (1935) *Great Barrier Reef Expedition 1928-29. Scientific Reports. Vol III, No 1. Ecological Surveys of Coral Reefs*. London: British Museum of Natural History

Yonge C M (1930) *A Year on the Great Barrier Reef; The Story of Corals and of the Greatest of their Creations.* London and New York: Putnam

Yonge C M (1929) *Progress of the Great Barrier Reef Expedition* Nature 123, 89-90 (1929)

A series of articles by Trisha Fielding, historian at James Cook University Library based on their archives about the Great Barrier Reef Expedition and especially C. M. Yonge's collection.

https://jculibrarynews.blogspot.com/2018/08/expedition-to-great-barrier-reef-1928.html

https://jculibrarynews.blogspot.com/2018/08/expedition-to-great-barrier-reef-1928_21.html

https://jculibrarynews.blogspot.com/2018/08/expedition-to-great-barrier-reef-1928_29.html

https://jculibrarynews.blogspot.com/2018/09/expedition-to-great-barrier-reef-1928.html

https://jculibrarynews.blogspot.com/2018/09/expedition-to-great-barrier-reef-1928_12.html

Michael Akam *Foreseeing Fates: A commentary on Manton (1928) 'On the embryology of a mysid crustacean Hemimysis lamornae'*
Philosophical Transactions of the Royal Society
19 April 2015
https://doi.org/10.1098/rstb.2014.0381

Biographical Memoirs of Fellows of the Royal Society. Vol 26. (1980) London: Royal Society. pp 327-356

Sisters make their mark on Venus New Scientist 7 November 1992

Ngaben-Hindu Funeral Ritual of Bali Wikipedia

APPENDIX

Reason for Sidnie's name; The first born child of George and Milana Manton was a boy called Sidney. Sadly he died of scarlet fever aged four. The next child was a girl: she was called Sidnie in his memory and both she and her younger sister Irène were given as good an education as if they were boys. Many people were surprised Dr Sidnie Manton FRS was a woman, not least those who had invited "Dr Manton and wife" to an event of some sort.

Prof Flynn (prominent Australian marine biologist and zoologist) – father to Errol Flynn who moved from Hobart to become a Hollywood film star.

Trove (Australian on line resource with digitised newspapers) -many articles from across Australia about the Great Barrier Reef Expedition in 1928-1929. Those by C.M. Yonge (expedition leader) and Charles Barrett (a journalist who frequently visited Low Isles) are especially interesting.

There is a magnificent model of the S.S. Mooltan in the National Maritime Museum, Greenwich in the 'Trade and Empire' gallery.

A diving helmet similar to the one used on the expedition is in the Museum of Tropical Queensland, Townsville.

We plan to make a website "Sidnie Manton: Letters and Diaries, Expedition to the Great Barrier Reef 1928-1929". We wish to upload more of her photos from the Barrier Reef and her travels across the East Indies. We hope people will be able to add comments for others to share.

We believe an exhibition to mark the centenary of the Expedition is being planned at the Royal Society in London.

Editing Notes;

[ ] denotes an editors comment or amendment.
*[ ]*conjectured reading of something illegible.

Printed in Poland
by Amazon Fulfillment
Poland Sp. z o.o., Wrocław